DATE DUE

Soft Core

Soft Core

Moral Crusades against Pornography in Britain and America

Bill Thompson

CASSELL

Cassell
Villiers House
41/47 Strand
London WC2N 5JE

387 Park Avenue South
New York, NY 10016–8810

First published 1994

British Library Cataloguing-in-Publication Data
A catalogue record for this book is available from the British
Library.

ISBN 0–304–32791–3 (hardback)
      0–304–32793–X (paperback)

Typeset by Fakenham Photosetting Ltd, Fakenham, Norfolk
Printed and bound in Great Britain by Mackays of Chatham plc

Contents

To Mo

about lying to the public about the magazines' contents and effects, and ideologically exploiting problems like sexual assault in order to vindicate statutory controls. While there can be no doubt that pornographic materials are sometimes utilized by people who wish to impose their sexual desires upon others, the fact that millions more consumers do not do this demonstrates that there is nothing innate to soft core that encourages coercion. I have, therefore, become convinced that as long as anti-pornography crusaders harp on about 'pornography', to the detriment of all else, the major reasons for sex crimes will not receive the study and consideration that they should. In highlighting this problem, I hope to encourage public debate. I am not the first to try to do this. During my research, I discovered the following news item in the *Hampshire Chronicle*:

> **Winchester: August 22nd 1885**
> The Bishop of this Diocese, in answer to an invitation to attend a conference held yesterday in St James's Hall has forwarded the following reply: I have to acknowledge the invitation to attend a meeting on the subject of the Prevention of Crimes Act. No one can feel a greater horror than I do of the condition of things in London and other great towns, a greater desire to protect the young and tempted, and to punish the monsters in human form who sacrifice them to their lust. But as one of the 'natural guardians of morality', in this country, I cannot join in public demonstrations, which I fear *are far more likely to increase and stimulate prurient and unwholesome curiosity in the young of both sexes, and so largely to create vicious appetites and encourage vicious indulgences*, than to promote healthy public opinion or to give strength to the administration of the law. [emphasis added]

Likewise, the purpose of *Soft Core* is to avoid unwholesome curiosity, and to promote healthy public opinion, by exposing the bogus 'debate' about pornography and sex crimes. Unfortunately, similar forms of misrepresentation tend to be a feature of the British approach to social problems. Again and again, moral crusaders, the 'politically correct', and politicians exploit issues to promote their moral agendas while doing little to alleviate suffering. As no mis-diagnoses ever lead to a cure, the only result will be more frustration and further stupidity. During October 1993, we reached the point where our foremost law enforcement 'expert' openly and sincerely advocated, on prime-time TV, the blitzing and laying waste of whole neighbourhoods if anyone had started using crack! This nonsense has to stop, and *Soft Core* is as good a place as any to start.

The battle over soft core's existence is not an elementary clash between the residents of 'sin city' and 'kill-joy Christians' – a naive misrepresentation at the best of times. The current dispute is essentially an attempt by two social groups to promote their ideals about female sexuality by limiting choice. Whatever label it likes to give itself, a society or ideology that is not premised upon enhancing people's opportunities to make choices is repressive. When people are not free to choose they cannot make an informed choice, and their subsequent faith or belief, action or vote, will be a poor one. No society can afford the consequences.

Acknowledgements

THIS book would never have been possible without the valuable time and attention given to me over the years by those who feel the issue is so important. Among those who have, without fear or favour, offered assistance are: Eileen Jones and Anne Whitaker of the Community Standards Associations movement; Ted Goodman of Campaign Against Censorship, and David Webb of the National Campaign for the Reform of the Obscene Publications Act; Avedon Carol and Nettie Pollard of Feminists Against Censorship; Bill Jeffery from the Soho Society; and Chris Tame from the Libertarian Alliance. Mary Whitehouse was also kind enough to point out a potential misunderstanding in an earlier draft. I suspect that they will all find some of the contents challenging, and will be disappointed at some of my conclusions; but I hope they will accept that I have striven to repay *their* sincerity and kindness with an attempt to salvage this debate from the machinations of the dishonest.

My ability to spend so much time considering the subject was originally made possible by Monica, and while Sean kept the computers running, Dan kept me rock 'n' rolling. Being a member of Leonore Davidoff and Ken Plummer seminars certainly helped; and it has been great fun working with Jason Annetts and Cecil Greek for three years. The ultimate academic debt, however, will always go to John Gagnon of the State University of New York at Stony Brook, who made it possible for us to talk about such subjects. Personal thanks to Mary Girling, Carole Allington, and Brenda Corti, who made my time at Essex University so special;

Dawn Clark, who read this particular version for me; and Cassell's Steve Cook. Regards to: Isabel and Zak; Francis de Theye; Eddy Holland and Dave Pittard; Betty Lavington; the Frosts and Bill Norton; Janet and Christina; and, finally to Remmy Ongala and Orchestre Super Matimila who put life into perspective in such a beautiful way.

Introduction

PORNOGRAPHY'S dictionary definition, much beloved by the ignorant, bears no relationship to its content, *and never did*. The fact that Victorians invented a new word to describe novels about men and women having sex, by sticking together two Greek words *porne* and *graphein*, which mean 'harlot' and 'to write', tells us far more about Victorian attitudes to sexually active women than it does about the contents of any books. Contemporary definitions of erotica, obscenity, and pornography suffer from a similar prejudice.

When used by 'educated' people, the three terms are heavily loaded: with rare exceptions, erotica are approved-of depictions of sexuality; pornography, by default, is disapproved images. Obscenity, a moral–legal term, is used to reinforce the designation pornography. To be obscene the picture or text has to tend to 'deprave and corrupt' people. Whether or not it does is determined in court, when juries, judges, and everyone else involved in the prosecution agree that someone else will be corrupted and depraved by what they have just seen, and accordingly pass a guilty verdict! Yet a guilty verdict does not mean that all copies are obscene. Each case is judged on its own merits, as two Portsmouth video dealers discovered in 1984, when in adjacent courts, on the same day, one was found 'guilty' and the other 'not guilty' despite renting out the same films.

For the rest of us, pornography is merely a very convenient term to describe magazines and videos which show naked bodies or people having sex, which may or may not be physically arousing; erotica is a convenient term to describe material which needs an 'expert' to tell you where the sex is; and obscenity rarely figures in our vocabulary, unless we want to describe the activities of a Pol Pot. And that means that in less than thirty years pornography has

lost the pejorative inference given to it by the British literary establishment in an attempt to distance their 'erotica' from the more
popular fare. Some people, however, like to make a distinction
between soft and hard pornography; and the arguments about
which is which go on and on.

Content

For all intents and purposes, however, British soft core consists of pin-up-style pictures of semi-naked or naked women and
men, close-up pictures of female genitalia, and couples or groups
simulating sexual contact. Typical examples are *Escort*, *Playbirds*,
Vulture, and *Women Only*. British soft-core videos consist of
women posing around in underwear and taking their clothes off,
such as Linzi Drew's *Striptacular* and the *Electric Blue* series.
Consequently the British tend to call magazines and videos which
show men and/or women having sex in various positions and com-
binations, like *Private* magazine and the video *Plaisirs Sauvages*,
which are commonly sold on the Continent and in the USA, hard
core. Americans and Europeans, however, often use the term soft
core to describe oral and genital sex, up to and including ejaculation; hence the description 'suck and fuck' movies. Hard core is
reserved to describe minority sexual practices, once known as 'perversions', such as anal sex or drinking ejaculate.

When I use the phrase 'soft core' in this book I will follow
the American convention, and add the prefix 'British' to refer to our
top-shelf magazines and videos. 'Hard core' will be reserved for
images which show more than vaginal and oral sex, and all other
minority-interest material will be designated by specific type. When
I use the word 'pornography', I am including everything.

Law

Of the many laws which exist to restrict public access to
pornography, five are particularly important. The 1959 Obscene
Publications Act (and 1964 Amendment) restricts availability of

most soft core and all hard core because it is deemed obscene. The 1984 Video Recordings Act makes it an offence to distribute videos that have not been censored by the British Board of Film Certificators, which is very restrictive. Apart from sex education videos which recently gained 18 certificates, sex has to be simulated to gain an 18R and be confined to sex shops. The 1876 Customs Consolidation Act prohibits importation of material deemed 'indecent'. To be indecent something merely has to disgust a police, Customs, or postal officer, and then a magistrate. The 1953 Post Office Act makes it a crime to mail an obscene or an indecent article. Any material featuring minors deemed to depict a sexual pose or sexual act is outlawed by the 1978 Child Protection Act.

Since 1959, these 'obscenity' laws were supposed to punish pornography and leave erotic art and literature alone. Between 1978 and 1986, however, the Customs Service had an unofficial policy of not seizing most items if they were for the individual's own personal use, or for professional study. Today, Customs officers will not only detain a person who has a couple of items, but with the aid of the police they will turn the person's house upside down looking for more, while the police go through the rest of your belongings taking anything they like in order to make you write dozens of letters asking for it to be returned before they will tell you they have lost it. The Post Office also like to rifle through people's mail looking for anything to do with sex, let alone indecent and obscene material. In 1986, for example, they decided to intercept a copy of the US Attorney General's Commission into Pornography Report I had ordered from the Justice Department through their official British agents. For five weeks the Post Office maintained that they had no knowledge of its whereabouts; but when the agent became involved, the Post Office miraculously found it, stopped breaking the spine (thereby revealing which sections they found most interesting), and made a very clumsy attempt to re-pack it. Between 1991 and 1992, several packets from the Netherlands, containing scholarly articles and reports printed in Dutch, sent to me by academics and the Justice Department, had also been 'examined'. Since then they appear to have become obsessed with seizing safe-sex and Benetton advertisements in French newspapers.

Technically, it is illegal to possess imported material, pass on home-made material, or even invite your friends round to see your collection; but Customs and the police rarely bother unless you have committed another offence, although they would like to.

Availability

Today most British soft-core magazines can be found in the thousands of newsagents which stock between six and two hundred titles. Many more titles, including many sexual fetish magazines, can be found in the sixty or so licensed sex shops, which also sell sex aids and 18R videos.

The size of the indigenous industry can be partly gauged by recent company returns and sales figures. In 1989, Congate, which publishes *Parade* (circulation 65,000) and *New Park Lane* (15,000) among many others, had a turnover of £7 million. Paul Raymond's businesses, which include *Club International, Escort* and *Men Only* (selling between three-quarters of a million and several million copies), earned £16 million. Northern and Shell, which produces *Penthouse* (100,000) and *Forum* (30,000), made less than £6 million; Galaxy Publications, which produces *Fiesta* (300,000) and *Knave* (150,000), was reported to be making £4.4 million.

Minority-interest and gay material is in a peculiar state of limbo. Gay pin-ups are generally deemed soft core, unless they contain an erection, or involve sexual penetration. Until recently, corporal punishment magazines and videos showing various acts of restraint and force, such as spanking, were freely available in specialist shops, but could not be imported because Customs considered them indecent. Consequently, while you cannot send for the passive *Three Hundred Bound Beauties*, you can buy magazines like *Janus* and videos like *The Sixth Formers' Lesson* which imply acts of force.

Because of various Supreme Court judgments, access to different types of pornography in the USA depends upon the community in which one lives. Major cities like New York and San Francisco have a large number of adult book and video stores supplying both soft-core and hard-core material. Until about four years ago, one could freely purchase almost any type of sexual imagery, except that featuring children, from these stores. Since then, material depicting acts of force and restraint has declined and is being replaced by a large amount of home-made videos. In other parts of the country availability is restricted to soft-core titles like *Penthouse*, available in convenience stores. Most European countries allow anything apart from child pornography to be sold anywhere. Although a lot of material will be found in special sex shops, their newsagents and video stores sell hard-core titles from companies like Copenhagen's *Rodox's Colour Climax* and Berth Milton's *Private* series.

People become pornographic models for many different reasons. In Britain, models can find work through agencies, by being approached by a freelance photographer who pays the model and then sells the pictures on to a magazine, by writing to the company or magazine concerned themselves, or by meeting an employer at a party. For the vast majority of those involved, it is a part-time occupation. In the USA, magazine work is similar, but the video industry involves approximately 100 models at any one time. A quarter of these are men, who tend to last longer but are paid half the rate. Far from being coerced or blackmailed into the industry, for most women it is a positive choice. In Europe, most companies are inundated with offers by enthusiastic female consumers who wish to appear in the magazines and films. Readers wanting a more extensive and completely reliable account of the international hard-core industry should consult Hebditch and Annings' *Porn Gold*.

Over the last 20 years a large number of second- and third-generation copies of Continental and American video cassettes, easily copied on VCRs, have been circulated in Britain. Since 1990, this stock has been boosted by copies of Continental satellite broadcasts. How many illegally distributed videos and magazines are now in circulation is anyone's guess. While tacky copies can be purchased under the counter in some Soho stores, those adverts offering 'Continental hard core direct from Copenhagen' are a 'rip-off'. The writer Paul Ferris, for example, once answered a full-page advertisement by a company with an address in Upper Montague Street, London. He received a six-page colour catalogue posted from Leighton Buzzard with ten explicit photographs purporting to represent the videos together with descriptions of the films. Although his cheque for £35 was cashed four days later at a Hemel Hempstead bank he did not receive a video; and nor will you, so don't bother. Buy your partner a present and tell them you love them instead.

Breaking the consensus

After numerous court cases during the 1970s, a compromise was reached in Britain; hard-core and 'suck and fuck' movies were prosecuted under section 2 of the 1959 Act; pin-up material far less so. As a result, the British industry concentrated upon the latter, and developed a style of its own. While various police forces, especially the Obscene Publications Squad, would frequently raid British soft-core warehouses and sex-shop stocks under section 3 of the 1959 Act (confiscation and destruction), to convince the public they were doing something useful, no one seemed too bothered.

Between 1988 and 1992, however, British soft core came under attack in the quality press's women's pages and tabloid TV programmes like *Dispatches*. Every report asserted that a group of 'feminists' had just discovered that soft-core content was becoming more violent, and that American social scientists had recently found a link between this material and sex crimes. Readers and viewers were then invited to rethink their attitude to British soft-core availability in order to reduce sex crimes and to support a new law which these 'feminists' had fortuitously put together to ensure that evil soft core could be eliminated without censoring harmless erotica.

Far from being news, these features and programmes had been promoted by the latest group to join the four-hundred-year-old crusade by the middle classes to label various kinds of sexual material 'obscene', 'offensive', or 'pornographic' in order to imply they possessed some innate and dangerous quality that spread immorality among the great unwashed, and must, therefore, be outlawed. During the nineteenth century, this 'obscene' material was accredited with 'corrupting' youth, which meant it encouraged them to fornicate. As fornication is now blamed upon the birth-control pill and the supplying of council homes to unmarried mothers, pornography is accredited with provoking sex crimes. In 1985, for example, serial rapist Malcolm 'The Fox' Fairley was told by Mr Justice Caulfield:

I am satisfied that you are a decadent advertisement for the evil pornographers. They will want to forget you as one of their worst casualties.

While such judgments about illiterate labourers have often been ideologically exploited by people like Jill Knight MP to outlaw soft core, after 1987 this pressure increased. From *Girl about Town*, in June that year, to the *Observer*, on 16 April 1989, a group calling itself Campaign Against Pornography, known as CAP, kept up a constant barrage of propaganda to convince us that soft-core magazines posed a serious social problem. The contents were supposedly full of crimes, like child pornography or women being tortured, mutilated and murdered, or incitement to crime like young women in sexual poses 'made up' (*sic*) to look like children; or they caused crimes. Not that the offending titles were ever named. Dozens of unlikely candidates, like the *Daily Express*'s Lynda Lee Potter, suddenly became born again feminists and urged their readers on.

But this was no tabloid sensationalism; the quality press women's pages also vied with each other to see who could make the most outlandish claims about British soft core. Top prize went to the *Guardian*'s report in February 1988, which included the suggestion that the inevitable result of British soft core's legal immunity was the distribution of videos containing real rapes, and snuff movies, where the raped woman was then killed. Likewise, without exception, the reports stressed there was 'new' and accumulating evidence that soft core, like hard core, produced callous attitudes in men which led them to commit sex crimes.

The Primarolo Bill

Following CAP's campaign, an Early Day Motion fronted by Dawn Primarolo was presented to the Commons in 1989. Apart from obfuscating the difference between British soft and international hard core, it made several unsubstantiated claims:

This House views with grave concern the continued rise in sales, both covert and overt, of pornographic and obscene material; notes that such publications have a grossly degrading and damaging effect, particularly in their depiction of women and children; notes the increasingly extreme cruelty and violence involved in such material; believes that the anecdotal evidence is now overwhelming and this kind of stimulus is an important factor in encouraging criminal acts affecting innocent victims; and calls on Her Majesty's Government to initiate an urgent study of the impact of pornography to update and supplement the limited research currently available and thereafter to implement urgently whatever measures are necessary to protect those who directly and indirectly suffer as a result of such perverse influences.

Another wave of adverse media comment followed, and in January 1990 Primarolo promoted a Location of Pornographic Materials Bill, which would have drastically curtailed sales of magazines like *Penthouse* and *Escort*:

1. (1) It shall be an offence to display, sell or otherwise distribute any pornographic material from any premises unless the vendor or distributor has a licence to sell or distribute such material from those premises; or, as the proprietor of such premises, to permit such unlicensed display, sale or distribution.

    (2) It shall be an offence to display, sell or otherwise distribute pornographic material to the general public from premises where any other goods or services whatsoever are sold; or, as the proprietor of such premises, to permit such display, sale or distribution.

    (3) A licence to sell or otherwise distribute pornographic material shall be granted only by the appropriate local authority for the area where the premises are situated, and a licence shall be granted only where the premises from which material is sold or distributed are used solely for the sale or distribution of pornographic material.

2. (1) Any person guilty of an offence under this Act shall be liable –

(a) on a summary conviction to a fine not exceeding level five in the Standard Scale or to imprisonment for a term not exceeding six months or both; or

(b) on conviction on indictment to a fine or imprisonment or both; and the court may order that the premises used for sale or distribution of pornographic material may be closed.

(2) Prosecutions for offences under this Act may be brought by the trading standards officers, and the rights and duties of trading standards officers shall be extended accordingly.

3. (1) Pornographic material means film and video and any printed matter which, for the purpose of sexual arousal or titillation, depicts women, or parts of women's bodies, as objects, things or commodities, or in sexually humiliating or degrading poses or being subject to violence.

(2) The reference to women in sub-section (1) above includes men.

The Bill's backers tried to secure more support by suggesting that it would 'only' restrict British soft-core material to sex shops. In reality, as there are fewer than sixty of these shops in the whole country, the Bill would drastically restrict soft-core availability. As the third clause also defined pin-up magazines as consisting of degrading images of women it would have enshrined in law the ideological belief that for a woman to pose nude or semi-nude was to demean herself. In doing so, this Bill was not just telling people how to act, but how to think; and it laid down very stiff penalties for anyone who disagreed.

Sex, censorship and society

The Primarolo Bill's third clause confirms that campaigns against pornography are to the twentieth century what prostitution was to the nineteenth: a means to promote and determine society's unofficial but 'public' attitude towards all sexual behaviour, especially that of women. Far from simply censoring material, such campaigns have always included inferences about, and attempts to prescribe, which sexual practices are desirable and undesirable. Irrespective of which 'dangerous' item was being targeted, these prescriptions have steadily moved from denouncing fornication for both sexes to the idea that no woman would voluntarily act like a lustful man and engage in sex merely for pleasure's sake; female sexuality was to be limited to expressing love and having babies. In saying so, crusades have been one of the most powerful influences in creating and perpetuating this stereotype. Today's campaign is no different. By saying women are degraded by posing for soft-core material, it suggests their sexuality has some other purpose. By suggesting women are being harmed, it implies women are being forced against their will, and have no choice. So although the rhetoric appears to concentrate upon what men should not be doing, the campaign has important implications for women too.

Chapter one

From Bad Manners to Pornography

FAR from highlighting a new social problem, CAP's campaign is merely the latest move in a four-hundred-year-old crusade to limit the British public's access to sexually orientated publications. The only thing new about the campaign is its justifications and claim to be a 'feminist' measure.

Reforming manners

The first recorded attempt to outlaw publications about sex was a 1580 Obscenity Bill which sought to outlaw licentious 'poesies, books, pamphlets, ditties, songs, and other works'. How many were in circulation we do not know. During the Reformation publications were controlled by the Stationers' Company, which licensed printing presses; but it was more preoccupied with unorthodox political and religious doctrines than sex, and the system collapsed amid a corruption scandal in 1695. Consequently, when James Read was prosecuted in 1707 for publishing the *Fifteen Plagues of a Maidenhead* he had to be acquitted because there was no law forbidding 'bawdy stuff not fit to be mentioned publicly'. Although Mr Justice Powell personally thought *Plagues* would 'corrupt good manners', he also believed that this was not a sufficient cause for punishment. At that point, most licentious books were of foreign origin and expensive. While the lower orders also utilized various forms of sexually orientated material, too few survive to enable historians to make a detailed assessment of content or quality.

This *laissez-faire* situation was eventually challenged by evangelical Christians, who created Societies for the Reformation of Manners to 'clean up' public prostitution, the theatre, fairs, masquerades, and 'obscene ballads', enjoyed by the non-churched. Apart from gaining pre-censorship of the theatre in 1735, these Societies helped create the climate in which secular prosecution of literature could begin through the creation of a new offence known as 'obscene libel': the crime of corrupting the King's subjects' morals.

The first to suffer was the printer-agitator Edmund Curll for publishing a copy of *Venus in the Cloister*, which was accused of 'weakening the bonds of civil society, virtue, and morality'. The prosecution was really an excuse to punish Curll for exposing a spy scandal a couple of years before; but his case led to a systematic clamp-down of sexual books between 1728 and 1757. By 1738 the Societies were so satisfied with the authorities' endeavours that they disbanded, their work done.

The Society of Vice

Towards the end of the eighteenth century several new forms of sex literature appeared. While the labouring classes read sex education pamphlets, 'gentlemen' read bawdy verses like *The Electric Eel*, collections of sexually explicit divorce trial reports, and novels like *Fanny Hill*, subscribed to a new breed of magazines like *The Bon Ton*, and consulted guides to city 'nightlife', including Harris's *List of Covent Garden Ladies*.

Little of this material would be deemed 'pornographic' today, but it upset devoted Christians, who were already dismayed that contemporary medical opinion promoted healthy sexual exercise; a 'Dr' Graham even held public lectures advocating the use of 'lascivious' prints to arouse the passions, before selling gullible couples a night in his 'celestial bed'. But what really angered the Christians was that members of the Government did not particularly care, probably because of their own proclivity to visit Covent Garden. So in 1787, William Wilberforce, who sensed that there was something different about George III, persuaded the King to issue a proclamation *For the Encouragement of Piety and Virtue*, *and for the Preventing and Punishing of Vice, Profaneness and Immorality.* Armed with this justification, Wilberforce founded the Proclamation Society with the aim to suppress all

> loose and licentious Prints, Books, and Publications, dispersing Poison to the minds of the Young and Unwary, and to Punish the Publishers and Vendors thereof.

A change of name to The Society for the Suppression of Vice a couple of years later coincided with members initiating a spate of prosecutions for obscene libel; and after 1802, the Vice Society, as it became known, waged a permanent moral crusade against the printers, distributors, writers and artists behind the cheap broadsheets, ballads, literature and prints, which owing to advances in technology were increasing in quality and falling in price. The Society's public justification was the existence of a gang of six hundred filthy-minded Italians who for some reason were determined to corrupt Britain's fair youth by provoking lust and encouraging 'deviations'; and that books like *The Quintessence of Birch Discipline*, prosecuted in 1809, 'incite and encourage indecent practices'.

Occasionally the Courts did not agree. The 1822 prosecution of William Benbow's *Rambler* magazine collapsed when the defence questioned the Society's motive. If they really were Christians, where was their forgiveness? Persecuting people and destroying them through expensive court cases was surely the action of a Pharisee? But such setbacks were not common.

Encouraged by a change in medical opinion which insisted that women did experience sexual arousal like men, the Society's activities effectively determined what was labelled 'obscene'; but that was not their only legacy.

The 1824 Vagrancy Act outlawing 'obscene displays' not only reduced the trade at provincial fairs and ensured that the mysterious Italians disappeared, but also cut the number of 'obscene' bookshops in London's Holywell Street from 90 to 23. It was the appearance of one of the Holywell booksellers, 'Smith', before Lord Campbell's court that led to his 1857 Obscene Publications Bill, which codified a definition of 'obscenity' in law. Obscenity was

> something offensive to modesty or decency or expressing or suggesting unchaste or lustful ideas or being impure, indecent or lewd.

This extremely loose definition led to an increase in targeted material. By 1870, the Vice Society claimed credit for the confiscation of 129,681 prints, 16,220 illustrated books, 5 tons of letter press, 16,005 song sheets, 5,503 cards, snuff boxes and similar items, and a 'large quantity of infidel and blasphemous publications' – which included anything from religious tracts denying the existence of the Holy Trinity and 'bawdy' limericks, to birth control material and French novels of the realist school published in the English language. Despite Campbell's parliamentary assurances that the 1857 Act would apply 'exclusively to works written for the single purpose of the corruption of youth' and of 'a nature calculated to shock the common feelings of decency in a well regulated mind', the Vice Society used it to prosecute anything they did not like.

Although the Vice Society's reluctance to prosecute the flagrant immorality of the high bourgeoisie led to charges of hypocrisy (Sydney Smith denounced them as the 'society for the suppression of the vices of those whose incomes do not exceed £500 per annum'), and reflected their failure completely to remoralize society, they were fairly successful. While Royalty brazenly paraded their paramours down Rotten Row, and St John's Wood became a bourgeois brothel, British erotic bibliophiles all agree that home-produced 'obscenity' virtually disappeared in the mid-nineteenth century. Building upon this success, the Vice Society took advantage of magistrates' forfeiture procedures and destruction powers to ensure novels became judged by the critics' assessment of the characters' morality; sin had to be seen to be punished. While great authors who sold on the strength of their work, like Bulwer Lytton, tried to fight back, Smith's and Mudie's, the major distributors, happily co-operated in promoting the sentimental pulp for which the period is well known. Drama and song degenerated into melodramatic symbolism and innuendo. Those who preferred to keep their integrity, or publish on sexual subjects, crossed the Channel.

In order to justify their personal crusade, the Vice Society promoted a myth that licentious literature encouraged aristocrats to seduce working-class women, who were then forced to become prostitutes. If only the flow of literature could be stopped, the crusaders reasoned, prostitution would disappear and all women would remain virtuous – as if urbanization and economics had nothing to do with it. This seduction myth reflected the bizarre theological marriage between the Protestant evangelicals' fear of sexual arousal and the Anglo-Catholics' sensibility regarding the Madonna, which turned Eve from the Genesis temptress into a helpless victim of debauched male lust, thereby inverting biblical tradition in favour of a secular rationale. The real problem women faced, of course, was that they were no longer protected by custom if they became pregnant, but not only did the prosecutions after the 1824 and 1857 Acts curtail the circulation of birth control and sex education, they also had a drastic effect upon public perceptions of women's sexuality.

Women were now supposed to be completely sexless; but far from promoting a double standard whereby men could sow 'wild oats', but not women, the crusades promoted a clear distinction between 'good girls', who avoided sex until marriage, and then made a procreative sacrifice, and 'bad girls', who if seduced had suffered a fate worse than death! These 'foolish' girls' only chance of instant absolution, like Dickens' Nancy, was a sacrificial death for a pure person! Meanwhile, men were supposed to overcome their 'urges', stop seducing 'girls' on packet-steamer day trips to France, and take to the poetry of Alfred Lord Tennyson and Henry Wadsworth Longfellow.

As often happens, history loves irony, and the test of obscenity to 'corrupt and deprave' emerged in the case of *R. v. Hicklin* concerning *The Confessional Unmasked*, a 'pornographic' anti-Catholic pamphlet supposedly exposing the sexual confessions priests extracted from female penitents. Complete with its cover illustration of the Pope setting a dragon upon a chaste-looking Britannia, this volume was designed to be consumed, as many copies had been, by evangelical Christians!

Despite this prurient hypocrisy, the new concept of the pure woman had such a dramatic and forceful influence on the language and interpretation of sexual practices in Britain that it is only just beginning to disappear.

Being vigilant

In the last third of the nineteenth century, British Christians became convinced, with the help of the American evangelist Reverend Moody, that sexual impurity rather than greed was the major sin of the age, and a third wave of moral censorship began. By then, new inventions and improved techniques had led to the importation of nude photographs and sexually explicit books, produced in France and Belgium by Carrington and other exiles, through the growing postal systems. The major crusades were run by the National Vigilance Association and the Public Morality Council, which drew support from revivalist missions; the White Cross, which secured celibacy pledges from working-class men with those tales of upper-class seduction of their daughters; the Salvation Army; the Protestant Truth Society; and the Gospel Purity Association. By the end of the century, three hundred local Vigilance Societies were initiating private prosecutions against homosexuals and obscene literature. These soon reached 200 per year. Like their predecessors, the Vigilance Societies had a wide definition of obscenity. Apart from securing new laws like the Customs Consolidation Act, which targeted the foreign mail-order corruption of public-school youth, great efforts were made to deny the working classes access to birth control, and completely clamp down on sex in print.

James Bradlaugh and Annie Besant were convicted of an obscene libel for distributing *The Fruits of Philosophy: An Essay on the Population Problem* in 1876, because it 'tended to create morbid feeling and lead to unlawful practices' – namely birth control. In 1888, the height of Jack the Ripper's reign of terror, the Vigilance Society was preoccupied with prosecuting Henry Vizetelly for publishing English-language versions of Zola's novels! Vizetelly was no back-street publisher either; he had been the first to put Longfellow and Edgar Allen Poe into British print. Apart from *La Terre*, he was also prosecuted for Flaubert's *Madame Bovary*, and

Guy de Maupassant's *Bel-Ami*. And to make completely sure the masses would not have their passions inflamed, the Libel Amendment Act forbade newspapers to quote any of the 'obscene' or 'blasphemous' passages read in court. The following year the Society's legal subcommittee drafted and secured the 1889 Indecent Advertisements Act in an attempt to prevent the distribution of birth control information once and for all. They then took over the London County Council's licensing committee, revoked numerous music hall licences, shut down art exhibitions, and censored bill posters. In 1897, the Association obtained its most effective proscription of the century by targeting Havelock Ellis's *Sexual Inversion*, a major study of homosexuality, denouncing it as 'a filthy and obscene book'. The prosecution of this 'pretence and shame at science' put British sexology into hibernation for over sixty years. Consequently, although the century ended with Britain's biggest 'corrupter of youth', Carrington, being prosecuted in Belgium, the nineteenth-century moral crusades had ramifications way beyond the censorship of obscenity.

Victorian standards and social purity

The combined activities of the crusaders left the legacy we now call 'Victorianism', the facade of moral consensus behind which many people hid their real proclivities and habits, but which many more felt compelled to adopt for fear of public shame. Despite the label, however, this phase in British history existed only between 1920 and the mid-1950s. As Cyril Pearl's study *The Girl in the Swansdown Seat* made clear, it was only towards the end of the crusades that the Societies' attitudes about sex, obscenity, and morality became the norm, as the State took over responsibility for obscenity prosecutions. 'Victorianism' really began when 1000 copies of D. H. Lawrence's *The Rainbow*, printed by Methuen, were destroyed by a Bow Street magistrate. All in all, this was probably a good thing, as Lawrence was a prat who claimed he could detect a difference between pornography and his art when there is none; but that was not the prosecution's rationale. Sex had to be harnessed for the benefit of race and nation rather than pleasure, and the masses would have to do as they were told.

Faced with this kind of pressure the emerging cinema industry quickly established its own censor – the BBFC. Domestic broadcasting was limited to the BBC and was tightly controlled by Lord Reith, who imposed 'Victorianism' on the air-waves but ignored it in his private life. Apart from 'dirty postcards', the 'blue book' trade became restricted to reprints of eighteenth- and nineteenth-century novels and smuggled copies of the works of European sexologists. Any insipid indigenous missive in this line, such as texts on prostitution, could be sold only to clergymen, medical doctors, or academics, who had to sign for their copies in the same way that one had to sign for 'dangerous' drugs. The Director of Public Prosecutions, Bodkin, was so obsessed with repressing sex that when he attended the 1923 League of Nations conference on the 'international traffic' in pornography, he argued against any attempt at a definition lest it restrict his ability to prosecute what he did not like. The cost of transgression was high: in 1937, William Hamilton, a Charing Cross Road bookseller, was imprisoned for three months and fined £100, with 10 guineas' costs, merely for selling *The Autobiography of a Flea* to an undercover policeman. But sexy books, films and music got off lightly compared to women.

Between 1880 and 1920, early 'feminists' joined the evangelicals in a Social Purity crusade to destroy birth control information and sex education, and abolish 'white slavery', then a euphemism for all non-marital sex, not just prostitution. In 1885 they enlisted the help of the publisher-journalist, William Stead, to help them secure an increase in the age of consent. Stead's sensational *Maiden Tribute to Modern Babylon* grossly exaggerated the coercive nature of, and failed to address the real causes for, prostitution. As a result, the Criminal Law Amendment Act, while sensibly raising the age of consent to sixteen, failed to dent the industry. So in 1898, the 1824 Vagrancy Act was amended in order to permit the flogging of the husbands and boyfriends of prostitutes, to dissuade men from ignoring the 'fact' that fallen women were 'ruined' for life. Eight years later, an Aliens Act was passed amid anti-Semitic slurs that all organized white slavery was controlled by Jews; and six years after that, the Jews apparently forgotten, the Suffragettes convinced themselves that 'Votes for Women and Chastity for Men' would be greatly enhanced by flogging Negroes, who were allegedly pimping white women. Parliament grabbed the opportunity to buy off the feminists; and the Home Secretary, Reginald McKenna, on the advice of the Obscene Publications Squad, passed a Bill which would send these 'animals' back home

> with the hall-mark of British muscle on their back, so that [they] will carry away some appreciation of the sentiment of Great Britain towards procuration.

Not surprisingly, the racist, anti-Semitic, and eugenic sentiments which lay behind the middle-class social purity movement have been edited out of feminist histories, which uncritically swallow and repeat the alliance's white-slavery urban legends, while covering up the real fate that awaited any women 'rescued' from prostitution: becoming the domestic servants or laundresses of nice middle-class feminists. Those who refused to be rescued had their children taken from them. Likewise, we hear little about the 'feminist' association for Moral and Social Hygiene, which aligned with the White Cross to vehemently oppose the opening of the first VD ablution centre in Manchester during 1920, because it would undermine 'racial hygiene', and stop the sinful from suffering before going to hell. The centre closed after two years, and the Government bowed to the crusaders' moral demands and blocked the public availability of VD cures for decades! The alliance's flirtation with Freudianism, with its message of sublimating sex for the benefit of society, was also a disaster for women. Freud's followers, such as Ernest Jones, created secular rationales for moral imperatives which were then used to justify incarcerating thousands of young women, who had been 'mad' enough to think they might enjoy non-marital sex, in mental asylums for decades. Some of these unfortunate women have only been released in the last ten years!

Women, teenagers, and members of the working classes were not supposed to think about sex as leisure. Gay men and lesbians never stood a chance. *The Well of Loneliness*, for example, was denounced because it

> glorified unnatural tendencies ... there was not one word

which suggests that anyone with the *horrible tendencies* described is in the least degree blameworthy. All the characters are presented as attractive people and put forward with admiration. What is even more serious is that certain acts are described in the most alluring terms. [emphasis added]

Fiction was still being judged on the morals of its characters; lesbians obviously did not have any, even in print.

Occasionally the crusaders' efforts backfired: in 1926, their endorsement of the sensational exposé film *The White Slave Traffic* failed to prevent its being censored by the BBFC on the grounds that the scenes were too arousing. But, by the 1930s, with local and national political authorities, the courts and police, and the BBC now behind them, the crusaders did not have that much to do. If publishers stepped out of line, or someone thought they had, it did not take long to rectify the situation. In 1938, the *Daily Mail* and the National Council for Public Morals quickly forced Routledge to withdraw the novel *I Beg to Be Ashamed*. During the 1950s, American thriller novels and magazines were prosecuted in their hundreds. The crusade which led to the 1955 Children and Young Persons (Harmful Publications) Act, outlawing American horror comics, was even led by the Communist Party.

These examples, and there are hundreds more, clearly show how censorship and social purity know no bounds. After decades of sustained and successful crusading, the moral crusaders' influence upon public morality, backed by the authorities, was so strong that the Vigilance Association voluntarily disbanded in 1953, believing its work accomplished. Sex was now something that women were not supposed to know about, let alone openly discuss. To do so was to lose the status of 'a lady'. Men, because of their baser nature, would always discuss such things; but a real gentleman would never do so in the presence of a 'lady', because 'ladies' did not think about such things. Immoral women who dared to enjoy sex, even in the confines of a marriage, were now called nymphomaniacs – a designated mental illness – and were tortured with electricity and drugs in the growing number of mental hospitals. Women amoral enough to quadruple their weekly earnings in a quarter of the time by prostitution were criminals and filled the prisons. Not surprisingly, women eventually began to police themselves: bad girls who stepped out of line were called 'slags' or 'tarts' by good girls. Knowing society would blame the woman, unscrupulous men took advantage of the situation, and the belief that promiscuity was dangerous for women became a self-fulfilling prophecy: the only viable option in the post-war period, unless one was wealthy, was to lie back and procreate for England, tidy the house for the husband, and bake for one's two children; and secretly dream of being ravished in an Arabian tent. Magistrate's courts, probation officers, teachers, and social workers all strove to ensure that any working-class youth who rebelled and refused to conform to this moral norm would be punished. Sexual knowledge and exploration were now socially as well as biblically sinful.

In this climate, a new double standard arose. Some men readily had sex with the 'slags', but sought to marry only good girls, who were closely inspected by their potential mother-in-laws. Respectable wives deluded themselves into believing that they had married nice men. Those who could not forget what they had done during the Second World War, or wondered what it would be like to do something a little different during the long boring British Sunday afternoon, felt incredibly guilty. Young women learned to keep quiet, worry endlessly, and despise themselves for their fantasies. Moral ideology had gained a material form. And then came 'porn'.

The Obscene Publications Act 1959

During the late 1950s, the official morality finally began to fall apart. Though no one cared when the police returning from the 1953 Oslo Interpol conference on sex crime began to seize thousands of cheap novelettes, the literati became very upset when Sir David Maxwell Fyfe's mainstream publications were declared no better, and the police went after Secker & Warburg, Hutchinson, and Heinemann in 1954. The Society of Authors asked Roy Jenkins to bail them out with a new Obscenity Bill, to exempt their 'serious' literature from prosecution, and rigorously to *strengthen* controls over the production and distribution of 'pornography'. It was the

Parliamentary select committee that finally established the existence of something called 'pornography' which was obscene, and 'art' which was not; or if it was, could be 'in the public good' when taken as a whole as opposed to turning down the corners of pages with 'the dirty bits' on them. Pornography, in contrast, was 'filthy stuff' and had no artistic merit. The major stumbling block at the time was whether or not nude pictures, sold as 'art studies', were pornography or art. As the Act did not say and juries became very confused, an Amendment in 1964 tried but failed to sort it out.

The history of the 1959 Act, and the moral crusades which followed, has gone through four phases which help to explain the inevitability of the contemporary campaign to banish soft core from the newsagents.

Between 1959 and 1970, individual crusaders attempted to maintain the pre-1959 definitions of obscenity, and to restrict access to it, through a series of private prosecutions or complaints to the police; the prosecution of a cheap paperback version of *Lady Chatterley's Lover*, to ensure that no man's wife or servant would read it, was only the most famous case. Though the crusaders enjoyed an occasional victory, they failed. In this phase, Art, Literature, sex education, and magazines featuring nudity became both legal and 'acceptable'. By 1970 millions of people had taken to British soft core; and the crusaders, who believed their coercive measures in the past had enjoyed widespread support, now blamed the law for the public's preference.

Having failed to maintain the old definitions, the crusaders changed their strategy in the second phase of the Act's history, which began with targeting the new 'sex supermarkets' in large towns, which threatened to make sex toys, lingerie, and pseudo-sexology respectable too. By 1971 there were a hundred or so, including thirty in Soho, turning over an estimated £3 million a year. Various local church groups lobbied their local councils, which in turn looked to the Conservative Government to prohibit the shops; but in May, Heseltine's Department of the Environment turned them down, arguing that 'the current climate of public opinion' was against more controls. Attempts by the Conservative MP Tom Iremonger to pass legislation giving authorities powers to control the opening and conduct of sex supermarkets, and a Sale of Offensive Literature Bill, merely revealed the division between pro-

and anti-censorship lobbies in Parliament. The 1972 Longford Report, designed to rouse Britain against this insidious threat, turned out to be a damp squib. In 1973, a Cinematograph and Indecent Displays Bill, which followed a spate of crusaders' complaints about advertising displays and the content of films, also failed to become law.

Crusaders managed to secure convictions against the 'underground' press with its mix of radical politics, sexual libertarianism, recreational drug use, and anti-war protests, because the 'Establishment' were unhappy too; their offspring not only brought this filth into the house, they even invited the authors home to raid the fridge. *International Times, Oz and The Little Red School Book* were declared obscene. Success, however, was restricted to material perceived to be a threat to children under the age of twenty-one. Juries were far less willing to convict 'men's magazines', mainly because two very clever barristers, Geoffrey Robertson and John Mortimer, utilized a group of doctors and psychologists whose justifications for soft core magazines and films sounded convincing. By the time this game had been restricted by the House of Lords' limitation on the public good defence, the crusaders' conception of obscenity now appeared on page three of the *Sun*, and gross depravity – pubic hair – could be bought in over 20,000 newsagents. Customs officers may have continued to restrict the import of more explicit material, but the 'sex supermarkets' remained unmolested, and general-release movies like *Emmanuelle* included simulated sex.

Soft core had made it, as long as penises remained limp and nothing entered an orifice. And that was the way it might have stayed, but for three events which ensured that pornography would re-emerge as a major 'social problem'.

The crusaders' belief that pornography was a communist plot had blinded them to the real culprits: the police. For over a decade, the Obscene Publications Squad licensed the growth of an unofficial 'red light' area in Soho, where, for a short period, the shops sold Scandinavian and Dutch magazines, and a number of sex cinemas screened uncertificated movies by taking advantage of the loophole in the 1954 Cinematographic Act. Once the Squad was exposed as the protection racket it was, the new force was determined to prove itself. The Labour Government, by appointing a Committee to review all obscenity laws, then ensured that pornography stayed in the headlines for two years. The most important factor, however, was the dramatic growth of Christian moral reform movements encouraged by the success of the National Viewers' and Listeners' Association, or National VALA.

Britain's moral majority

National VALA, which lobbied Parliament, initiated court cases, and collected petitions through churches and their media monitoring groups and churches, was joined by the Nationwide Festival of Light (NFOL), which sought to promote the 'regeneration of British moral standards', and the Community Standards Association movement, known as CSAs. Started in Cornwall by Ms Whitaker, CSAs quickly expanded as local single-issue campaigns became permanent groups promoting a mixture of both Christian and secular imperatives in their public rationales for opposing 'permissiveness', Cornwall's aim, for example, was

> to promote and explain the positive value of traditional Christian Standards and warn of the consequences of permissive values and practices threatening to take over our culture. . . .
> In spite of the increased material prosperity figures of violent crime have soared in the last 20 years.
> Rape, robbery and child molestation are all increasing.
> It has been established by nearly 750 pieces of scientific research that there is a link between violence on the television screen and in society. Violence, including sexual violence, on television and in the cinema, in 'girlie' magazines and now on video cassettes is contributing to tragedy in the lives of many.
> Children are being encouraged in early teenage sex by a 'you may do as you choose as soon as you can' message, sometimes reaching them through material taught in schools, certainly what they read in teenage magazines.
> You may be careful what your children see and hear, and the friends they make. But what is being shown and taught

to other children – and adults too for that matter? Soon they will all be adults together.

CSA members would appear on radio phone-ins and TV studio debates, and become prolific protest-letter writers and petition collectors, in order to raise important questions like Cornwall's about moral attitudes and developments in society. A single letter sent by a Devon CSA member led to the removal of pin-up magazines from a local Travellers Fare bookstall; and Cornwall CSA raised 27,000 signatures for National VALA's 1977 ABUSE campaign. Films refused local showings following CSA protests included *Caligula* and *The Life of Brian*. Sex education material from *Make It Happy* by Jane Cousins to gay-orientated material were constant targets. Teachers were encouraged to take alternative material from organizations like Family and Youth Concern. Portsmouth CSA even produced their own audio cassette, *Sex and Personal Relationships*, for distribution to several hundred schools. The most novel way of promoting family values, however, was the 'Family Seal of Approval' awarded to local newsagents who did not stock soft core.

In the long term, the NFOL proved to be the most important of the new groups. Established in 1971 after an evangelical 'Rally against Permissiveness' in Trafalgar Square, the NFOL enjoyed steady growth under Raymond Johnston, a member of the Church Assembly and the General Synod, but became transformed during the early 1980s under Lyndon Bowring, an Elim Church minister, and took the new name CARE: Christian Action Research and Education.

Adopting the American organizational approach, CARE pumped a lot of effort into providing sophisticated resources and expertise in a wide number of fields, mobilizing thousands of fundamentalists from its own local branches called 'Core' groups to those already in the medical, teaching and social welfare professions. Regular newsletters, 'Parliamentary Updates', campaign posters and leaflets covering everything from pro life issues to pornography constantly updated a massive crusade manual and set of Briefing Papers, which bettered anything ever produced by a political party, providing everything required to run a very professional campaign.

It was an alliance of these Christian groups with the Conservative Party's Lawyers Group that proved to be decisive in putting pornography back on the reform agenda. Since 1971, the Lawyers Group had been trying to convince the party that there were votes in moral issues; but while Heath, Whitelaw, and Heseltine were in power, this was unlikely to be successful. All that was to change with Mrs Thatcher, who saw the value of morality votes, and helped initiate the third phase in the history of the 1959 Act.

The third phase

The turn of the tide began with apparent defeats. 'Not guilty' verdicts against *Inside Linda Lovelace* in 1976, and *Libertine* magazine a year later, effectively ensured that textual 'pornography' would rarely be prosecuted again. Conservative Members began to complain that this was a scandal; and given what is written in *Inside Linda Lovelace* it was easy to see why they thought so. Their protests grew louder after Bogdanov's production of Howard Brenton's *The Romans in Britain* with its sodomy scene, and came to a head when Labour's Attorney-General failed to prosecute *A Thought in Three Parts*, which coincided with the publication of Mary Whitehouse's new book, *Whatever Happened to Sex?* The NFOL also waded in against the Government's proposal to abolish the right of private prosecutions against cinema obscenity.

Faced with these demands to 'clamp down' on 'pornography' in print, on cinema screens, and the stage from the Opposition benches, the Labour Government attempted to side-step the issue by appointing a Committee of Inquiry into obscenity legislation headed by Bernard Williams. With the Conservatives beginning to think that there might be something in moral votes after all, the scene was set for a symbolic battle over permissiveness with soft core as the main scapegoat.

For the sake of the children

Faced with the inevitable prospect of the decriminalization of pornography by the liberal Williams Committee, Mary Whitehouse did not panic; she created one. Like Stead before her, Mary Whitehouse brilliantly orchestrated a national scandal.

Contrary to her claims that the 1959 Act had so debauched the nation that perverts were now turning to child pornography, photographs of naked children were *not* new, and had nothing to do with a search for a more 'depraved kick' for those jaded by soft core. Sadly, the sexploitation of children is as old as the world, and child pornography as old as the photographic industry. In the late Victorian period photo-sets of 'green fruit', as pre-pubescent children were known, accounted for up to 30 per cent of the pornographers' catalogues. Whether this materialized into 30 per cent of sales to the high bourgeoisie who were the only ones who could afford them, we do not know. Nor do we know whether child sexploitation existed then because of the Victorian obsession with virgins, because it served as a means of avoiding sexually transmitted diseases, or because it amounted to an interest in paedophilia as we know it today. What we do know is that despite proliferating between 1900 and 1910, commercial child pornography had all but disappeared by 1975; and a short-lived attempt to create a market in the late 1970s failed, as active paedophiles were, unfortunately, more than capable of making their own.

What *was* really new was the emergence of a small public pressure group, the Paedophile Information Exchange, known as PIE; Mrs Whitehouse took advantage of PIE's stupidity and the public loathing of 'peds' to justify the silly ideas that child pornography was the inevitable result of sixties permissiveness, that it was widespread, and that *all* pornography should be outlawed to stop it.

PIE exposé articles peaked in September 1977, with the *Daily Mirror*'s 'Children in Sex Shock'. Popular anger boiled over; trade unionists threatened strike action if the British Psychological Association conference at Swansea even discussed the nature of the proclivity. National VALA quickly launched Action to Ban Sexual Exploitation of Children, known as ABUSE, and promptly repeated several fantastic stories about international 'kiddy porn' dreamed up by an American crusader, Dr Densen-Gerber, who had launched a similar campaign across the Atlantic some months before.

Three days after the Williams Committee met for the first time, Mrs Whitehouse met Margaret Thatcher, who promptly demanded that the Labour Home Secretary initiate immediate legislation. Mrs Whitehouse was reported to have seen magazines featuring girls of 'six, seven or eight years of age', some of whom were British. The *Daily Mirror* backed Mrs Thatcher and asserted that the police had just seized £200,000 worth of 'pornographic books and films showing young girls in sex acts' as a result of a *Mirror* investigation.

In reality, the police had merely undertaken another of their periodic raids on soft-core warehouses; and no prosecutions followed. Not surprisingly, no details about the 'kiddy porn' appeared in *The Mirror*'s article either; their proof that distribution was rife amounted to being 'disturbed by the recent trend of involving children in X films', such as Jodie Foster's role as a thirteen-year-old prostitute in *Taxi Driver*, the unsubstantiated claims of a 'sex shop assistant' who claimed that 'kiddy porn' was 'being shown' at 'trendy private parties', a reference to a defunct US magazine *Lollitots*, and half a dozen Letters to the Editor condemning PIE. This sensationalism even spread to *The Times*, whose leader the following morning, 6 September, gave its unqualified support to Mrs Thatcher's demands.

When Parliament resumed, the Conservative Opposition were determined to embarrass the Government, as MPs like Edward Gardener QC fell over themselves to demand that Labour's front bench 'stamp out the growth of this abominable industry' and not wait for the Williams Committee. Mr Rees's desperate attempts to assure the Commons that both the material and the offences leading to it could easily be prosecuted under existing legislation did not satisfy National VALA, whose rebuttal revealed their true target.

Mrs Whitehouse insisted that the 1959 Act was useless given that soft-core magazines in newsagents already 'featured obscene and indecent photographs of young women dressed as children'. Without supplying one title, Mrs Whitehouse suggested that:

> Such material surely amounts to incitement to commit offences against children? This vogue has inevitably led to the use of real children. The truth is that *in the whole area of public decency there has existed* in the Home Office, the Office of the Director of Public Prosecutions and the Office

of the Attorney General *a consistent unwillingness to take effective action*. It is this attitude which had finally put the Home Secretary at such a disadvantage now that he, the Government and the country are face to face with a form of exploitation which deeply shocks us all. [emphasis added]

Whatever they thought about the sexploitation of children, National VALA were clearly after soft core too. The public panic they helped create, with a circular letter to 270 provincial newspapers, was now so great that any attempt to suggest that the problem was being exaggerated in order to target soft core met with media condemnation. By then, an ABUSE petition had gathered over one and a half million signatures.

When Cyril Townsend, the Conservative MP for Bexley heath, and Chairman of the St Christopher's Fellowship, presented a Bill outlawing child pornography, he publicly distanced himself from ABUSE, but did not object to their lobbying on the Bill's behalf, or to flying in Dr Densen-Gerber to meet the Obscene Publications Squad. William Whitelaw, Sir Michael Havers, and Baroness Ellis, whose task it was to ensure that the Bill passed in the Lords. The good Doctor played her role as 'expert' to perfection, waving around magazines *unavailable* in Britain, and quoting grossly inflated statistics about the number of missing and sexploited children in the United States, all uncritically repeated by the media. Everyone seemed impressed by the ridiculous assertion that as Densen-Gerber had just cleaned up the USA, only Townsend's Bill stood between morality and Britain's becoming the centre of the 'paedophile movement', although this new rationale in effect admitted that previous statements about Britain being awash with the material were untrue. Face was then saved by a dramatic eleventh-hour 'confirmation' by James Anderton, the Chief Constable of Greater Manchester, who alleged that five per cent of his Vice Squad's seizures the previous year (which I worked out at 162,581 items with an estimated value of almost £500,000) were 'hard-core child pornography', and that a quarter were produced in Britain. This came as a surprise to the soft-core wholesalers whose distribution centre had just been raided and made up the bulk of the Manchester figures; but over four hundred MPs now attended the debate, which was a complete farce. Rational discussion was impossible, and the vote a foregone conclusion. Townsend played upon fears of an exodus from the USA, and wooed Labour back-bench support by suggesting children from low-income, Indian and West Indian families were most at risk – the first politically correct speech in Britain.

The origin of these fantasies was revealed when Townsend admitted that though it *was* impossible to prove that photograph-ing children for commercial purposes was on the increase in Britain, everyone he 'consulted' believed that it was. What he did 'know' was that legal soft core led its consumers to illegal hard core, which in turn led to sexual deviations, then on to the 'vile combination of violence and sex', then murder, and inevitably child porn. A lucra-tive market had been established in Britain, and would be exploited by pornographers filling the gap caused by American legislation. Proof of all this? The existence of PIE. David Young then reminded the House about Anderton's invisible haul, and Sir Michael Havers repeated Gerber's fantasies, which not only ignored the real cause and nature of child sexploitation, but have long since been debunked by American criminologists, legal scholars, and the US Government's own statistics.

Proof that the Act was unnecessary was then amply demon-strated by the police's ability to raid PIE members' houses looking for child pornography with warrants issued under the 1959 Act. The first prosecution under the new Act, involving a former sex cinema manager who possessed a dozen foreign films, could just as easily have been dealt with under the 1959 Act too. The trial of David Joy and Peter Bremner, which finally destroyed PIE, was also on an obscenity charge.

The real value of the Act was not, however, in its stated aim. Apart from casting a shadow over the impending Williams Report, by giving the crusaders their first real victory in a decade, the Act encouraged them to abandon their public morals rationale against commercial sex in favour of the highly emotive protection of chil-dren approach, and to abandon the attempt to utilize the 1959 Act in favour of gaining alternative legislation which outlawed material without the need to go to court. This new strategy ensured that the third phase of the history of the 1959 Act was a success for the crusaders. Within a decade they had obtained the Indecent Displays (Control) Act 1981, which curtailed sexual advertisement; the

Cinematographic Acts 1982 and 1985, which eliminated sex cinemas; the Video Recordings Act 1984, which reintroduced the concept of pre-censorship into Britain; and Clause 28 of the Local Government Act 1988, forbidding public funding of any art form deemed to be promoting homosexuality. Prosecutions and prohibitions under these Acts were then extended beyond the 'pornographic' to include nuclear war survival manuals, rock records, computer games, and women's wrestling. The most important measure, however, was Clause 3 of the Local Government (Miscellaneous Provisions) Act 1982, which closed hundreds of sex shops and ensured that newsagents became the major suppliers.

God's design for sexuality

The fact that Christians have been running a four-hundred-year-old crusade against sexually orientated material before finally forcing it to ground in newsagents means that there is something lacking in all those situational explanations offered by commentators about particular campaigns in the last twenty years: there must also be something common too. The most banal suggestion is that Christians have 'sexual hangups'; but as millions of others who suffer from 'hang-ups' do not join campaigns, this cannot be the sole reason; and in any case, explanations that do not take account of faith are disingenuous, because the Christians' first and foremost motivation is their belief. It always makes sense, if you want to know why people do something, to listen to what they say.

The major complaint on both sides of the Atlantic is that pornography promotes lust and promiscuity; but while this once depended upon simplistic rationales about 'original sin', these have since been replaced with more sophisticated theologies about God's design for sex. As this has been defined in numerous, but similar, ways, that of Morality in Media will suffice:

> Human sexuality was made by God and is good as long as it is used according to God's design. In Genesis we read of God creating man in His own image and likeness, ... then God joined the first man and woman together and blessed them and said: 'Increase and multiply and fill the earth; thus sex

was designed by God to be used only within the context of matrimony. It is something sacred and is necessarily related to the origin of human life as well as an expression of conjugal love and unity.

Humans, even in ignorance, are not supposed to tamper with any of God's designs, or this will have serious consequences for both the individual and for society. Pornography, however, is not ignorance; it is seen as a *deliberate* challenge to God's wish for monogamous marriage and procreative sex, because of its display of 'perversions' from His design; the most important being the negation of a necessary spiritual dimension, expressed through love. As the 1974 Lausanne Congress of World Evangelism made clear:

> Sex is ordained by God in the context of Love, which is essentially a spiritual factor. Christians must not underestimate the damage caused by over-emphasis on sex by adultery and promiscuity to the individuals involved and to society itself. Overemphasis on sex goes together with the loneliness of the young. There is a preoccupation with physical sexuality and this tends to heighten the loneliness felt by young people. Christians must not let go unchallenged the flood of pornography which involves the exploitation of the weakness of man and the corruption of his spiritual and moral nature. By attacking man in this way he is made an object of lust rather than a person made in the image of God. Pornography, in attacking the image of God in man, is an attack upon God Himself. In short, pornography is a destructive dehumanizing trade which exploits the weakness of consumers.

In other words, by emphasizing physical pleasure as opposed to love, pornography, like all other instrumental desires which do not conform to God's design, must be promoting lust. The sophistication ends there.

David Caton, head of the Florida chapter of Donald Wildmon's American Family Association and author of *Overcoming the Addiction to Pornography*, takes us back to procreation:

Oral sex and anal sex fit the category of 'sexual impurity for the *degrading* of their bodies.' God did not create our mouths or our rectums to be directly engaged with sexual organs. The eyes, ears, and nose are no more of a sex organ than is the mouth or rectum. Additionally, God did not give our mouths or our rectums a sexual reproduction purpose.

People like Caton still equate lust with sexual arousal; and he insists that 'there is no way you can look at a porn magazine without the intent to lust'. Others point to Scripture such as Matthew 5: 27–28 where Jesus proclaims that 'anyone who looks at a woman lustfully has already committed adultery in his heart'. Either way, pornography is condemned because it elevates physical feelings above the spiritual only obtained in marriage; and crusaders extrapolate from there into tautologies.

As all non-marital sex is a 'crime' against God's design for sex, it follows that pornography promotes 'sex crimes'. Pornography *must* likewise degrade and de-humanize people, because we are only truly human and in a state of grace by being created in God's image – unlike 'bestial' animals. Pornography *must* have an effect on people, because, being innately sinful, we simply cannot help being tempted. All similar criticisms follow from the belief that God *designed* sexuality to be expressed in marriage and to involve a relationship with a 'whole', God-created person.

Though these claims are often couched in secular terms, and are frequently backed up with references to apparently secular research, like Victor Cline's 1974 addiction model (according to which readers of pornography become addicted, escalate consumption, become desensitized, and then act out what they see); the conviction comes from religious faith, and the knowledge that God gives Christians greater insight than the non-churched. Be it when God speaks to them directly, through Bible study, or having been blessed by the Holy Spirit, evangelicals are convinced that their analysis of the world must be superior to that of others like criminologists who rely upon 'imperfect' and 'corrupt' secular reasoning. For example, the addiction model, which is used to suggest that it is futile merely to oppose hard core because soft core starts the craving for the 'harder' stuff and 'acting out' fantasies in the first place, must be true because that is the nature of sin. Judith Reisman, whose *Soft Porn Plays Hardball: Its Tragic Effects on Women, Children and the Family* has become a second Bible for Christians and the wrong one for separatists, denounced *Playboy* because it is 'gateway pornography', and leads to a desire for snuff movies, while leaving 'the spiralling rates of impotence, divorce, child abuse, and a host of other sadosexual tragedies' in its wake. Reisman is convinced that soft core deliberately sets out to subvert marriage and family in order to sell more pornography.

This anti-family theme, however, is merely a secular metaphor for God's design, as when Scott's *How Pornography Changes Attitudes* draws attention to the fact that

> pornography focuses almost exclusively on chance encounters between strangers, who suddenly arouse themselves to heavy, immediate sex, but without kindness, and without enduring emotional relationships. Never, in pornography, is there a hint that sexual intercourse produces children, whose rearing requires commitment and financial sacrifice on the part of the parents.

This threat to married love through husbands' 'unrealistic' expectations of their wives, who crusaders believe never view the material, is seen as an extremely dangerous trend, not just because the family is supposed to keep instrumental sexual desires under control, but, as Raymond Johnston argues in *Who Needs the Family*, because it is also the major social bulwark against all forms of godlessness from lesbianism to one-parent families.

For Christians, the best proof of these adverse effects, like the truth of Christianity itself, comes from the testimonies of the converted. Caton, for example, claims to be a saved porn addict, and so knows the dangers of this temptation; and his definition is a wide one. Pornography appears to be anything Caton finds sexually stimulating:

> Any magazines, catalogues, and even newspapers which could cause you to stumble must be removed from the home ... Feeding the eyes on such magazines as *Swimwear Illustrated* will cause the porn victim to desire more explicit material.... Newspapers often print brassiere, swimsuit,

and other advertisements which could spark an unhealthy desire for pornography.... Cable television should, by all means, be cancelled or at least all cable movie channels should be locked out, including MTV. Failure to remove this media will result in unnecessary temptations to watch the more liberal R-rated cable shows. The porn victim should stay away from television during the rehabilitation period. In other words, NO TELEVISION. It is not worth taking the chance of a sexually oriented advertisement or news flash causing the porn victim to stumble.... The movie cinema should also be avoided unless the movie to be watched can guarantee no skin scenes, including swimsuits.

Once one understands this applied theology, and the fear that ungodly sexual arousal will evoke in a Christian, it is easy to see why Christians are adamant that a link between pornography and sex crime *must* exist. Pornography, once it has enslaved enough people, not only destroys virtue and consideration for others, but weakens a country's resolve and opens it to attack from Satan.

The Christian critique of, and mobilization against, pornography, therefore, has far less to do with individual sexual hang-ups than with their applied theology. Pornography is perceived as an anti-Christian philosophy that deliberately seeks to undermine God's design and in doing so promotes sex 'crimes' ranging all the way from masturbation to rape. But why do Christian crusaders worry? Why not let the sinful and the perverts get on with it and receive their comeuppance on Judgement Day? Crusaders know they are not allowed to do that.

The Ezekiel factor

Crusaders are crusaders because they worry about God's 'collective judgement' upon sinful people, cities and nations. Clifford Hill, who rose to fame during the 'video nasty' campaign, thinks that:

It is worth remembering that of the 27 civilizations the world has so far known each one has collapsed through moral decay and corruption. The foundations of law and order in the Roman Empire were already crumbling long before the armies were defeated by the Huns. . . .

The same fate will overtake Britain in the near future with the systematic perversion of our children and the corrupt personal morals of large numbers of our citizens.

When God is displeased, he sends a sign of judgement in the form of economic, political, or social problems. If these signs are ignored the situation becomes worse, as the evangelical Gardner warned:

The Bible clearly shows that when one form of judgment fails to bring a people to repentance, God has to visit them with another judgment – of a more severe kind. And often he has to continue with another, and yet another. Each visitation takes a more serious form than the previous one, whilst all the time God is pleading with his people to return to him.

When the leaders and people of a nation such as our own stubbornly refuse to heed the warnings which have repeatedly been given and deliberately choose to ignore them, then God has to resort to far more stringent methods to bring them to their knees.

Yet Christians are not allowed to stand idly by while the ungodly suffer. The Book of Ezekiel warns them that no matter how devout they are themselves, Christians have a duty to alert the faithless to the dangers of their life-styles:

The word of the Lord came to me: 'Son of man, speak to your countrymen and say to them: "When I bring the sword against a land and the people of the land choose one of their men and make him their watchman, and he sees the sword coming against the land and blows the trumpet to warn the people, then if anyone hears the trumpet but does not take warning and the sword comes and takes his life, his blood will be on his own head. Since he heard the sound of the trumpet but did not take warning, his blood will be on his own head. If he had taken warning, he would have saved himself. But if the watchman sees the sword coming and does not blow the trumpet to warn the people and the sword comes and takes the life of one of them, that man will be taken away because of his sin, but I will hold the watchman accountable for his blood." '

It is this attempt to avoid further judgement, upon believers and non-believers alike, which encourages Christians to 'blow the trumpet' even louder on moral questions, by launching moral crusades. The 'Ezekiel factor', by linking private morality and the collective public good, means that salvation cannot be a private concern; it has to be public, collective, and national. And this is one of the reasons why the crusade against pornography has lasted so long, irrespective of situational factors or justifications.

Here we go again

Given their fears about collective judgement it is easy to see why most moral reformers in the past have come from the ranks of evangelical Christians.

The Societies for the Reformation of Manners made no secret of their moral imperative; as non-procreative sex was a sin and an act of rebellion against God, and as Government power ultimately derived from God, they had to police sex because

> the open and avowed Practise of Vice might provoke God to withdraw His Mercy and Blessings from Us, and instead thereof to inflict heavy and severe judgements.

The Societies' initiatives made sense to them because as judgement was collective, one had a right to ensure one's neighbour did not bring down God's wrath on everybody. Unfortunately, those who followed began to stray from that path.

The Vice Society, despite wishing to avoid collective judgement, played up fears of biological imbalance. Their concern that licentious publications were 'particularly fatal to the unsuspecting and unguarded minds of the youth of *both sexes*' was motivated by fears of working-class procreation, an economic concern – fears that non-marital sex drained people physically. Obscenity was becoming too 'democratic':

> it flies to the remotest corners of the earth – it penetrates the obscure and retired habitations of simplicity and innocence, it makes its way into the cottage of the peasant, into the house of the shepherd and the shop of the mechanic.

The activities of the Vigilance Associations towards the end of the nineteenth century also included secular sentiments, as this attack on H. G. Wells's *Ann Veronica* demonstrates.

> The loathing and indignation which the book inspires in us are due to the effect it is likely to have in undermining the sense of continence and self-control in the individual which is essential to a sound and healthy State.... Unless the citizens of a State put before themselves the principles of duty, self-sacrifice, self-control and continence, not merely in the matter of national defence, national preservation and national well-being, but also of the sex-relationship, the life of the State must be short and precarious. Unless the institution of the family is firmly founded and assured, the State will not continue.

This duality, whereby collective judgement was entwined with sexual fears like racial impurity and military defeat, while attempting to harness female sexuality to serve the state rather than God, continued well into the 1960s, and obviously raises questions about that kind of faith; but more importantly it shows how religious imperatives are confirmed by what crusaders perceive as God's signs.

The secular aspect of this rhetoric has fooled numerous historians like Jeffery Weeks, and hundreds of scatty feminists, who like Sheila Jeffreys are scrabbling for their non-existent antecedents; yet a cursory glance at the propaganda masquerading as science in that period will quickly reveal the moral judgements that lay behind them. It certainly did not fool contemporaries, as the archives of humanist journals like the *Freethinker* demonstrate.

A temporary return to more overt religious rationales by

crusaders after the Second World War followed from their need to maintain their identity as a religious group, and they can be seen clearly in the Clean Up TV campaign manifesto in the 1960s, despite Mary Whitehouse's recourse to secular causalism in public.

1. We women of Britain believe in a Christian way of life.
2. We want it for our children and country.
3. We deplore present day attempts to belittle or destroy it, and in particular we object to the propaganda of disbelief, doubt and dirt that the BBC projects into millions of homes through the television screen.

The reason why such sentiments were rarely heard in Parliament or the media at the time was because the crusaders moved away from *moral* rationales whereby the material condemned is innately wrong for one religious reason or another, to *causalist* rationales which place the emphasis upon the alleged adverse social effect of an action or idea. People simply did not think in terms of righteousness and sin any more; and the crusaders sought to accommodate to that fact. This did not so much reflect a decline in the influence of religion, but was a question of tactics: the crusaders knew that causalism had been used to justify permissive legislation from the mid-1950s onwards, and were replying in kind. The three most important causalistic rationales advanced by crusaders during the 1970s were: avoiding violence, which along with sex crimes became a metaphor for immorality generally; the concept of sex-ploitation, a metaphor for lust; and avoiding 'offending' femininity, the metaphor for spirituality. These worked rather well to begin with, because, as we saw, women's attitudes to sex and fear of sexually orientated materials had been shaped by the moral crusaders' campaigns.

Behind these secular rationales, however, crusaders are collectively attempting to apply biblical standards to contemporary society; while individually, they are merely promoting values and beliefs that have been taught and which are maintained by their church community.

The Christian critique and opposition to pornography, therefore, has nothing to do with alleged content or 'new' and 'scientific' evidence about effects; it follows from Christian belief about God's design for human sexuality, and the Ezekiel factor: God's judgement upon a community. In the last decade this factor has also been reinforced by a belief that the contemporary ills facing society are a sign that the end-time of the Book of Revelation is upon us, and that Christ's arrival is imminent.

Summary

The earlier crusades against sexually orientated material reveal that campaigns do not necessarily highlight their real rationale, and that they frequently feature bizarre horror stories to raise public fears. Despite constant claims that the material has an automatic adverse effect, the crusaders believe that no one should read or see material that arouses them anyway, as this may lead them to engage in sexual practices crusaders disapprove of. Core complaints about the nature and ascribed meaning of soft core, such as degradation, objectification and so on, follow from religious beliefs about the relationship between humans and God. Likewise, one can clearly see how many so-called 'feminist' rationales are really religious, and that their proposal for a new law also follows the preceding crusaders' practice of attempting to codify their beliefs into law.

History, however, demonstrates that once the crusaders achieve legislation, the range of material targeted suddenly increases beyond the original stated aim. Without exception, obscenity laws have been used to promote private as well as public sexual standards. These standards were used to stigmatize and persecute not only homosexuals, lesbians, and other sexual minorities, but any unmarried sex. Far from controlling men's lust *per se*, the crusades sought to enforce the idea that female sexuality was restricted to procreation. As the possibility of pregnancy could lead to female reticence, the crusaders then deliberately restricted sex education and birth control material in an attempt to ensure that women who dared to risk a sexual encounter would get pregnant, while the social purity crusades sought to punish those who might do so out of wedlock.

The ultimate aim and effect, until recently, was to induce women to conform to the crusaders' beliefs about female sexuality.

As a result, women have always suffered more than men from crusades. As an overt Christian message in the age of feminism has as much chance of success as insisting that the end of the world is nigh, recent rationales have concentrated on fear of marital breakdown, and the protection of children, to suggest that the price of pornographic sex is too high.

Chapter two

Soft Core and Sex Shops

FAR from reflecting a feminist concern over content or effects, soft-core magazines suddenly became a focus of attention at the turn of the decade because newsagents were the only readily accessible legal outlet for pornography left in Britain. The Christian crusaders' victories against sex cinemas, sex shops, and video nasties made the dispute about the 'top shelf' inevitable; and to understand why, we need to go back to Soho.

Soho

The half square mile between Regent Street and Charing Cross Road known as Soho has always been associated with commercial sex; but though Soho's first known record in history is the 1641 trial of a 'lewd woman', the extent of prostitution has always been exaggerated, and the association with pornography is very recent. In the nineteenth century the 'obscene' book trade was centred in Holywell Street, and the interwar under-counter trade was dissipated across London. Give or take the Windmill Theatre, Soho's reputation as Britain's sex capital was a media creation.

Between 1950 and 1970, media exposés, court cases, films and novels like Victor Russell's *People of the Night*, hyping the Maltese pimps, clubs, and clip joints, acted as a self-fulfilling prophecy, drawing potential customers and hence more suppliers to the area. Wortley's description of the late 1960s in *Skin Deep in Soho* gives some indication of the result:

> Trip up and down the Soho wooden staircases . . . for
> camera clubs and their models, strip clubs and their strip-

pers, prostitutes and their clients, film editors and their star-let celluloid belles, sex films and dull bedroom clichés on hot afternoons, blue films where penis entering vagina marks them from implied intercourse, duos male (rare), duos female (not so rare), the smell of oil paint on canvas, life classes at St Mary's School of Art, display cases of home movies with June Palmer and Harrison Marks still King and Queen, vast supplies of sub-literature with cheap covers, small club cinemas, like the Cameo Compton, Old Compton Street, and the Dilly, Old Windmill Street, or the more general cinemas in the Charing Cross Road that switch rapidly and confusingly between Art and Tart, and the ancient commercial trick of changing titles, *The Girl from the Dead Sea* converted to *Seduced in Sodom*.

But while the media found the misdeeds of the Maltese Messina brothers, Frank Misfud, and Bernie Silver good copy, the residents were more worried about the threat of redevelopment.

Sohoites were proud of their cosmopolitan tradition based upon generations of immigrants from the Huguenots to the Chinese, who all brought unique trades, crafts, and restaurants. This is where Ministers of the Crown came to dine, and where Orwell's hero Gordon Comstock blew his royalties. Those wishing to entertain at home could find fresh goat's milk at the Oxford Express Dairy, fresh pasta from Lina Stores, choice coffee and French delicacies from Madam Bourbon's, and Chinese fare in Gerrard Street. Numerous specialist shops, housed between the craft workshops, sold the products of jewellers, gold- and silver-smiths, watchmakers, lace makers, bookbinders, gunsmiths, cobblers, and musical instrument makers. Each shop or craft had its own history contributing to the folklore of Soho, which also boasted the birthplaces or residences of the famous from William Hazlitt to Karl Marx, the anecdotes of the Bohemians, Shaftesbury Avenue based theatre-land, 139 film production companies, and institutions from Smith's Hospital for Women to the British Board of Film Censors. The compact sex industry which had grown up around Paul Raymond's Windmill Theatre, the bars, and the prosti-tutes added even more colour.

Once they realized this way of life was in danger, residents founded a Soho Society to oppose numerous redevelopment plans threatening to destroy everything including listed buildings under a ton of concrete, offices, and car parks. Soho would become an after-five ghost town.

By 1975, the Society had forced several developers to a compromise, and hustled the local Westminster Council to provide better community facilities; but block after block was still falling to development corporations who were not adverse to deliberately cutting off services, making property dangerous, and even physically threatening tenants. The crux of the problem was Use Class Orders.

Under the 1971 Town and Country Planning Act, and subsequent amendments, every British building could be given a Use Class Classification, known as an Order. Once an Order was granted, the nature of any business in the building was not supposed to change without new planning permission from the local council, and a new Order. A company buying residential accommodation, for example, was not supposed to turn it into offices without the correct authorization.

Compared to this threat, 'the Vice', as the sex industry is known locally, was hardly a problem; but once the grandiose plans to transform Soho into a profitable business centre – with its vicious circle of demolition, increased rents, amenity decline, depopulation, increasing opportunities for redevelopment, demolition – were abandoned after the property crash, 'the Vice', by willingly paying high prices for short-term run-down sites, became embroiled in the three-cornered clash between the Society, the developers, and Westminster Council, which was not averse to hiking up their rates and seemed to resent the residents' opposition to the destruction from Piccadilly to the Charing Cross Road.

Between 1976 and 1982, almost anything was available in Soho, at a price determined by the customer's shrewdness. There were 54 sex shops; 39 sex cinemas and cinema clubs; 16 strip and peep shows; 11 sex-orientated clubs; and 12 licensed massage parlours. At least 18 establishments contained two or more different operations. A single building could contain a club in the basement, a sex shop at ground floor level, nude photographic models (Polaroids provided) on the next floor, and a prostitute or two above. Sex shops and peep shows would invariably contain film or video booths too. Many of the premises were in blocks where the buildings were interconnected by corridors, enabling a convenient exit for a manager, doorman or sex workers who wished to avoid the law. There were also numerous other premises, providing other services accessible only to those in the know; but that's another story.

The battle between the Society and 'the Vice' began when the Society went to court to stop evictions and the four hundred per cent increases in rent demands by developers designed to encourage standing tenants to leave. A local trader seeking a rate reduction because the sex club next door was allegedly losing him trade had his appeal turned down when the Council brazenly insisted his premises' rates would be higher if a sex club took over his business. Though the real villain was the Council, which was freely dispensing massage parlour licences at the time, 'the Vice' now found itself in the front line. By hogging leases, being obsessed with super profits, and riding roughshod over the local community, they foolishly began to replicate the sins of property speculators; and once the threat to Soho could be presented as a battle against erotica-filled windows rather than finance capital, everyone suddenly wanted to preserve the old Soho – everyone, it seemed, apart from the Council.

The Council dismissed the residents' appeals for a change in the planning law, by claiming it was helpless until government acted. While there was some truth in this, some Westminster councillors were turning a blind eye to broken Use Class Orders in their own premises.

Although several 'Vice' premises were legally taking advantage of a loophole in the law, most of the premises were illegal. Buildings with retail Orders could change the items sold without new planning permission. There were exceptions to this rule, but sex shops were not one of them. So all it took to legally open a sex shop was to secure the lease of a retail Order shop, fill it with stock, and open the door. Unless another law, like the 1959 Act, was broken, owners could trade anywhere. Many of the sex premises, however, were opening in buildings without the appropriate Order. As owner of some of these properties, the Council could have taken immediate action; but, according to Society members, it did not even check the covenants!

The Conservative-run Greater London Council was not much help either. Its much-lauded anti-vice campaign in the late 1970s failed to materialize, being no more than the latest in a long line of vote-catching promises; when the police finally did take action, raiding several cinema clubs, like *L'Erotic* in Frith Street, at the behest of GLC Arts Committee moral crusaders, it had nothing to do with Soho's real problems. Committee members were scrabbling for the moral high ground: the Conservatives in another attempt to embarrass the Labour Government's 'inaction' on obscenity, and Labour members in order to prove they were equally 'concerned'. The police took advantage of this to continue their favourite sport: persecuting soft-core film maker, John Lindsay.

Several of Lindsay's movies had been acquitted at Birmingham Crown Court in 1974. He then opened a shop in Soho at 37 Berwick Street which retailed the acquitted films. Annoyed at the Birmingham fiasco, the London police raided the store, and took 16 films to the Old Bailey in 1977. Lindsay was acquitted for a second time. In 1981, the same films were then taken before Ealing Magistrates, who ordered forfeiture. Before the appeal was heard, Lindsay was raided eight times in an effort to close him down; but he won again, and Judge Cassel severely criticized the police's actions, ordered the films to be returned, and awarded him costs. Rather than accept this decision, the police promptly set up five separate trials at Knightsbridge Crown Court before Mr Justice Babington. The first trial produced a hung jury; and the second: not guilty. Once again, costs were paid out of public funds; the judge denounced the prosecutions as 'vexatious' and a 'shocking waste of public money'. The real point to note, however, was that contrary to natural justice, Lindsay was repeatedly being tried for the same films and offence – a typical example of how the police will use censorship laws for their own purposes. Judge Bruce Campbell was in no doubt: Lindsay was being harassed by the police. Given that the GLC was contemporaneously ordering 5400 canes for London schools from a sex shop, these kinds of raids could also be considered somewhat hypocritical.

Finally running out of patience with the authorities, the Society stood its own candidates in the 1978 local elections. Despite a hasty Conservative-arranged media tour of Soho complete with headline sound-bites about eradicating 'the Vice', and the sudden

Planning Committee 'discovery' of a dramatic increase in sex shops, the Society's candidates topped the poll. Unfortunately outsiders did not know what was really going on.

In 1979, when Hugh Rossi promoted an Indecent Display Bill, Soho was everyone's excuse; yet when future Heritage Minister Peter Brooke alluded to the displays found there, few realized that they existed courtesy of Council inaction. Likewise with the 'gravely offensive' displays facing the children's playground, which so 'disgusted' MPs. The Society then discovered that the Council *had* enforced a sex shop Closure Order: but on Ram Books in the Victoria Road, Westminster. Rumours that Westminster Council and the new Conservative Government, despite their pledge to return to Victorian standards, were quite happy to leave Soho to 'the Vice' were rife. Many believed the Conservatives were turning Soho into offices by day, and a red light zone at night to solve the pornography problem. True or false, it might have happened if the false confidence that Westminster Council's inaction generated had not led to 'the Vice's' attempt to expand, and led to the fatal mistake of picking Portsmouth.

'Heaven's light our guide'

While National VALA were running their ABUSE campaign, and the Soho Society were pulling their hair out, residents in a quiet residential street in Portsmouth were demanding that their local council close the makeshift, 32-seat, Apollo cinema club. Operating in a disused shop, showing the hard-core *Swedish Erotica*, the owner kept the Planning Department at bay between 1977 to 1979, when three local churches and almost 100 members of the Portsmouth Association for Community Standards, known as PACS, threw their weighht behind the protest.

PACS was founded in 1977 to oppose a new sex shop in Queen Street. Despite lobbying PTAs, Townswomen's Guilds, and Church groups, writing numerous protest letters, and local radio coverage, PACS was unable to persuade the council, and switched its attention to local newsagents and other typical CSA issues. Having gained experience and strength there, PACS helped gain a

DOE inquiry which established the cinema's change of retail use during August 1979.

Incredibly, it was at this point that the Soho-based Holloway family sought to open a sex cinema club in the city; and if that was not dumb enough, their choice of building was the crassest move ever made by a pornographer. The former Royal Sailor's Rest is not only an imposing building on the corner of Edinburgh Road, adjoining the main shopping area and facing Queen Street, which leads past the Catholic Cathedral and naval shore bases towards the dockyard and HMS *Victory*; it was also the post-war flagship of Aggie Weston's hostels, the Christian alternative to the brothels, gin houses, pubs and bawdy entertainment once found in this seaport. Although recent use had been restricted to Billy Graham film shows, and the doors had closed in 1972, the 'Rest' obviously held a special place in the hearts of many Portsmouth service personnel and evangelical civilians.

Early in 1980, the Holloways' Bardengold Ltd acquired the lease, and applied for permission for a private cinema club. Uproar ensued. Protest letters in the local newspaper alluded to the fact that no one wanted to live in another Soho; and several letters to the Council, which safeguards the city's motto, 'Heaven's Light Our Guide', told it that it had a responsibility to the parents of young students and sailors to ensure they would not be corrupted. Moral objections, however, are not good enough grounds to refuse planning permission when properly applied for; and as movies had been shown in the building there was not even a change of use, let alone an illegal one like the Apollo.

Cynics might have thought that as two other city cinemas, The Tatler and the Palace Continental, had been showing soft-core sex films for a number of years without complaint and that the former also featured an afternoon strip show, why worry about the 'Rest'; but a flood of letters to the media and the Council encouraged the latter to find a reason to justify denying Bardengold's plan.

Scanning the relevant sections of the Williams Report provided no excuses; but then a junior officer came up with three possible objections: the adverse effect on adjoining shops and premises; the proposed new shopping centre; and the residents in the nearby students' hotel. Given the existence of a gay bar with transvestite staff next door to the 'Rest', an infamous 'disorderly' public house, and a night-club better known for its fist-fights than its music less than two minutes away, these objections seemed somewhat curious. Planning rejections usually rest upon traffic problems, lack of parking, noise or nuisance; and there was no proof that a private club of 300 members would cause any of these problems.

Councillor Williams, however, had had enough. Someone had to call a halt and represent the growing public protest; and he persuaded the Planning Committee, which he chaired, to turn down the application. After hearing a delegation from PACS argue that the cinema would attract sexual deviants, putting both women and children using a nearby park at risk, the Committee agreed an 'adult' cinema would 'potentially' have a degrading effect on a proposed shopping centre. These moral undertones were then seized upon by Terry Wallis, Bardengold's local design consultant, who lodged an immediate appeal.

Councillor Williams, however, was not to be denied; determined to keep a mini Soho out of Portsmouth, he ignored the Planning Officer's advice that it was hopeless to resist and began a search for an academic or a doctor who could prove that sex cinemas led to sex crimes. In these circumstances, the local constabulary's refusal to join the dispute was a serious blow. The only good news was that the protest campaign was snowballing, because the Holloway family had a death wish.

Instead of simply continuing to the inevitably favourable appeal, the Holloways pulled a typical Soho stunt and made a second application using a front company called Stonerealm Ltd, which wished to show 'minority interest films'. But Soho scams do not work in Portsmouth; and by provoking a company search it transpired that one of Stonerealm's major shareholders was a Ronald Braverman, who crusaders knew was linked to Dr Johnson's Enterprises, the world's largest suppliers of sex toys, which had been subjected by American crusaders to rumours of association with 'organized crime'. Apart from having their second application turned down, the Holloways now found themselves subject to two exposés in the local paper on 16 and 17 September. The first, 'Dossier on Film Club Plan', revealed the nature of the Holloways' premises at 8–10 Brewer Street and 9 Greek Street, and exacerbated popular fears of the Soho to come if the appeal failed.

If that did not work, the second feature, 'The Sex War', did. Covering the Soho Society's perennial battle with 'the Vice' in general, and Stonerealm's complete disregard of planning regulations in particular, it convinced many readers that the Holloways were moving out of an overcrowded Soho, lock, stock and barrel, to Portsmouth, and that others would inevitably follow.

With PACS maintaining popular protest, the appeal under Mr Miverton, at the local Guildhall on 25 November found Bardengold, despite good grounds for appeal, on the defensive. All their homework about comparative problems concerning the City's rowdy pubs, including a new one built right in front of the war memorial, being ignored by the Conservative Council went to waste. The Council played the Soho card to the full with the Planning Officer alluding to the 'positively appalling' threat posed to the new centre's shoppers running the gauntlet of sex shops and cinemas. Backed up by supplementary evidence from Westminster's Assistant Planning Officer, Bardengold's fate was sealed. The description of the demise of traditional Soho placed solely on 'Vice' planning irregularities climaxed with the revelation that the Holloways' six premises were among the worst offenders and target of Westminster's 'vigorous enforcement policy'! PACS and the City's senior solicitor then welded a link between moral and commercial objections, and the inspector was handed the protest letters and petitions, along with a list of Stonerealm's previous prosecutions. The Holloways' Soho past had caught up with them, and it was almost inevitable that the Inspector would refuse the appeal, though the official reasons made far less sense than the moral objections. It was decided that the cinema would be 'incongruous and quite out of place' with the shopping centre, client noise would affect the sleep of local residents, and that there were not enough parking facilities. Yet the shopping centre did not materialize for a decade; the Council was flagrantly ignoring the desperate appeals of Southsea residents' requests to control the noise and damage caused by the night-club users in that area; few people lived near the proposed cinema; after the appeal, the Council promptly stuck a new student hostel next door to its own concert hall; and the Commercial Road area boasts a computer-controlled parking scheme for several thousand cars. As the Inspector failed to comment on the main argument – previous Holloway activities in

Soho – it is impossible to say how far the moral objections impressed the DOE; but the application failed.

The Holloways' blunder meant that not only was the loop-hole enabling sex cinemas to spring up anywhere closed by the 1982 Cinematographic Act; sex shops were next.

Sex shops

After 1972, when the campaign against sex supermarkets was quashed by Heseltine and the Conservatives, sex shops enjoyed an unmolested growth until October 1980, when Pimlico residents obtained a writ stopping a new outlet from trading. Then David Sullivan decided everyone should hear about them. This ex-LSE student had made a fortune turning soft-core magazines into an explicit display of female genitalia and exploiting the lack of hard-core material in the UK by constantly changing his titles and using several that sounded like well-known Continental products to maintain profitable confusion. As well as producing several feature-length simulated sex films, touted as 'hard core' to his gullible readers, expanding mail-order services, and becoming a power within Soho, Sullivan had been expanding his provincial operations for some time.

The methods were simple: find a town, persuade local news-agents to stock material on extremely favourable sale or return agreements; and, where viable, obtain a retail lease, stock it with magazines and vibrators, inform the local press you are about to open, and ask the readers to comment. The effect was predictable. Following the initial front-page story, editorials, the letter pages, and further features provided Sullivan's Congate company with thousands of pounds' worth of free publicity for the cost of a postage stamp. The tactic was even repeated in some towns without a shop! Between 1978 and 1981 over a hundred sex shops from Alton to Whitstable were opened in this way. The atmosphere produced in each locality is illustrated by the tone of provincial press comment: 'Demo at Sex Shop' (*Bristol Evening Post*); 'Churchman in Anti-Porn Action against Sex Shop', 'Fears of Rape if Shop Opens' (*Bedford Times*); 'Council of Churches Join the Protest against Sex Shop', 'Sex Shop – a Step Backwards' (*Hitchin*

Comet; 'Churches Attack Sex Shop Plan' (*Wolverhampton Express & Star*); 'Degrading to Have Sex Shop in Town' (*Lancashire Evening Telegraph*); 'War on Porn Hots Up' (*Southampton Evening Echo*); 'City Leaders Say "No" to Sex Shop' (*Salisbury Journal*); 'Sex Shops the Target as Porn Storm Grows' (*Press and Journal*, Aberdeen); 'Fury Grows in Sex Shop Row' (*Romford and Havering Observer*); 'Unsavoury Shop Will Degrade, Protect the Vulnerable' (*East Essex Gazette*); 'Sex Shops Exploit Females, Honour Must Be Restored' (*Colchester Evening Gazette*); 'Sex Store Plans in Bad Taste' (*Lytham St Anne's Express*); 'Storm Rages over Sex Shop Cinema' (*Lancashire Evening Telegraph*); 'Churchmen Rap Sex Shop Plan, Degrading to Women and to Family Life' (*Camberley News*); 'Dean's Attack on Sex Shop' (*Surrey Comet*); 'No Sex Shop Please – This Is Guildford' (*Surrey Daily Advertiser*); 'Over 6000 Sign against a Sex Shop in Clacton' (*East Essex Gazette*).

Sullivan may have been laughing all the way to the bank; but the engineered high profile of his Private or SVEN shops in High Streets drew attention to all sex shops, many of which had been trading quietly for a decade or more. The row that blew up in Barnsley proved crucial. For the first time a local protest made national headlines.

The shop opened on 3 January 1981, opposite a school in Doncaster Road, Ardsley. Despite the obligatory ritual raid by the police, the Council found itself powerless: there was no change of retail use. A picket and petition lasting several months by a moral action group got nowhere; then patience snapped. Paint was sprayed on windows, slates ripped from the roof, signs smashed, walls daubed, and locks filled with glue. But if it was the violence which drew the media to Barnsley, the manager ensured they persisted with the story by threatening to 'swamp' the town with sex shops:

> If they think they have a problem now, they will not know what has hit them soon ... We will turn Barnsley into a sex shop centre until the town is synonymous with Soho!

When juxtaposed with baby-carrying mothers of local schoolchildren, who according to the headmaster had no other topic of conversation, such fighting talk spells disaster; even Sullivan's unprecedented conciliatory noises failed to stop the rot. Sex shops were national news; and this was just the boost the CSA movement had been hoping for.

CSAs *and sex shops*

Sullivan's publicity ensured that CSAs could now call upon the newly aware to kick-start their previous campaigns back into life. Though they were not the only groups involved, Christians and CSAs were the most prominent and effective. Guildford fundamentalists flooded the *Surrey Advertiser* with letters. Harwich evangelicals ensured that a shop would not open there. Another evangelical mission achieved the same result in Sutton. The Elim Church led public protest in Rochdale. All denominations joined in Camberley's campaign. Canon Richard Gregory led hymn singing and prayer outside Keighley's shop. Following Congate's letter, the moderator of Bedford Baptist Church launched a campaign against pornography in general, suggesting that people locally had turned their backs on God. The Hitchin Council of Churches protested against another sex shop proposal. Derby's Christian Trade Union Association petition collected 3000 signatures. Paisley's Campaign for Common Decency, including pickets, petitions and hired solicitors, was the work of National VALA supporters. Whether or not these protests had some bearing on Congate's decision not to open shops, they were skirmishes; the ultimate victory against Congate belongs to the dedicated persistence of CSAs.

Typical was the 1980 protest against the Wavertree sex shop on Merseyside, where Charles Oxley got the local Action Group to lobby residents and maintain a daily picket. One Wavertree petition of over 11,000 signatures was presented to Downing Street on 16 July, and another, eight days later, to Parliament. The group's publicity leaflet summarizes standard objections:

> . . . sex shops are now being opened in towns and cities throughout the length and breadth of the land causing great offence and concern to right-thinking members of society;
> . . . a private company already claims to be engaged in a

multi-million-pound expansion programme to establish a chain of at least one hundred sex shops throughout the UK;

... such shops sell pornographic literature, large colour posters of a lewd and indecent nature, obscene articles used to stimulate sexual activity and encourage sexual perversions, films and video tapes showing explicit sexual scenes, perversions and sexual violence;

... such shops offer contact services for prostitution and sodomy;

... the presence of such shops is highly offensive and [they]

(1) are a temptation and a danger to young persons who become addicted to pornography,

(2) are an insult to young children who see obscene posters through open doors of such shops,

(3) attract people of undesirable repute to the areas of these shops,

(4) are a source of evil which damages respect for womanhood, degrading the sanctity of sexual relationships within marriage, undermining family life.

In the early 1980s the CSAs made most of the running. Merseyside 'bought out' the St Helens sex shop for £5,000. Enfield CSA initiated petitions and protest letters to present to Tim Eggar MP – the shop did not open. In Poole and Christchurch, East Dorset Family Concern collected 1500 signatures from twenty local churches and held a demonstration at the Bournemouth sex shop to show Congate what to expect. Two hundred people from twelve local churches joined forces to protest against the shops in Bristol. Worthing CSA, prepared in advance by spotting an advertisement for the future shop's manager, called a public meeting attended by three hundred when the shop opened in 1981. A petition with 5,398 signatures was then sent to the local MP and shop pickets were organized.

CSAs were convinced that new planning controls and a special Use Class Order were required, and on 23 March 1981, three Scottish MPs – Dundee's Gordon Wilson and Ernie Ross, and Angus South's Peter Fraser – backed Scottish sex shop protests and attempted to amend the Local Government (Miscellaneous Provisions Scotland) Bill along these lines. The House divided 163 to 114 against – a close vote given the Scottish Under-Secretary Malcolm Rifkind's argument that sex shops defied definition, that the existing law was sufficient, and that licensing made more sense. Three days later, National VALA's Dr Mawhinney's Early Day Motion on planning law secured the support of 68 MPs.

It was in this climate that Portsmouth made its move. Encouraged by their victories against the sex cinemas, PACS returned to the sex shop issue, targeting Sullivan's new SVEN – the city's fifth. Councillor Williams, who swopped ideas with Barnsley Councillors, was convinced that the level of protest demonstrated that the climate of public opinion, used to dismiss action in 1971, had now changed and he sought a meeting with Mr Heseltine at the DOE to tell him so. Giles Shaw, replying for the Minister, told Councillor Williams that planning controls should not be used because morality was involved – the same rationale Heseltine had used a decade before; and no, a delegation would be useful given that sex shops were a local issue. This was not the complete truth.

The Government, clearly worried by CSA protests, had already decided to deflate the issue by using the GLC to introduce a licensing system in Soho, and revealed as much on 7 May to Teddy Taylor, a CSA supporter, who had wanted to clarify Mr Ryman's statement during the Indecent Display debate which had rejected licensing for giving sex shops respectability. PACS and Councillor Williams were not going to accept the Government's brush-off; and Providence ensured they did not have to. Hampshire County Council, like the GLC, was also in the process of preparing a General Powers Bill; and as part of the county, Portsmouth was entitled to include clauses. Planning controls on sex shops were an obvious choice.

Sexual licence

The Government's sudden conversion to controls came as a surprise to the Soho Society. Once they uncovered the Ram Books decision they had vigorously lobbied Peter Brooke, and lambasted Westminster Council for leasing property opposite the school playground in Great Windmill Street to a Nude Encounter Parlour. This

Council inaction was put in perspective by Sutton Estates, which had no problems evicting a cinema club from 30 Great Windmill Street ten days after it had opened in February 1980, by gaining an injunction, with the police carrying out the eviction. Society members then packed a local Conservative Party meeting where Mr Heseltine was speaking and demanded to know what he was going to do. The Environment Minister gave the usual reply about moral judgements and Use Class Orders, before passing the buck: as sex shops were a national issue they were the Home Secretary's prerogative. Given Shaw's rejection of Portsmouth's requests on the grounds that sex shops were a local issue, the Conservative Government were up to something; but what? The mystery deepened when Soho councillors, surmising that planning controls were a non-starter, wrote to Mr Whitelaw requesting licensing, only for the Home Office to reply that such control was not needed as present legislation (i.e. planning law) 'adequately' covered existing situations. This merry-go-round could not go on for ever; something had to give.

The Society's councillors had started the ball rolling by opening up the hitherto closed Westminster Planning Sub-Committee, and could now ensure their concerns were taken seriously. This was matched at national level by Tim Sainsbury's Indecent Display Bill. Its easy passage not only demonstrated that controls could and would win Parliamentary support; it worked. Most of Soho's displays disappeared or were toned down within days. The implications were not lost on the Government. In April 1981, as the provincial pressure for sex shop controls mounted, the Home Office and DOE agreed to meet a London delegation. The Society backed the planning law option. Mr Whitelaw offered licensing, and tried to buy them off with the promise that despite only covering sex shops, a GLC Bill would slip through the House faster than a national scheme. Given the Government's large 'Victorian standards' majority, this was a ridiculous suggestion; but the GLC readily agreed, and by May 1981 had an appropriate clause for their Bill drafted by the Home Office. But the Government had not bargained for the persistence of Councillor Williams and PACS.

The Government's licence scheme for Soho seriously threatened Williams' plans, because the Conservative Hampshire Council began to soft-peddle on their Bill's sex shop planning provision.

Other Portsmouth Councillors balked at the expense, and an embarrassing incident involving the Fawcett Road sex shop threatened the whole enterprise. Once the owners realized they did not possess a correct Order, they sought to 'regularize' their status and won because no one had objected before February 1981. Without PACS stepping up their campaign this defeat could have convinced Portsmouth Council to follow the Government proposals; but a huge public meeting in July 1981, and more petitions, kept the campaign alive and enabled Councillor Williams to approach the DOE again: licensing in Soho would mean Portsmouth being swamped with sex shops, so it could not be a 'local' issue.

The Government pulled out all stops to block him. A Ministerial statement during the 23 June Adjournment Debate backed licensing, and on 22 July the Association of District Councils came out against planning controls because of the moral issues and backed the Soho plan. The DOE rejected the second delegation request, by now suggesting that a Portsmouth delegation was futile given that sex shops were a national issue! And the Home Office did likewise, on the grounds the GLC scheme would provide a test for licensing systems *before* the Government decided on a national method.

Something very odd was going on. Everyone was being led to believe that the Soho licensing scheme was a dummy run for national licensing, in order to stop any alternatives gaining an airing. John Wells' proposed Sex Bookshop (Control) Bill, for example, was blocked by another DOE anti-planning statement in July, on the erroneous grounds that changing planning controls would take longer than introducing licensing. As monitoring the GLC scheme and implementation of a national Act would take at least four years, the statement was untrue; especially as the GLC scheme did not really exist. The London boroughs had not been officially informed, let alone consulted, and the earliest a GLC decision would be made was 13 November. But while things looked bad for Councillor Williams, it is always darkest before the dawn.

GLC officers had accepted the licensing scheme only because the Government promised an easy passage, but once the CSA campaign pushed other councils, like Lancashire's into backing planning too, the GLC began to reconsider its position. The Home Office were now stuck, and hastily granted Portsmouth a delegation on 8 October. Though the aim was to shut them up, the Home Office were in for a shock.

No council was prepared to ditch planning unless the Government introduced national legislation. Councillor Williams also had an answer to all the previous excuses, including the 'need' to monitor the GLC experiment. Raising the spectre of provincial 'Sohos', he suggested that several different schemes could be monitored. The DOE were without an argument. And the Government was facing defeat in Parliament. Trying to justify singling out Soho with the threat of an exodus to the provinces in the face of the County Bills may just have been possible by offering an easy passage for a GLC Bill; but this was no longer guaranteed either. David Webb's National Campaign for the Reform of the Obscene Publications Act, or NCROPA, had uncovered the little-known right for individuals to petition against County Bills, and they had done just that with the GLC Bill. Once an objection has been recorded an inquiry *must* be held; and this would have forced the Government to justify themselves in public. A taste of what that would be like emerged during the Second Reading of the Local Government (Miscellaneous Provisions) Bill, on 25 November. Facing a barrage of protests and demands to do something about sex shops, the plea by Giles Shaw to leave the issue to the Soho licensing went down like a lead balloon.

Realizing the game was up, the Government hastily rushed through national licensing to avoid a debate over planning. The crusaders were far from happy. Although they were able to secure amendments and changes in the Lords, Mary Whitehouse thundered against the 'sharp political practice on the part of those permissives at the Home Office who have consistently resisted all attempts to tighten up the obscenity laws', and followed this up with half a million signatures to the Prime Minister. Bernard Braine, a national VALA stalwart, warned that licensing implied social and parliamentary approval of 'a fundamentally corrupt and corrupting enterprise'. The legislation was not even compulsory. But a victory it was.

PACS backing for Williams in Portsmouth, and the CSA campaign nationally, had forced a reluctant and devious Government to act when they preferred not to. By mobilizing the public, CSAs not only undermined the Government's 1972 excuse that public opinion was against further controls, they had extended controls beyond Soho and gained a means to shut down most of the shops; and there was not a feminist in sight.

The 1982 'Sex Shop' Act

The Local Government (Miscellaneous Provisions) Act came into force on 13 July 1982. Its numerous provisions gave local authorities wide, but discretionary, powers; all a council had to do was pass a resolution of intent, advertise that fact, and everyone who wanted to run a sex shop had to apply for a licence. Though many councils did not take up this opportunity, most containing sex shops, like Liverpool, did. Several councils without sex shops, but with active CSAs, like Fareham and Gosport, also initiated the scheme, to ensure that any action taken by neighbouring councils would not rebound upon them. Weston-super-Mare's crusaders celebrated their victory by turning the sex shop into a Christian bookstore. Like the Bill itself, success in the crusade against granting licences rested with the CSAs. CARE even sent every Council in the country a copy of *Community Standards and Public Responsibility*, detailing how to close sex shops and sex cinemas too.

Sullivan was the only sex shop owner big enough to fight the 'Sex Shop' Act. Kicking off with a huge £8000 advertisement in the *News of the World*, contrasting the freedoms of millions of Private Shop customers to 'the puritanical minority' who would use the Bill as the first step in 'restricting your right to choose', he got shop managers to organize counter-petitions, tried to take advantage of the clause granting existing sex shops priority, and brought in Lord Grey to improve the company's image. If shops failed to secure licences they were turned into 'five percenters' a common Soho tactic, whereby a shop reducing the number of sex articles to below 'a significant level' negated the need for a licence. Hence those grotesque stores where remaindered books and magazines are piled high from floor to ceiling with a few sex magazines, books, lingerie and equipment behind the counter.

Sullivan's major weapon, however, was the Act itself. By fighting the clauses and definitions one by one through the courts, his shops could remain open until the procedure was exhausted.

Many increased their trade because smaller owners without resources for the Law Courts closed down. This cost Quietlynn, the shops' new holding company, a considerable fortune; but by being the only national company in the field, and by building court costs into its price system, Quietlynn ensured that every adverse decision could be taken to a higher court. It seems incredible that a House of Commons containing some 200 lawyers, a huge Home Office Department, and countless parliamentary agents, not to mention local council legal departments, cannot draft a Bill to reduce disputes to a minimum; yet the Government's desperate haste to avoid the Portsmouth proposals in the Hampshire Bill meant that three judicial reviews were required to settle the issue.

Several points worried judges, not least the process of making illegal a business which before the Act was legal. Most of the appeals against council judgements centred upon lack of hearings, denying 'natural justice', and the deliberate misuse of paragraph 10 of the Act which contained 20 sub-paragraphs outlining the methods of granting, renewing, and transferring licences. Birmingham and Swansea, for example, failed to insert the proper notice in local papers. Others had denied licences when no one objected, or refused to see or hear representations by the applicant.

The biggest single issue, however, was the question of 'appropriate' numbers of shops in an area. A Lords' amendment allowed councils to set it at nil. Obviously, if this was established after applications had been made, owners lost their non-returnable application fees for no purpose. Likewise, councils could claim that one area in town was not 'suitable' without saying which one was, merely insisting the present site of the shop was unsuitable. Yet the mere existence of a school or church was frequently used, even though this is a moral decision. The law, however, held no views on the character of a locality: quite the reverse. Mr Justice Woolf and Mr Justice Forbes, in a series of decisions, ensured that councils could turn down applications because of a locality's character without a need to define what that character was. Consequently, as long as the procedures laid down in the Act were followed carefully, a licence could be refused for an undefined reason, which obviously prevents rebuttal. Once Quietlynn's judicial reviews in 1983 and 1985 were also lost on the grounds that much of the Act was 'directory' not 'mandatory' in law, which meant that appeals were denied because the councils did not have to do what they actually did, the Catch-22 was complete. Adding insult to injury, not only were Quietlynn's occasional victories negated by councils simply reintroducing the Act, but local magistrates were not averse to fining the shops open legally while awaiting the review decisions, for trading without a licence. This effectively meant that Sullivan was being punished for trying to clarify a poorly worded law and, in some cases, opposing what amounted to council illegality; while taxpayers met an even higher bill for official incompetence. When the Court of Appeal met, in March 1984, Quietlynn were refused leave to take their case to the Lords; and another review, in July 1986, proved equally fruitless.

After four years Quietlynn had obtained licences for only a fifth of Congate's previous empire. Allowing for those still trading in areas not requiring licences, just over a quarter were legal sex shops. Scotland lost every one. Sullivan's typical response was more dial-porn services and the *Sunday Sport*, which incredibly was launched on the presses of Portsmouth's *The News*, which had consistently backed the PACS campaign to drive him from the city.

The major losers in all this were the Soho residents. 'The Vice' had already been dealt a blow there when a DOE inquiry turned down 15 appeals against planning enforcement orders, using the Ram Books precedent whereby shops introducing other facilities, such as video booths, placed sex shops outside planning law and legality. The shop at 39 Frith Street was typical. The basement below the ground floor shop housed a number of coin-operated booths where customers could view soft-core clips from hard-core films. A surreptitious survey revealed that 50 per cent of the shop's customers did just that, enabling Westminster Council to contend that the basement was effectively part of the shop, and that the installation of booths contravened proper retail use. The Council immediately issued another 180 enforcement notices. But when Westminster met to determine its policy and number of sex shops, the Society were in for a shock. The Council suggested issuing 44 licences! Given the number of other sex-related premises, Soho might as well be an official red-light area; was that the real aim all along?

A vigorous Society campaign, however, forced the Council to reconsider, and 'the Vice' searched around for new loopholes.

Out of 61 shops still trading, 24 made applications for sex shop licences; 9 applied for cinematograph licences under the 1909 Act, hoping that an outstanding application would make them immune from prosecution; 3 converted to topless bars; and 12 converted to peep-shows or Nude Encounter Parlours (not covered by the Act). One became an amusement arcade. In all, 37 shops continued to trade, 13 of them illegally. By June 1983, 100 applications for cinematograph licences had also been made to the GLC. But once that of the 'manager' of Continental Blue Video Club in Old Compton Street had been dismissed on the grounds that he was not the leaseholder, a contravention of Licensing Regulation Rule 3, most others withdrew too. Only 7 premises received licences.

When the licence subcommittee finally met in August to hear the shop applications, the Metropolitan Police's Clubs Office provided damning 'evidence' about most applicants. The only winners were the Ann Summers lingerie chain. Eighty unlicensed premises then faced inspections and prosecutions. The Sin Cinema and Bookshop in Peter Street, for example, was fined £5000 for the first day of illegal operation, and £7000 for the second. A real 'clean up' had begun; but it was not as successful as many had hoped. 'The Vice' exploited the legal process for all its worth: apply for a licence, any licence; when refused, appeal to the courts, or when the appeal was dismissed, appeal to the appropriate higher authority; when denied, apply for another type of licence and start the appeal procedure all over again. Once this means was exhausted, simply transfer the ownership, and begin again. If transfer failed, the Council would still have to initiate an enforcement notice, subject to yet another set of appeals.

As far as Soho was concerned, the 1982 Act was a useless means of control, forcing the Council back to the unchanged planning law. Success, and once again only partial success, had to wait until the GLC General Powers Act 1986 Section 12 – which authorized licensing of all sex-related premises. There was a blitz during June 1986 on the 16 peep-shows, 4 male revue bars, 2 Nude Encounter premises, 3 lingerie model shops, a photographic 'studio' and 15 near-beer bars, and this temporarily contained 'the Vice' to the Tisbury Court area.

As a result, between 1982 and 1986, Soho's visual environment became distinctly shabby as the felt pen signs on paper, card or windows replaced the professional neon and plastic facades of the tatty 'five percenters', and numerous 'For Sale' signs reproduced the urban blight of the early 1970s. Then came the body blow: just before the 1987 General Election the distinction between light industrial and office Use Class Orders was abolished, following a request by Westminster Council. Landlords were now free to convert premises without planning permission, and the craft workshops could not compete. Residents were also faced with massive rent increases by the impending abolition of rent controls. The Society's efforts had ensured that Soho would not become a *de facto* red-light area; but the old crafts and businesses have made way for the trendy cafes, expensive boutiques, restaurants and bars much beloved by yuppies. Within less than five years, the traditional Soho has been replaced by a fake. In reality, 'the Vice' had merely filled a gap in the market caused by the collapse of the property boom, and the long delays in redevelopment. The demise of Soho's 'Vice' is no great shame as it was always a rip-off, but the bigger crooks are clearly to be found elsewhere, and they got away with it.

The major effect of the 1982 Act, therefore, was merely to ensure that many more newsagents stocked British soft-core and minority-interest material like rubber fetish magazines; and that is why newsagents would inevitably become a crusader target. The only reason they did not do sooner was the huge popularity of horror movies.

Video nasties

At first sight the 'video nasty' furore of 1982 to 1984 appears to have nothing to do with soft core; but that is precisely the point. As the campaign against the 'nasties' generated and gave a spurious respectability to crusader claims that 'pornographic' videos were becoming more violent, the fact that horror movies have nothing to do with soft core is very important. Yet Graham Bright's Act not only 'banned' 40 horror video cassettes, it outlawed any video cassettes not submitted for censure by a new statutory body, and so blocked the loop-hole enabling the importation of American and European soft-core video cassettes; and behind the *Daily Mail* campaign against the 'nasty' horrors stood a four-year campaign which had targeted soft core.

The campaign against sex videos began back in 1980, when crusaders realized that undermining the Williams Committee's proposals and gaining the Sainsbury Act were not enough to defeat pornography.

The crusaders feared the video. The demand for machines was high. Between 1976 and 1982 imports increased from 12,000 to two and a half million per year, and lack of 24 hour and cable television gave Britain the largest per capita ownership in the world. This twenty per cent market penetration was paralleled by a rapid growth in video rental outlets providing films not on general release, and uncensored versions of those that were. The demand for material was so great that garages, newsagents, and corner stores got in on the act. This fascination with free choice threatened to make regulations controlling pornography in print or licensed cinemas irrelevant. Apart from watching thousands of mainstream movies from all over the world not offered by the two cinema chains, VCR owners could secure soft- and hard-core tapes from various sources because they could be copied easily, quickly, and repeatedly, and circulated without difficulty.

Despite numerous attempts to include pornographic videos within the wider campaigns following 1979, such as national VALA's 1981 StoPorn campaign which collected over 2 million signatures, crusaders made little headway for three years.

The so-called 'nasties', however, involved much more than sex, and it is easy to understand the crusaders' reaction: if pornography was permissive sex, 'nasties' were permissive violence. From their perspective, here was the decadence of Rome, not in the Colosseum, but in every British living room; a completely corrupt society now appeared to regard mutilation, murder, and worse – the blasphemous rise of the undead – as popular entertainment. By adding children to the equation, as they had in 1977, the crusaders hoped to gain wider support, provide rationales for increased censorship, and save Britain's future generations. It worked.

Numerous groups queued to ideologically exploit the 'nasties' for their own purpose; and the TV and cinema lobbies saw a chance to control the video boom which undermined their stranglehold over viewing. National VALA, the CSAs and CARE were all involved, but the switch in emphasis from sex to violence began when the NSPCC, yet to uncover 'real' Satanic abuse, joined forces with Gareth Wardell MP, who tabled a Bill controlling pornographic and horror tapes in December 1982, on the grounds that working-class children preferred them to Noddy and Big Ears.

The term 'nasties' gained popular currency after it was used by the *Sunday People* to describe a *pornographic* video in December 1981. The transfer was almost complete when the *Sunday Times* gave the horror cassette the once-over in May 1982, eight months before it published National VALA supporter David Holbrook's 'Seduction of the Innocent'. The 23 May exposé warned that:

> Uncensored horror video cassettes, available to anybody of any age, have arrived in Britain's High Street ... They exploit the extremes of violence, and are rapidly replacing sexual pornography as the video trade's biggest money spinner ... [they] are far removed from the suspense of the traditional horror film. They dwell on murder, multiple rape, butchery, sadomasochism, mutilation of women, cannibalism and Nazi atrocities.

Having thrown in the snuff movie legend, Peter Chippendale implied that the Home Office was backsliding: video availability to adults left the law 'far behind'. A second article a week later referred to Scotland Yard's impending prosecution of *SS Experiment Camp*, a title named the previous week, and quoted Detective Superintendent Kruger from the Obscene Publications Squad, who propounded his worry that the police would be unable to secure obscenity convictions, and bemoaned, as the Squad always do, the alleged delays in taking cases to court.

It was piffle: pornography had never been the trade's major money spinner; the horror films were rarely new, many having been screened at the cinema; real sadomasochism never featured at all; and the plots rarely involved rape. These so-called 'nasties' were merely cult slasher films, spaghetti zombie movies, or low-budget American drive-in gore that would only shock someone who had not been inside a cinema in two decades. The gross inaccuracy of crusaders' claims is damningly illustrated by their assertion that

Palace Video's award-winning, all-time masterpiece of spoof horror, *The Evil Dead*, the video of which was no different from its BBFC 18 certificated cinema version, was accused of being one of the nastiest of the lot. Having featured in no fewer than forty court cases from Exeter to Leeds, where, despite constant acquittals in the Crown Courts, it was constantly declared obscene by dozens of inane magistrates, Judge Staple QC, sitting in Snaresbrook Crown Court in July 1985, castigated the police and the DPP when finding in favour of Palace Video, and told them to put an end to this nonsense. Others were not so fortunate.

If there was a problem, it was that some unsupervised working-class children were watching the equivalent of 18-certificated films which graphically displayed the result of violence that their fathers were about to experience in the Falklands for real; and that the fears generated among the middle classes increased the campaign's dishonesty.

Kruger's complaints about the inability to gain convictions and prosecution delays were bogus. True, the DPP had dithered over what part of the 1959 Act to invoke against the cassettes. However, as both the Attorney-General's Reference No. 5, 1980, and a 1981 Court of Appeal Ruling defined a video as an 'article', the necessary designation for an item to be covered by the 1959 Act, that meant that the September 1980 Willesden Magistrates' decision to label a case of violence as opposed to sex on video 'obscene' could now be applied to any cassette. Far from having their hands tied, the police had already seized 22,403 videos in London alone during 1982; and a spate of trials were heard in 1983. Mrs Whitehouse, who had attempted to force the DPP's hand back in 1981, had already taken her opportunity to turn the original complaints against pornographic videos into a wider fear of child desensitization to violence. Despite some crusaders' honest worries about children's access, the fact that some parents were being irresponsible hardly justified powers placing the videos outside the vagaries of jury decisions under the 1959 Act, and giving a censorship board the right to outlaw them by refusing certificates. Likewise, as the complaint supposedly concerned gore, there was no justification for limiting the content of soft-core cassettes when juries were clearly giving explicit sex the green light by constantly returning not guilty verdicts in court. By making all videos illegal without a certificate, the public were being denied their right to decide for themselves both in the High Street and in court.

Once again, the crusaders' role in provoking others into action was vital. In Portsmouth, for example, the 'Sex Shop' Act had only just received the Royal assent when the council was faced with protest letters about pornographic video tapes; video shops had 'erupted' all over the city 'like a disease' and were a cover for selling pornographic videos.

This was not correct; the real source in the early days included the nice man who installed the VCR, and video 'clubs' within three of the city's major employers. At first, the Council considered using the 1982 Act, then the provisions of the Children and Young Persons Act, but dismissed these in favour of lobbying the Home Secretary, pointing out that as even liberal Sweden had video controls, Britain could too.

PACS, whose integrity was maintained by always expressing a rational concern about the dual danger of children's access to pornographic and horror cassettes, mobilized local MPs Bonner Pink and Peter Lloyd. They wrote to Patrick Mayhew, who promised that the Government intended to keep tight control on the booming video trade, although they wanted to assess the impact of the British Video Association Working Party (which was considering voluntary certification, before taking action that might be difficult to enforce). In other words, another attempt to avoid legislation.

PACS's campaign, which culminated when a local company's documentary was broadcast in TVS's *Seven Days* series during May 1983, sought a comprehensive law which would cover video, cable TV, existing broadcasting systems, films and pornography. PACS also compiled a list of video titles subject to prosecution, sent it to dealers, and called a successful meeting with numerous traders to discuss the merits of inhibiting children's access to such material. If this kind of initiative had led to a healthy public debate all could have been well; but someone had picked up their phone.

On 15 September 1982, the local Vice Squad raided 'Greetings', a very popular greetings card and video rental shop just outside Portsmouth. Acting on 'several complaints', the Squad removed 60 titles including *Driller Killer*, *I Spit on Your Grave*, and *Cannibal Apocalypse*, and a number of simulated sex films. At this stage the police did not have a clue what they were really looking for – a problem common elsewhere in the country, making the final list of designated 'nasties' a very hit-and-miss affair. *Bogeyman* was prosecuted, while *Bogeyman 2*, which starts with highlighting the gore from the previous film, was not!

But they learn fast in Portsmouth. On 15 November, the haul at Porchester's Video Library, following another complaint, included *Driller Killer*, *Last House on the Left*, and *Cannibal Holocaust*. Similar 'tip-offs' led to fourteen more raids during the next seven months, culminating in coordinated raids on the Network Video chain, making Portsmouth's shelves clear of 'nasties' and soft-core cassettes long before the country heard of them. The trials on 25 November 1983 made national news because of their contradictory verdicts, which crusaders exploited to justify their demand to bypass the 1959 Act.

Many other local initiatives were paralleled at national level by National VALA and the Parliamentary Video Inquiry. Determined to gain legislation, Mary Whitehouse took her campaign to sixteen marginal constituencies during the 1983 election, sent letters to 150 provincial papers, held 'nastie' preview sessions at the Conservative Party Conference, and appeared on television to explain her case. The attempt to ban 18R sex films, proposed by Sir Bernard Braine during the Committee stages, also came from National VALA.

The Video Inquiry then set about finding the evidence to justify the crusaders' claims by employing a methodologically dodgy questionnaire which inevitably produced exaggerated figures of children's access to the material. When Britain's foremost media researcher, Dr Guy Cumberbatch, replicated the procedure using a methodologically sound questionnaire, he found that most children were claiming to have seen horror movies that did not exist.

Given the make-up of the parliamentary inquiry, the result was inevitable anyway. Lord Nugent had a history of promoting moral legislation in the Lords; Raymond Johnston was CARE's Director; Lady Watherston ran Christian Unity and soon became President of the National Council for Christian Standards in Society; Lord Swinfen was a veteran anti-porn campaigner; and Tim Sainsbury, with fundamentalist connections, had the Indecent Display Bill under his belt. The Director was Dr Clifford Hill, who had already published two books on the moral dangers and dilemmas facing society, and ran an evangelical mission in London. Along with Mrs Whitehouse, the inquiry organized the Parliamentary preview on the eve of the Bill's Second Reading. Irrespective of the methodology and validity of the group's interim report, its sensational conclusions, uncritically repeated by the popular media, neatly summarized Dr Hill's previous prophecies about society: 'moral pollution' in the form of obscenity produced permissive attitudes towards violence; videos desensitized children to violence; the moral laxity of parents justified parliamentary intervention to protect the moral welfare of children. The report, therefore, had far less to do with children's viewing habits than it did with confirming the validity and necessity of the contemporary evangelical Christian message for adults. But it was also the height of the Christian crusaders' influence; for although the Bill passed, questions began to be raised about increasing censorship.

Although crusaders gained the support of the popular press and non-feminist women's magazines, the reintroduction of precensorship was opposed by the quality press. While the *Daily Telegraph* reversed its initial support, because it did not want 'a state playing heavy hand with censors and policemen', the politically correct *Guardian*'s 'Where Do You Draw the Line?' series could only find Polly Toynbee, who seemed desperate to exorcize the demons of her Williams Committee past, to defend the Bill.

Critics were in general agreement: the Bill censored all material under the guise of protecting children from two score horror films which were already covered by the Obscene Publications Act; it reintroduced pre-censorship; and placed dealers in 'double jeopardy', a concept frowned upon in English law, as even certificated films would still be subject to the obscenity law. The attack on Hill's research was so strong that Graham Bright had to distance himself from it.

Even though they secured the Bill, the crusaders were not completely successful. The BBFC, blamed by crusaders for certificating cinematographic permissiveness since the 1960s, now became the state's recognized censors, and soft-core sex videos like *Electric Blue* gained 18 certificates, and simulated sex, 18R; and thereby, like sex shops before them, gained legitimation.

Meanwhile, the British public faced another drastic reduction in choice as the major film and distribution companies regained control of video distribution, which further ensured that the stocks of soft core in local newsagents would take on increased importance.

Page Three & TV

When Winston Churchill got in on the morality show with a December 1985 Private Member's Bill to place television broadcasts under the 1959 Act, and impose drastic limits on the contents of soft core, he, like Primarolo, tried to define what was *de facto* obscene, and take the decision away from juries. Soft core would be automatically prosecuted if:

(a) it depicts visually, and in actual or simulated form, acts of masturbation, sodomy, oral/genital connection, oral/anal connection, the lewd exhibition of genital organs or excretory functions, cannibalism, bestiality, mutilation or vicious cruelty towards persons or animals; and

(b) it is published in a place to which persons under 18 years of age have access or it is published through the medium of television broadcasting.

Given the vague definition of 'lewd', and clause (b), this would not only have driven the magazines from the newsagents but have restricted everything, even topless pin-ups, and seriously restricted TV news and arts coverage.

All the initial signs pointed to a repeat performance of the 'nasties' crusade. National VALA released a study claiming that one in four TV programmes contained scenes of violence. Individual Conservatives and the Party's Central Office backed a TV 'clean-up' following political disputes over BBC news coverage and documentaries. In December the Home Secretary, Douglas Hurd, launched an attack on TV violence and bad language; and Norman Tebbit in the Disraeli lecture demanded a 'tightening' of the obscenity laws. TV was in trouble, and soft core would be caught up in war.

Churchill, however, committed a serious blunder. Subjecting

TV to the 1959 law was one thing; changing the definition of obscenity with a 'laundry list' and threatening the contents of news broadcasts with the reference to violence was another. The Bill effectively reversed the 1959 Act's justification by once again comparing serious *art* to *pornography*. The literati exploded, and opposition mushroomed. A public forum, including BBC Controller Michael Grade and obscenity law specialist Geoffrey Robertson, lambasted the proposals. Old foes like Michael Winner and Jeremy Isaacs found common cause, and scores of organizations from the British Academy of Film and Television Arts to the Royal Shakespeare Company were united in total condemnation. Whereas the film and broadcasting lobbies realized that soft core and foreign gore would detract from their own pap, they supported heavily censored videos as these would provide no competition to TV viewing, or undermine the cinema industry and the BBFC's existence; the Churchill Bill was a direct threat to them.

Sullivan's Sheptonhurst, which apart from running sex shops, organized the distribution of his soft core to over 10,000 newsagents, waded in with a critique of Churchill's rationales; using the Government's own figures they demonstrated that sex crimes had increased after indecent display and sex shop controls had been introduced. The Campaign against Censorship, chaired by Ted Goodman, were very busy. Their Secretary, Mary Hayward, demonstrated brilliant polemical skills in the press and letters to MPs. David Webb's NCROPA, which had laboured almost single-handed against National VALA since 1977, issued a critique which tore the Bill apart, and suddenly found itself in friendly company. Labour MPs, mindful of recent attacks on gay literature, requested draft amendments from NCROPA to talk the Bill out. Conservative members who had supported the Video Bill because they had interests in television now invited Mr Webb into the private visitors' box on the floor of the House, a privilege once reserved for Mary Whitehouse, who had to take a place in the public gallery. *The Times*, which had backed National VALA since 1977, now denounced the Bill and its supporters as Mrs Grundys, and went to great lengths to expose the contradictions between the Conservatives' economic and moral philosophies, directly addressing Mrs Thatcher in the process. Neither the inclusion of the words 'Protection of Children' in the Bill's title, nor dropping the 'laundry list' in favour of shrink-wrap covers, or tedious reference to 'the violence' in *Jubilee* or the 'sex' in *Sebastiane*, shown on Channel 4, could detract the opposition.

But what ultimately killed the Bill, when, ironically, it could have saved it, was Clare Short's amendment attempting to outlaw topless models on Page Three of the *Sun*. Conservative MPs saw this as a political attack upon Rupert Murdoch. Several, including Mr Bright, posed with Page Three models, and Churchill could not accept an amendment which would have caused havoc in Labour ranks by forcing them to choose between their arty friends and a politically correct amendment. Only Joe Ashton was brave enough to dismiss Short's silly assertions about a correlation between topless models and rape. Either way, Churchill's opportunity had gone; the Bill was lost.

In April 1987, Gerald Howarth tried again. Mindful of Labour votes, he claimed that the increase in rape and crimes of violence over the past 30 years 'started with soft porn and went down to a deep cesspit of filth at the bottom'. David Mellor, then better known as a Home Office Minister than as a befriender of out-of-work actresses, concurred: the existing law had failed to protect TV viewers from gratuitous violence and explicit (*sic*) sex scenes, and *some* people must be influenced by the 'extreme and sadistic violence, especially extreme and sadistic sexual violence, of which far too much was depicted'. The Opposition spokesman on Home Affairs, Alf Dubs, soon to secure a sinecure with the Broadcasting Standards Council, rallied the Labour benches with a politically correct version to avoid upsetting the art lobby. The 'real problem' was not any individual episode or programme; these were not offensive; violent behaviour followed the cumulative 'drip, drip effect' of such programmes. Wets were obviously not confined to the Conservatives.

The Bill failed only because an election was called; but the Conservative Party made a manifesto commitment, and after their third victory rewarded National VALA with one of their original aims: subjecting TV to the 1959 Act. Not that it has ever been invoked.

These two Bills had, however, taught some crusaders two lessons. First, success in extending definitions of obscenity that went too far was not guaranteed. Second, future success against soft core was going to be determined by feminists in the Labour Party, as much as Conservative morality. As a result, some began to consider the unthinkable, an alliance with their long-term opponents over abortion and family stability.

Conservative sexuality

The real lesson the crusaders should have learned from the Page Three issue was that ideological exploitation of social problems like rape, rather than promotion of their theology, to obtain short-term gains was ultimately working against them. But the alliance with the Conservative Lawyers Group to change obscenity's legal test from 'corrupt and deprave' to one based upon 'community standards' had undermined the Williams Committee, and convinced Conservatives that there was mileage in morality; once in power, the Conservative Party conned the Christians.

Despite paying lip service to crusader demands, and offering a single reform per Parliament, Conservative Ministers had shown great reluctance to deal with sex shops and were really in favour of the video retailers' voluntary code. Anyone following events over a decade would have begun to smell a rat, and taken a hard look at both Mrs Thatcher's display of support for the Video Bill, and National VALA's gushing praise for David Mellor's work, in complete contradiction to their annoyance at the sex shop fix. Someone, somewhere, was trying to horse-trade; and they had to. CARE not only avoided Party affiliation, in 1983 they had advised supporters to vote for the most moral candidates, irrespective of party; and whatever political scientists think about important issues, two thousand fundamentalist votes can make a lot of difference in marginal constituencies. While certification of videos, like licensing sex shops, can keep the moderately moral happy, and removes obscenity cases from the courts – where acquittals demonstrate that we live in a pluralistic society – no real crusader could be satisfied with this game.

Even if it did not dawn on CARE that gaining a sex shop clause and the Nasties Act was no big deal, given their desire for a complete overhaul of the 1959 Act, their prioritization of moral imperatives over Party must have worried Mrs Thatcher. A real

Christian would not be slow to realize that the Conservative Party can afford to support action against kiddy porn, indecent displays, unlicensed cinema clubs, uncontrolled sex shops, and violent videos, without bringing the numerous contradictions between the free market and 'Victorian morality' into the open. By giving way on symbolic moral issues, the Government could avoid a serious confrontation over more vital Christian issues such as teenage contraception, divorce, Sunday trading, and family tax law, all of which have a greater social impact than the sight of naked breasts. But once their ability to palm the crusaders off while not offending other vested interests fell apart during the Churchill Bill, Conservative hypocrisy was more exposed than *PlayBirds* labia lips. The Government could not even guarantee symbolic moral legislation, and some people began to wonder if they really wanted to.

Those 'permissives' at the Home Office have been getting away with a double bluff for years. Despite all the ballyhoo over a decade, nothing has been completely outlawed, and contrary to all 'informed' opinion the Home Office *had*, albeit slowly, been introducing various sections of the Williams Report into each new piece of legislation:

The Indecent Display (Control) Act 1981:
restricted public display, and introduced warning signs: recommendations 8(a) and 8(b).

The Local Government (Miscellaneous Provisions) 1982 Act:
licensed sex shops making material available in separate premises with no access to people under eighteen years of age: recommendation 8(b).

The Child Protection Act 1978:
recommendation 19(a), 20, 22.

The Video Act 1984;
established a statutory body to review films and video cassettes: (effectively) recommendations 35, 36, 37, 38, 39, 41, 42, 43, 44(a) (b), 51, 52, 53, 54.

The Cinematograph Act 1982 and the Consolidation Act 1985: 45, 49.

In reality, far from promoting 'morality', the Conservatives have been laying down a framework for control and distribution of sexually orientated material while not appearing to impose total censorship. Though these restrictions made sense to the Williams Committee only because the Committee also recommended decriminalizing all soft-core material at the same time, it is feasible that if British soft core is ever allowed to expand to American-type content (which is possible given numerous jury acquittals of hard core, and the BBFC's 18 rating for sex education videos), there will now be a system of distribution and revenue control in existence. And that means that National VALA will have lost the moral war for short-term strategic gains. No wonder some crusaders looked instead to an alliance with the feminists and the Labour Party; for they had just wasted fifteen years.

Summary

On top of the lessons to be learned from the four-hundred-year crusade against sexual arousal in print or on screen, the third phase of the 1959 Act puts the current attack on newsagents into perspective. Far from initiating a serious assault on pornography by overhauling the 1959 Act, the Conservative Party cynically took the crusaders' votes, while possibly considering turning Soho into an after-dark red-light area. The Labour Party will bend in the wind; having backed the liberal Williams Committee they now think they can gain 'feminist' votes in the same way as the Tories attempted to secure those of the Christian crusaders.

The Christians' contemporary attack on newsagent soft core is clearly an extension of their previous crusade against all sexual material. Claims that the material was becoming more violent after the 'video nasties' campaign and the failure of the Churchill Bill make an alliance with politically correct 'feminists' very appealing. So it is now time to take a look at the 'new' players in the soft-core morality war: the feminists

Chapter three

Good Girls and Bad Girls

THE only thing that is really new, or feminist, about CAP's 1987 crusade against newsagent soft core is that the separatists have changed their tactics. While Christian crusaders made all the running in the past, 'feminist' opponents dragged far behind, and even kept their distance from the Christians. To see how the feminists suddenly became major players, and why they readily took to an alliance with Christian crusaders, we need to go back to the mid-1970s.

From sexism to separatism

Complaints against soft core, like pickets of Miss World competitions, were an integral feature of the early women's liberation movement's attempt to oppose 'sexism'. Unfortunately, although these complaints raised important questions about women's role in society and the nature of inequality, many activists did not listen to the answers. Compared to other more vital issues, pornography was a marginal one; the motives and meanings of nude representations were constantly changing as more women took on the challenges of equal rights and responsibilities. Feminists of both sexes used to know this, and even the most radical feminist publications, like *Shrew*, realized that 'bourgeois pornography', with its particular 'role' in capitalist society, would take on a new meaning 'after the revolution'.

After the ABUSE crusade, however, the small 'separatist' wing of the women's movement, which rejected 'reforming' men and the patriarchal state, promoting a form of gender apartheid based upon the idea that all women should avoid men, instead began to push for the prioritization of an anti-pornography campaign. Back then, this had far less to do with allegations about content than their revolutionary means to overcome the perceived failings of the 'reformist' wing of the women's movement.

Back in 1977, British feminism faced several problems. The economic recession threatened to undermine the state welfare provisions upon which its middle-class-orientated programme depended; the effects of equality legislation were delayed by the re-orientation of British industry; and deep ideological differences within the movement, previously glossed over, were coming to the surface. Yet the most serious 'threat' was its success in other areas. Far from welcoming public interest in issues like rape and sexual harassment, the separatist wing became a victim of its own propaganda and saw media coverage as a sign that rape and sexploitation were increasing. To make it worse, men were becoming concerned too, and that did not figure in the separatists' plans. As a result, soft core, being highly visible, became a symbolic target for the separatists' frustrations; and given the attention paid to pornography by the authorities, defeating soft core looked easy. The separatists, however, were to the women's movement what Marxism–Leninism was to communism: all revolutionary rhetoric, but only fascist tactics.

The gender war

Behind the separatists' 'transitional programme' against soft core lay their long-term 'revolutionary' agenda. By mobilizing women in a 'united front', the separatists hoped to convince women that their interests lay in gender warfare rather than piecemeal reforms, and embracing the separatist solution to oppression: the total exclusion of men from their lives. This feeble feminist version of Trotskyism, complete with its 'that's a post-revolutionary issue' answers to the 'what do we do with the males' questions, was not even indigenous, still less original. It had blown across the Atlantic from America, where two groups, Diana Russell's Los Angeles-based Women Against Violence Against Women, and the New York-centred Women Against Pornography, co-founded by Susan Brownmiller, were already promoting similar theories. Nor would it ever have succeeded if the separatists had not found such a soft option for all those who baulked at the arduous trials and tribulations of serious campaigns for equality.

The major British organizations flying the separatist flag were the Leeds-based Women Against Violence Against Women – known as WAVAW; the itinerant Women's Information, Resources and Education Service – called WIRES; and the *London Women's Liberation Newsletter* collective. Their simplistic theories and *Animal Farm*-inspired slogans appealed to polytechnic and university women's groups whose members were taking sociology or the burgeoning Women's Studies courses on which American separatist publications were compulsory reading and whose lecturers frequently believed that political correctness, then known by its detractors as being 'right-on', was more important than developing the students' critical faculties.

The three organizations' middle-class converts, unlike many working-class women, exhibited a tendency to confuse sexism with sexual desire and display, and found it far more exciting to daub bikini advertisements with 'sexist crap' graffiti than to engage in the hard slog for equal rights, or even study; and readily took to WAVAW's apocalyptic promises that:

> A Feminist attack on porn would not just be reformist. As the frightening realities of sex-war and sex oppression which are exemplified in porn come into focus, the class consciousness of women will be built. A main object of action around porn would be to mobilise that anger and hate of all women in the fight against male supremacy. Until now the natural horror and disgust of most women at porn has been labelled puritanical and prudish and derided by the ruling male ideology of sexual revolution. Now we must validate that disgust, identify its real cause (the obvious humiliation and degradation of women in porn, which each woman knows applies to her) and enlist the 'prudishness' of all our sisters in the struggle.

This single-issue short-cut to the women's revolution would impress anybody when the only alternative appeared to be the SWP, which required its rank and file members to get up in bad weather at six in the morning to sell the Party's paper outside some factory gate, only to find the *Militant* had got there first. As feminism is egalitarian, and has no leaders, everyone could stay in bed.

Female students who were not impressed by WAVAW's dreams of remoralizing society through the 'expressive' virtues of womanhood, precisely because it sounded like the Christian discourse, were denounced by women's action groups as suffering from false consciousness. Males who dared to point out that WAVAW were abandoning feminism's tenet that genders did not possess innate character traits, or who suggested that if 'patriarchy' had oppressed women for so long, women's 'expressive nature' would be a product of oppression rather than a natural state, were castigated as porn-reading rapists. Gender traitors who wore make-up, dated male students, and scoffed at the separatists' discovery that high heels were deliberately invented by men to make women more vulnerable to rape, were vilified and written off. Sensibly, real lesbians tended to keep their distance. It would all have been laughable if it were not so serious: a whole generation of women were turned off feminism. Not that WAVAW supporters cared: they knew they were right, and could make themselves excited by jumping up and down outside sex shops, screaming at the odd sandwich-degree student who bought the *Sun*, or fantasizing of the final victory in the sex war.

Direct action

What kept WAVAW going for so long was the nature of their propaganda, and their ability to avoid, or refusal to engage in, the democratic process.

To raise women's consciousness they would produce a slide show at women-only events, consisting of obscure hard-core pictures alternating with some of billboards, record covers and advertisements. The hard-core pictures were presented in a sequence so that they appeared to be getting more and more violent, and the everyday representations with vague decontextualized similarities were slipped in between. The aim was to 'prove' that pornography was deliberately produced to be consumed in a soft-core-to-violent continuum, and that all male media were secretly promoting the same 'message'. The show climaxed with a scene from a horror movie showing a woman being murdered with blood everywhere. As the pictures were displayed, the presenter would read out accounts of rape, culminating in the assertion that the final picture was not a fake; the woman was really being killed for male sexual gratification. The result on the audience of gullible and uncritical students, with little knowledge of pornography's content, conventions, and imagery, was inevitable; pornography *was* a new holocaust.

But if anyone was emulating the Nazis, it was WAVAW; for they deliberately misrepresented the content, ideologically exploited the problem of sex crimes, and recontextualized everyday images like advertising to promote nothing less than an incitement to gender hatred.

That those present frequently failed to see that sticking a designer jeans advertisement, where the model's body is cut off at the knees by the photograph's frame then cut in half by the seam, between two hard-core shots from a female-domination magazine does not prove that pornography, let alone advertising, reduces women to pieces of meat and is merely self-serving propaganda, reflects badly on the UK's intellectual resources; though I have noticed that the strength of many people's 'opinions' about something is always in inverse proportion to the amount of research they have accomplished.

The other reason this nonsense was not exposed at the time was that WAVAW avoided the test of public debate by claiming women were so intimidated by men that it was unfair to expect them to justify themselves. Instead, they got supporters elected as 'women's officers' in women-only elections for women-only posts, justified on the bizarre grounds that the middle-class daughters of wealthy parents were somehow less privileged than the working-class male engineering students paying their own way through sandwich degrees; and they were allowed to raid Union funds to subsidize their curries and beer – the only male habits they agreed with. In any event, WAVAW reasoned that 'direct action', such as harassing strip-tease artists and censoring charity rag-mags, achieved far more than democratic debate: it showed men that 'wimmin' meant business, and the lack of progress which followed could always be blamed on the masonic male conspiracy.

In 1978, WAVAW members began defacing underground posters, moved on to pickets of W. H. Smiths and John Menzies, and then organized American-style Reclaim the Night marches. On Halloween 1978 and on 20 January 1979, between 500 and 1000 young women, mainly from the National Union of Students, whooped their way through Soho. The marches, designed to link the media-induced fear of unsafe streets to consumption of pornography, were only the beginning; for as Sheila Jeffreys reasoned:

> If all women decided that porn should not exist and smashed and destroyed it on the news stands, billboards, in the windows of sex shops, on the streets of Soho, and demanded their right never to be insulted in public again, then at least it would be driven underground.

The problem was, nobody took any notice. So after a WAVAW Sexshops and Strategies workshop in 1981, a group calling themselves 'Angry Women' took to terrorism, and fire-bombed sex shops in Manchester, Keighley, and Leeds to 'hurt men in a way that laws and restrictions can't'. In May 1982, a small number of provincial initiatives culminated in two weeks of pornographic-book burning, dozens of obscene telephone calls to sex shops, and another Soho march. At this stage, WAVAW and the WIRES network controlled the anti-pornography campaigns within the feminist movement by default; few dared to challenge their Stalinist authority because if you did, the outcome could be unpleasant.

The success of WAVAW's crusade against sex shops has always been grossly exaggerated by commentators who knew nothing about the Christian crusade; and WAVAW were happy to take the credit; after all, that was the idea. But to claim as Colin Manchester did that 'the feminists' were the *major* crusading force against the shops is laughable, especially when he can only cite Reclaim the Night and two shop pickets in Leeds and Oxford. The Soho demonstrations were totally ignored outside the women's movement and the *Guardian*; WAVAW's headquarters were in Leeds; and Oxford's sex shop, despite being opposite the local

Women's Centre, did not see an inhabitant cross the road until *after* a year-long protest by local Christians. Yes, many separatists held protests outside sex shops, but only once the 1982 Act was inevitable. Yes, several separatists and their 'right-on' friends in local councils implemented the Act; but look at the results. In their rush to prove their token feminism, the councils made elementary legal mistakes thereby enabling the shops to remain open until the judicial review. Newham, for example, botched the requisite public announcements, invalidating the whole procedure. Lambeth introduced the Act against an Asian newsagent, and by fighting the issue all the way to the High Court helped establish the viability of 'five-percenters' as a result when the Lords ruled that 53 magazines, being less than five per cent of total stock, did not constitute a sex shop. WAVAW did not really delude themselves either; they knew the evangelicals were making the running, and much of WAVAW's anger during this period arose from the fact that the Christians were far more effective than they were.

To say WAVAW achieved nothing would, however, be incorrect. In less than ten years they turned feminism into a crippling form of victimology comparable with ME ('the yuppie flu'), inhibited serious debate about sexuality among women through intimidation, and drained support from more important and pressing issues by their obsession with pornography.

Men, sex, and political lesbianism

From its inception, feminism spent a lot of effort researching and debating the origin of women's social subordination. While sociologists critically examined the idea of biological differences, and historians trawled the past to consider the effects of social institutions like marriage, the less scholarly created hypotheses about the effects of man-made 'culture'. No consensus emerged and progress was slow, not least because most of the 'causes' accredited to an amorphous abstraction called patriarchy could only ever have applied to a section of the bourgeoisie and were far more recent than many had assumed. It was also twenty years before Davidoff and Hall finally laid to rest the new myth of the historically passive woman in their *Family Fortunes*.

Meanwhile, the separatists, like all ideologues and religious sects before them, were more preoccupied with getting their theory or creed correct than with understanding what was really going on, and simply 'pick 'n' mixed' what appealed to them from the speculations of women's 'writers' like Millet and Ortner, in order to 'prove' their patriarchal conspiracy theory, whereby 'the media' and 'socialization' brainwashed women into accepting their oppression. This was naive enough, for the roles people hold has always more to do with economics and survival than any post-hoc rationalizations; but the separatists finally ended up insinuating that women's brains were located in their vaginas by insisting that male power was 'reproduced' on a daily basis by penetrative sex, which allegedly shaped women's character structure!

Proof of this male penile plot could supposedly be found in the 'pornographic' novels of D. H. Lawrence, Henry Miller, Norman Mailer and Jean Genet, whose hidden themes of domination and subordination 'really' reflected the male's cultural control of the female. How these novels, rarely read by the degreeless classes, had brainwashed the masses was never explained. Then Susan Brownmiller came up with the answer: they did not. It was *hardcore* pornography. Far from an expression of women's sexploitation by men, *hard core* was an expression of male hatred against women, and its purpose was to humiliate, degrade and dehumanize the female for the male's erotic stimulation and pleasure. Women, 'naturally', did not like pornography for the very reasons separatists asserted men did: it showed women as 'anonymous, panting playthings, adult toys, dehumanized objects to be used, abused, broken and discarded'.

For the separatists, this explained everything: just as Karl Marx had discovered the hidden force in history – the economic motor behind cultural change – now women had the hidden mechanism in herstory: inequality had nothing to do with biology and culture, as the married reformist feminists thought; male power followed the systematic physical subjection of *all* women by *all* men through the practice of penetration/rape. And this meant, according to Susan Griffin, that rapists, far from being oddities, really raped women on behalf of *all* men, and that women let them get away with it only because patriarchy deliberately socialized them to be 'victims'. Knowing that rape was the only alternative, women readily accepted becoming another man's property by getting married to them.

It also explained the biggest conundrum bothering the separatists: how come women preferred men to them?

Despite their public obfuscations, the obvious inference that heterosexual intercourse even in marriage *is* rape became a separatist truism – one among many self-referential and validating explanations to emerge from a phase of 'women's-centred analysis' that advanced 'feminist theory' by the sophisticated process of simply inverting the more ridiculous male assumptions about women in the past, so that what boorish males considered to be innate female weaknesses were automatically celebrated by the separatists as virtues. It got worse.

As most women were obviously being kept in the dark about this historically hidden role of rape in patriarchy by the men they associated with, the separatists decided they must re-educate the still oppressed through 'consciousness raising' groups which 'explored' how women could redefine their personal experiences, in order to 'discover' how they were being exploited as a 'class' by patriarchy. For those women who remained blinded to the fact that it was their ideology-packed degree courses that had failed to prepare them for the equal responsibilities that equal opportunities bring, this was ecstasy; all their personal failings, mistakes, and the inevitable downsides to life could now be explained away as a disadvantage forced upon them by all those male *Sun*-reading sandwich students who were now reaping the reward of securing vocational qualifications.

Not surprisingly, this 'exploration' involved ditching 'male' standards of 'proof', like empirical data, in favour of drawing upon women's 'feelings', which supposedly consisted of a universal truth or life force. The authenticity of women's testimony was born; and once a 'woman-identified woman' emerged, such women were separated from their victimized sisters by their freedom from male-engendered rationality. If only all women could transcend the personal barrier of 'self-hatred' erected by men to inhibit women's natural 'lesbianism', patriarchy would collapse. This 'lesbianism', however, was not defined by anything so base and vulgar as sexual proclivity, but by being emotionally in tune with one's true 'feelings' and 'emotions', long suppressed and denounced as illegitimate by evil male science. As scientific rationalism had brought bombs and pollution to the environment, this recovery of 'wimmin's' memory of their innate maternal knowledge was going to be the first step to saving the planet.

Unfortunately, no amount of consciousness raising seemed to make much difference either, not least among sexually orientated lesbians who knew exactly how to get in touch with their feelings without the need to ditch rationality. So separatism's neo-Maoist phase began with the creation of collectives of 'wimmin' who, being free from all male ties, could engage in revolutionary acts – like changing their surnames to Laura*daughter* – to eradicate the influence of the patriarchal chain. Knowing that changing one's name would pose such a serious threat to patriarchy that a male backlash was inevitable, separatists reasoned that authentic 'lesbian wimmin' would also need the protection of 'safe spaces' within the wider women's movement, to ensure that those with advanced consciousness could organize the downfall of male authority without being murdered or having to pay their own way.

These obvious parallels with Marxism's hidden oppressive mechanisms, the role of consciousness, Leninist united fronts vanguardism, and now Maoist guerrilla tactics, did not stop there: history had to be Stalinistically rewritten too.

Victimology

The belief that all women would embrace 'political lesbianism' if only they had not been raped as children, forced into the sex industry, or coerced into marriage was complemented by an assertion that patriarchy had hidden this fate from women by deliberately 'silencing' women's 'voices'; and because 'political lesbianism' was the only means by which women would ever discover their 'real' sexuality, it followed that 'wimmin's' sexuality must also have been 'stolen' from them by men. Griffin postulated as fact that men 'turned women into pornography' because they so feared women's real passions they had created a sadistic civilization to repress it. Fearing they would lose control over their own body and mind, and thereby self-image, men bonded together through pornography, turning women into manageable 'sex dolls', which in turn deprived females of their natural spirit, and destroyed their soul.

One way to mirror-image male victimization of women into a positive force involved rejecting early feminism's critique of familial duties in favour of a reverence for motherhood, the one gender-specific advantage women had always possessed, but divorce it from 'rape', and its 'aftermath', marriage, through artificial insemination. Others, having bumped into the New Age Movement, began the search for 'wimmin's' lost mystical and spiritual powers from the days when we all supposedly went around venerating Moon Goddesses. But the majority, being fascinated with violent sex, wanted to know more about that; so Mary Daly and others began to tell them stories.

Once upon a time everyone was happy because they worshipped Moon Goddesses. Then horrible men raped all the women and imposed Sun God worship and patriarchy. After a little while the Christian Church became the main agency of patriarchal control and violently and viciously suppressed the last vestiges of natural reverence for the life-giving Goddess through 'sadomasochistic' Christ worship. And everyone lived unhappily ever after.

This 'sadomasochistic torture of women' can apparently be traced from the great European Witch Hunt to the dispensing of birth control pills in the 1960s; though what that has got to do with the Church is anyone's guess. Be that as it may, the only solution for 'wimmin' was to exorcize their oppression and bond together; patriarchy could not be reformed. Drawing upon Morgan's assertion that pornography was a deliberate act of male sexual terrorism – 'pornography is the theory, and rape the practice' – separatists began to see anti-pornography campaigns as an excellent means whereby women-identified women could undermine male bonding, and initiate some of their own. To this end, American WAVAW members began to apply their lunar-induced insights and feelings to the world of pornography. Once they did, pornography turned out to be worse than they had thought; far from 'merely' invoking aggressive acts against women from battery to rape, Barry's *Female Sexual Slavery* revealed that it was really a sadistic sex manual, training men in all forms of systematic misogynistic violence, from mutilation to 'gynocide' – the mass murder of women. Hence their obsession with snuff movies.

The misogyny of metaphor

The obvious problem with all these masochistic speculations, which have no basis in historical fact and only a little in the development of human ideas, is that they all infer cause from perceived consequence. While there is a legacy of Christian flesh hatred in twentieth-century Western culture, a thousand authors have alluded to this before: though admittedly none of them realized the inevitable conclusion, namely that women would all be 'political lesbians' otherwise. What these 'theories' do prove, however, is that the separatist charges against contemporary soft core have little to do with alleged changes in content or growing evidence of a link with sex crimes.

The separatists' 'analysis' ultimately rests upon a series of tautologies which enable them to move from their theoretical belief that men have stolen the essence of women, to a metaphoric claim that pin-ups 'annihilate' that essence, to their fantastic assertion that all over the world men are sitting down to watch snuff movies while their wives are out doing the shopping. This is achieved by reductive reasoning, so that Leidholdt, for example, having realized that objectification is often used by powerful groups to justify their control over others, simply asserts that objectification is the 'standard mechanism' of power imbalance. Likewise having found a couple of examples whereby a powerful group gave itself human attributes and the powerless group animal-like characteristics, Leidholdt surmised that this inevitably means that they have also created a reason to fear, ridicule, and hate the other group. Finally, having asserted that objectification was then *institutionalized* by powerful groups, Leidholdt then flips the circular proof to 'demonstrate' this quality in pornography too. As women are oppressed by men and 'objectified' in pornography, it followed that they *must be* presented as bestial in pornography, because men hate women, and wish to be violent towards them. Given this definition, of course, even the humble pin-up can be defined as animal pornography.

If both penetrative sex and pornography's pivotal roles are the mechanisms by which patriarchy controls women, it would inevitably follow that soft core *must* be harmful and that it *must* 'affect' male consumers; because that is how *all* men learn how to oppress *all* women. Having thereby defined heterosexual sex as a harm to women, a 'crime', pornography *must* promote sex crimes. It's easy when you know how.

As with the Christian version, the separatist critique of, and convictions about, pornography, preceded rather than followed an examination of the contents and effect studies. No wonder Susan Brownmiller, when asked by the *Boston Globe* what her evidence was, told them: we supply the ideology, it is other people's job to gather the data. The top prize in theoretical and tautological proof, however, must go to Andrea Dworkin, whose contribution to the growing self-referential separatist herstory of the world, *Pornography*, added a touch of psychology, or rather a feeble inversion of Freudianism.

According to Dworkin, male readers will be surprised to learn, fathers supply pornography to sons to deflect the inevitable Oedipal clash and to focus the son's violent tendencies upon women. Sons then readily ally with the father against women because they have no wish to become a victim of their father's violence in the meantime; and they learn quickly because pornography says that women enjoy violence.

Pornography for Dworkin, however, does not just refer to *Escort* or *Fiesta*. Any textual representation of a woman not created by a woman amounts to a negation of women's existence by men and is 'pornography', because only women have 'the right' to represent themselves; and because men really hate women, it follows that all male texts and artefacts representing women reflect this hatred. As women have also been 'silenced' and excluded from 'all cultural dialogue', it follows that all man-made art, religion, law, literature, philosophy, psychology, and films are 'pornography'. Consequently, women can only become themselves, be real people in their own right, when they are not bound and defined by men's pornographic representations of them; and women can only know that they are free when pornography ceases to exist. It could not be otherwise because, as Dworkin's *Intercourse* reveals, women who have sex with men are either collaborators who gain pleasure in their own inferiority, or are 'occupied territory' even if there was no force and the woman thought she wanted sex.

Far from demonstrating the danger of pornography, the only thing this nonsense proves, apart from Dworkin's rather limited understanding of sexual relationships, is that the parallel crusade against date rape has a theoretical origin too. The British WAVAW, however, swallowed this twaddle wholesale, and began to repeat it.

From USA to WAVAW

Being already convinced that they were a threat to patriarchy, and that a backlash was inevitable, WAVAW readily promoted the American assertion that pornography had become more violent since the birth of the women's movement. They did not despair though. This blatant male move in the Revelation* of the gender war signalled men's desperation at the emergence of the woman-identified woman and the arrival of the 'feminist revolution which will eventually bring down the whole of the male ruling class'; for violent pornography is to patriarchy what the declining rate of profit was (in a Marxist view) to capitalism – the 'internal contradiction' which ensures its inevitable demise. All the separatists had to do was alert women to this fact.

The link between these American theories and British demands to outlaw soft core can be found in many of WAVAW's early arguments. Rachael Adams set the scene:

> Pornography could never on its own be responsible for the way men treat women, as it does in itself symbolise the fear, contempt and aggression which all men feel for all women and which permeate our culture. However, its universal availability does legitimise each man's feelings. When porn was under the counter, men might have reason to feel guilty

---

* The biblical analogy here refers to the separatists' view that we are living in the end-time period of patriarchy. This point is elaborated in my forthcoming book *Sadomasochism*, to be published in this series.

over their rape fantasies, which were apparently socially disapproved of, and guilt can be inhibiting.

Now a generation of male British youth has been reared and weaned on full page spreads of female genitals and of vile sadistic practices which are apparently approved of.

Having convinced themselves that patriarchy used to conceal pornography under the counter to hide it from women, rather than admit one obvious contradiction, they ignored another as Ginrod and Katyachild then denounced pornography for incitement to violence:

> Feminists' analysis of pornography is now well established – it shows porn to be a dangerous form of propaganda that deliberately incites men to carry out acts of violence upon women.
> ... In short pornography is about power, the sexual power that men seek to inflict upon women.

This feminist 'analysis', of course, was completely self-referential, but easily 'proven' for adherents to it by a correlation between the theoretical content and overt rape figures:

> the sadistic and cruel images of women being tortured, mutilated, raped and killed are rising steadily, and along with this increase with the pornography, rape incidents multiply steadily.

To suggest that one would have to weight any figures for population increase, not to mention estimating the covert unreported rapes of the past, before such a claim is even viable is just another part of the male plot to silence women. As is the suggestion that such melodramatic claims do not even square with WAVAW's rather inclusive public definition of what pornography is:

> pornography ... ranges from page 3 in the *Sun*, through to *Penthouse*, *Les Girls*, and finally terminates in the horror of Snuff movies. Each magazine and booklet is full of images of women that are objectified, fetishised, violated, dehuma-

nised and always degraded ... Snuff movies are films where women are actually killed as the ultimate climax in the pornographers' 'sick plot'. Cases have been discovered in California.

Not surprisingly, WAVAW asserted that as long as the male definition of sex ruled, women would never find their own sexuality:

Pornography is male defined sexuality. Women cannot reach a self defined sexuality while surrounded by the male view of what sex is and of what women are. The prevailing view of sex in porn is that not only can sex be separated from love, but from humanity. Rife at the moment are features of female genitals with no face or even body attached. At the same time sex is presented as a package, separate from the rest of our life and human experience. The view of women in pornography is that they are passive, depersonalized objects of male aggression, content for experimentation.

Apart from recourse to the snuff myth to avoid their claims about soft core's content looking foolish, this implication that the planet is not big enough for more than one sexuality in the market-place of ideas sounds very similar to the Christian inference that there are only two kinds of sexualities – the good and the evil.

As WAVAW had no need to convince a wider public at this stage, such arguments did not have to be tailored to fit a general audience; but once the need arose, it is easy to see how the contemporary version still only makes sense in terms of WAVAW's *a priori* beliefs.

Women v. women

Given the separatists' failure to explain just exactly what kind of sex they did approve of, while their complaints against pornography clearly implied what sexual practices were unacceptable, a lot of women, both lesbian and heterosexual, began to call the separatists' bluff, and opponents in the women's movement began to emerge. Beginning in America and Canada, the ensuing rift took several years to permeate into Britain, though when it did it took a similar form: for despite their anti-male rhetoric, separatists hate women who disagree with them even more.

The American WAVAW and WAP (which always struck me as a strange acronym for an anti-violence group) became extremely angry when they discovered that several lesbian groups' discussions on 'sexual politics' were covering issues like women's fantasies, pornography, and fetishes rather than stick to the catechism of male oppression. When one group, SAMOIS, dared produce a lesbian guide to SM sex it was the final straw. WAVAW then attempted to deny the group's ideas wider circulation in the women's movement, because SAMOIS' very existence undermined all WAVAW's tautologies about 'male' sadomisogyny and pornography. If women, as SAMOIS members did, also enjoyed dressing up, using dildos, and spanking each other, twenty years of theorizing 'male' sexual desire also went down the pan. Already frustrated by the failure of American women to throw away their see-through baby-dolls or lap dance, the attack upon SAMOIS became obsessive.

The first public division in the movement occurred in April 1982. The Women's Centre at Barnard College was hosting the Scholar and Feminist Conference 'Towards a Politics of Sexuality', organized by academics to discuss all facets of women's sexuality and experience, and swop ideas about what issues should be covered before feminism could fully develop a sexual theory and politics. To this end, invitations were extended to a variety of perspectives that cut across, and went beyond, academic disciplines; it was going to be one of the most exciting academic conferences in years.

WAVAW, however, were not happy. The academics would inevitably examine current feminist orthodoxy, and would invariably consider the possibility that there was more to women's sexual experience than male violence.

Being the authors of the orthodoxy, WAVAW and WAP were faced with the prospect of having their babble put under the microscope by serious rational academic feminism; and that was more than they could stand. Having spent a couple of months failing to get prominent feminists to denounce the conference, and then telling the college administration it was a forum for perverts, child abusers and snuff movie makers, WAP supporters turned up on the first day distributing a libellous leaflet making absurd insinuations about individual participants who collectively were also supposed to be encouraging sexual torture and murder of women, having all internalized patriarchal woman-hating values. The denunciation of the organization No More Nice Girls, a New York abortion rights group, for promoting pornography was typical. WAP had a personal grudge against No More Nice Girls because one of their number had opposed WAVAW publicly in the past.

Having their conference organization disrupted by the college authorities and then losing their Helena Rubinstein Foundation funding because of the publicity stunned the academics. So-called anti-pornography campaigns were now trying to censor other women's views about sex in general. And once WAVAW's denials did not square with their tendency to raid feminist bookstore shelves and burn any SAMOIS literature they found there, the women's movement began to divide between those who believe all tactics in the gender war are viable, and those who do not accept that a utopian dream justifies fascistic ends. Civil rights activists and Libertarian feminists joined with the academics to denounce WAVAW's determination to use violence *against* women themselves. At first this led to a re-examination of WAVAW's politics, victimology, and claims about pornography content; but once they also formed an alliance with the Moral Majority, women's organizations were formed to oppose directly WAVAW's stranglehold on the 'feminist' approach to sex.

The ordinances

Within a year, WAVAW and their acolytes, being unwilling to face open debate within the women's movement, revealed their lack of principle and joined Andrea Dworkin and Catherine MacKinnon's appeal to the patriarchal state to force every woman to accept their theories about pornography.

American soft core's protection as a form of free speech under the US Constitution's First Amendment depends upon the lack of evidence of direct harmful consequences; so Ms Dworkin and Professor MacKinnon spent the 1980s trying to establish a legal judgment that soft core did indeed cause harm, and thereby bypass the protection offered by the Constitution.

MacKinnon developed her feminism from seeing how the Black Panthers had adopted Marxism for their cause, and she became convinced that sexuality was to feminism what work was to Marxism. As we have already seen, men supposedly steal women's sexuality through intercourse just as capitalists extract surplus value from workers; and women become alienated from their sexuality as workers are alienated from the product of their labour. But being a little smarter than the average WAVAW member, MacKinnon took the analogy further. Dehumanizing women not only stole women's consciousness, it involved money: selling pornography being one example. Having made her name fighting sexual harassment cases, MacKinnon then realized that if she defined pornography as a form of sex discrimination, men stealing women's sexuality to sell it on to other men, maybe the law should give women the right to sue to get it back. She was very pleased with herself.

Dworkin, who was invited to speak at one of MacKinnon's University of Minnesota classes in 1983, was not so sure at first; but convincing themselves over a coffee that they were the feminist Lenin and Trotsky with a herstoric role in securing the revolutionary overthrow of patriarchy, they continued to swop ideas. Because most women are not yet fully conscious they would never sue; so why not frame the law so that the middle-class 'woman-identified woman' vanguard could sue male pornographers for millions of dollars on behalf of women as a class, especially those bimbo models who do not know what they are doing. Just think of what the vanguard could do with all that money. Perfect; much better than that useless obscenity law, concerned with morals, which furthers the purpose of patriarchy. Yes; if pornography is illegal, you cannot sue it. But by suing after production, we make lots of money, and the politically correct will not have to choose between censorship and ending exploitation either. No, better still, why not insist that such a law was akin to providing black Civil Rights legislation? They will have to agree with us.

By equating the contemporary position of women to southern blacks in the 1960s who were physically denied their civil rights despite the Constitution, the dynamic duo were hardly being original, but it sounded good. By being sexually 'abused' – having sex with men and losing their identity in the process – women too were being physically denied their rights, despite the Constitution. This took two forms, either covert, as in marriage:

> In the common fabric of everyday life, women are in a sense, forcibly integrated, intimately integrated, with society so organized that women's reproductive capacities have been controlled by men. Women have been kept out of the market place to be kept in the home, or kept in the bed, or kept in the kitchen, or kept pregnant. Social institutions, patterns, and practices force women to fulfill the sexual and reproductive imperatives of men.
>
> Because so much of women's inequality centers on forced sexual and reproductive compliance, the ways in which women are debased in rights and in personhood center on issues of bodily integrity, physical self determination, and the social irradiation of forced sex or sexual abuse ...;

or an overt form of violence:

> Systematic violations of women's rights to safety, dignity, and civil equality take the form of rape, battery, incest, prostitution, sexualized torture, and sexualized murder, all of which are endemic in this society now.

But either way, all heterosexual sex maintained women's inequality:

> The second class status of women is justified in the conviction that by nature women are sexually submissive, provoke and enjoy sexual aggression from men, and get sexual pleasure from pain. By nature women are servile and the servility itself is sexual ... violations of women are seen as part of normal human nature, not the result of a coercive system that devalues women.
>
> Women need laws that address the ways in which women are kept second class. ...

To redress this rape/sex in marriage, MacKinnon sought a law which would undermine the male 'right' to women's sex, and the male 'right' to speech which enforced female silence: pornography. Assuming that no one freely gives up their rights, MacKinnon also warned that change would not be peaceful, but would have to follow 'sustained and bitter rebellion' against every social institution of male authority over women:

> The state is one institution of male authority. The rapist is another. The husband is another. The pimp is another. The priest is another. The publisher is another. ...
>
> Resistance to male authority requires far more than resistance to the state or the authority of the state. For women, the authority of the man extends into intimacy and privacy, inside the body in sex and in reproduction. In worshipping a male God, in conforming to social codes of dress and demeanor, even in using language, women defer to the authority of men.

But while taking on the whole edifice of patriarchy would be a tall order, a concerted effort at undermining its foundation would speed its destruction. Undermining the Constitution's protection of male 'rights' would force change. A new obscenity law was not the answer, because laws concerned with moral regulation rather than exploitation merely maintained patriarchy; but the issue of immoral display could provide a link to the new law, which once in operation could be used to expose the existence of women 'trapped in sexually toxic marriages' or forced sex outside, because law – the courtroom – would become the forum for demonstrating the 'harm' of all male pornographic/sex/rape/marriage practice.

The end result was the Ordinance, which did not so much attempt to set 'wrongs' right, as define what they were, by declaring the 'harm' of pornography at the same time:

> The harm of pornography includes dehumanization, sexual exploitation, forced sex, forced prostitution, physical injury, and social and sexual terrorism and inferiority presented as entertainment.
>
> The bigotry and contempt pornography promotes with

the acts of aggression it fosters, diminish opportunities for equality of rights in employment, education, property, public accommodations, and public services; create public and private harassment, persecution and denigration ... demean the reputations and diminish the occupational opportunities of individuals and groups on the basis of sex ... contribute significantly to restricting women in participation in public life ... damage relations between the sexes, and undermine women's equal exercise of rights of speech and action...

Although this perspective clearly rests upon Dworkin's wider definition of pornography, they were careful to narrow down their stipulative definition to appear merely to target sexually explicit material in order to increase their chances of success:

Pornography is the graphic sexually explicit subordination of women through pictures and/or words that also include one or more of the following: (i) women are presented dehumanized as sexual objects, things or commodities; or (ii) women are presented as sexual objects who enjoy pain or humiliation; or (iii) women are presented as sexual objects who experience sexual pleasure in being raped; or (iv) women are presented as sexual objects tied up or cut up or mutilated or bruised or physically hurt; or (v) women are presented in postures or positions of sexual submission, servility or display; or (vi) women's body parts – including but not limited to vaginas, breasts, or buttocks – are exhibited such that women are reduced to those parts; or (vii) women are presented as whores by nature; or (viii) women are presented being penetrated by objects or animals, or (ix) women are presented in scenarios of degradation, injury, torture, shown as filthy or inferior, bleeding, bruised, or hurt in a context that makes these conditions sexual.

As well as this section, which lists sexual practices that are *de facto* oppressive in such a way that a court would have to accept that such pictures and text were a discriminatory act, the Ordinance's other sections were likewise carefully crafted in an attempt to slip past every Supreme Court ruling and definition which might get in the way and make the Ordinance unconstitutional. This was tricky, given some ambiguous rulings, but the Ordinance's wording always attempted to imply direct harm. Consequently, the Ordinance contained: a coercion section, asserting that pornography systematically denied women the autonomy the law prohibiting restriction of free speech assumes; an assault section, defining sexual depictions as an assault on the model; and a discrimination section, making availability of pornography an act of discrimination.

Ultimately, all that MacKinnon and Dworkin were doing was attempting to codify the separatists' self-referential validations as a legal test, which would contain their stipulative definition of pornography and provide the means to enforce that definition upon everyone else. Under these sections any woman could file a civil suit against the sale, exhibition, or distribution of material she deemed pornographic; or file a suit following an assault or physical attack she believed was provoked by material she deemed pornographic. This right was not restricted to the model or the victim; on the contrary, anyone could attempt to secure damages for the model, *with or without her consent.* Consent was meaningless anyway; the 'limitations of action clauses' made it impossible for a defendant to use a model's consent, complicity, or contract as proof that the woman had not been coerced into posing or performing; and if another woman brought the law suit, even the model could not claim she consented! The almost immediate effect of the Ordinance once a law suit was filed would have been to drive all sexual representations underground. The separatists were so determined to do this that gay men were deemed to be substitute women for the purpose of the Ordinance.

The most bemusing aspect of this approach was how both Dworkin and MacKinnon firmly believed that a court conviction is sure proof the prosecution is correct – an untenable position for real civil libertarians. Yet they had such an awe for advocacy that they deluded themselves into believing that their argument was invincible. Typical was MacKinnon's conviction that as the concept of gender itself 'emerges as the congealed form of the sexualization of inequality between men and women', all heterosexual relations would inevitably involve dominance and submission, and all representations of this sexuality were therefore eroticized violence. They were, however, desperate for a successful suit not only to undermine male power, but to prove their theories were true; and there was a lot at stake here.

As the claim that violent imagery was increasing was based not upon content, but their own definition of pornography, whereby the image's forcible extraction of the women's integrity made everything, including the simple pin-up, an act of violence, and because their claims about models always being coerced rested upon the belief that no woman could be free to choose in a patriarchal society, real proof was going to be hard to find. Throwing around the odd picture culled from sadomasochistic magazines was a cheap way to illustrate a philosophical point, and would never suffice. Ultimately, both MacKinnon and Dworkin thought it irrelevant whether or not a link between pornography and harm could be demonstrated, because they had defined pornography as systematic harm:

> The presumptions that underlie the First Amendment do not apply to women. The First Amendment assumes some kind of social equality. ...
>
> In the context of inequality between the sexes, we cannot assume that that is accurate. The First Amendment also presumes that for the mind to be free to fulfil itself, speech must be free and open. Andrea's work shows that pornography constructs to enslaving women's minds and bodies. As a social process and as a form of 'speech' pornography amounts to terrorism and promotes not freedom but silence. ... Pornography terrorizes women into silence. Pornography is therefore not in the interest of our speech.

This blatant attempt to replace the kind of proof required by law that acts of violence arise directly from harmful attitudes with a mere tautological assertion was likely to convince only the ideologically committed. History, however, demonstrates that 'proof' of an ideology exists for as long as it can be imposed upon others. No wonder Dworkin and MacKinnon would do anything to ensure that someone somewhere would accept their law, and gain a conviction.

A feminist law?

The first version of the Ordinance appeared in Minneapolis, whose City Council was desperately looking for a means to deal with residents' complaints about aspects of red light zoning. A councillor, Hoyt, brought in Dworkin and MacKinnon as consultants; but although two local neighbourhood groups took this opportunity to press their case over zoning, few others welcomed these feminists' appearance. The Ordinance was passed only because it was railroaded through the Council over normal procedures, as all the 'public' demonstrations, midnight vigils, lobbying, and those present at the hearings consisted of the same fifty to one hundred women bussed in from MacKinnon's classes. The opposition this invoked was incredible.

Ironically, given its pretensions to be a civil rights measure, not only did the procedure adopted break the city's own civil rights guidelines but the civil rights officers were not even consulted. Nor was the black community, which was most put out by the subsequent analogies between the 'wimmin's' Ordinance and the fight against racism. The gay community denounced the measure as 'sexist' once they discovered that MacKinnon had defined them as substitute women. The most damning fact about Dworkin and MacKinnon's approach to civil rights, however, is that their appointments violated the city's affirmative action guidelines, which required open competition for all posts!

City employees were not happy either to see every formal procedure and democratic safeguard being broken. What annoyed the city's Assistant Attorney most of all was the bizarre situation whereby the lobbying advocate, MacKinnon, was being paid as a simultaneous consultant, which meant the Council was paying thousands of dollars to lobby itself. As awkward questions mounted, MacKinnon sought to mislead the Council that everything was consistent with First Amendment precedent and principle. Though some, rather than seek independent advice, were bamboozled by her status as lawyer and professor, the three feminists on the Council were not convinced, and opposed the Ordinance.

Local feminist activists who were not consulted became

more upset when attempts at discussion proved impossible. Like crazed millenerians, Ordinance supporters went to any length to avoid any. Theresa Stanton, for example, claimed that its passage was an act of survival because it was increasingly difficult and dangerous to be a feminist in the USA. (She was obviously a member of the vanguard.) MacKinnon simply denounced the opposition as 'not real feminists', and insisted that calling the Ordinance censorship amounted to calling the prevention of murder censorship, a definition culled from Dworkin's *Pornography*, which declared that 'eroticization of murder is the essence of pornography'. The hearings before the vote were also a farce, as the failure to invite countervailing evidence was excused by Dworkin and MacKinnon because 'this opportunity for our speech is a rare and unprecedented achievement'. This typical attempt to avoid debate went so far as misinforming potential opponents where and when the hearings were; and although gay activists, librarians, and a member of the civil rights commission did manage to get to speak, they were drowned out by the carefully vetted audience, who booed, hissed, moaned, and cried on cue. The 'victims of pornography' and the female 'experts', were then cheered and applauded for every line, for they were also 'women-identified women' like themselves, and repeated the tales of woe and assertions from WAVAW's *Reclaim the Night*. Oddly enough, given the importance placed upon the evidence linking soft core's link with sex crime offered by 'effects' expert Donnerstein at the hearing, MacKinnon excused the lack of a second opinion on the grounds that 'Andrea Dworkin and I did not waste the City Council's resources with outdated and irrelevant data and investigations'. The City Council members then voted for the Ordinance.

The Mayor, however, mindful of the huge opposition and concerned about the Ordinance's legal status, promptly vetoed it. Although it was passed again, the Federal Court promptly struck it down because it obviously constituted 'viewpoint discrimination', favouring one social group against another; and, ironically in doing so, effectively elevated pornography to a class of ideas, which meant that Dworkin and MacKinnon had actually furthered its First Amendment cause!

If the bully-boy tactics in Minneapolis encouraged American feminists to be wary of the separatists' motives, their next attempt also proved that MacKinnon's feminist credentials were completely suspect.

Indianapolis was the largest Republican-run city in the USA. Before they even heard of the Ordinance, the council had been systematically closing down its sex bookstores and massage parlours, but had since become bogged down with legal appeals, and hoped an Ordinance would avoid disputes over free speech and zoning. Unlike as in Minneapolis, however, Dworkin and MacKinnon could not hide behind any neighbourhood complaints about zones; the Ordinance's sole backers were Ezekiel factor Christian crusaders. The biggest group, Citizens for a Clean Community, was led by Baptist pastor Les Hickson, a co-founder of the Moral Majority who believed pornography was a humanist plot to undermine Christendom; and MacKinnon's employer was the conservative Republican, Ms Coughenour, an anti-feminist, who had led the successful Stop ERA campaign in Indiana. Coughenour insisted that Dworkin keep away and wanted a more pragmatic version of the Ordinance too. Only eleven of the twenty-nine Council members supported the Ordinance at first, and reservations had appeared in local conservative newspapers. Success, therefore, also depended upon keeping MacKinnon's neo-Marxism hidden from Council members. MacKinnon complied, and few Councillors realized that MacKinnon was anything other than an ultra-conservative until afterwards.

The hearings invited only anti-pornography witnesses, and when the local civil liberties union and the Equal Opportunities Advisory Board managed to submit 'public testimony' the CDL found others. The Ordinance gained a twenty-four to five majority. Women's groups were conspicuous by their absence; the audience on this occasion consisted of local Baptists bussed in for that purpose. Councillors were later to complain about being pressured in an open meeting facing TV cameras, and a big score-board to record the votes; and no wonder. In this atmosphere they also foolishly voted down a resolution limiting their fiscal ceiling for defending the Ordinance through the Courts. It was to cost the Republicans' flirtation with feminism dear.

The American Booksellers Association, backed by the Civil Liberties Union, took the Mayor to court on the grounds that the Ordinance went beyond the Constitutional standards, not least by making a person liable without requiring that said party to have any knowledge of the nature of the offending material; and in November 1984, the feminist Judge Barker struck it down. Apart from reiterating that it granted special group preferences, she dismissed key Ordinance terms as being 'excessively vague'. All the enforcement actions were then declared unconstitutional. In August the following year, Judge Frank Easterbrook upheld Barker's decision in the Court of Appeals, and denounced the Ordinance as

> thought control. It establishes an 'approved' view of women, of how they may react to sexual encounters, of how the sexes may relate to each other. Those who espouse the approved view may use sexual images, those who do not may not.

The Supreme Court took one look at its clauses and refused to hear the case: the law had to exhibit strict neutrality in speech pertaining to politics.

At each stage, the Council had to foot the bill, which ran to millions, and all for nothing. Some people never learn. When the Winchester City Council in Indiana had a go, they were unable to publish the Ordinance's clauses in the local newspaper because the proprietor deemed the wording to be obscene!

MacKinnon, however, was determined to press on. At another attempt in Cambridge during October 1985, MacKinnon finally let her real beliefs out of the bag by arguing that yes, even paintings of female nudes by female artists would be subject to the Ordinance; and, in replying to a lesbian's question regarding her views about porn-reading women, MacKinnon replied: 'If pornography is part of your sexuality then you have no right to your sexuality.' Far from saving the day, this was the final nail in the coffin of feminist support for the Ordinances.

Back in Britain

Incredibly, despite the coverage of the Barnard College débâcle in *Feminist Review*, news of American developments was slow to permeate Britain. When I gave a lecture on pornography perspectives at Essex University in 1984 to a packed room, none of the dozens of feminists present had even heard of Barnard, let alone the Ordinances! But the British WAVAW knew, and kept their eyes open for any dissent here, and over-reacted when the American feminist *Heresies* magazine's 'Sex Issue', which carried a balanced debate on anti-pornography arguments began to circulate; fear turned to fright when a dozen or so lesbians calling themselves SM Dykes also began to organize meetings; and when an arts magazine *Square Peg*, which had denounced Silk Cut advertisements as images 'of violation and hatred of women like every pornographic image', gave the Dykes and others six pages to put their case, WAVAW flipped, provoking a British split.

The SM Dykes had expected to be censored by the 'separatist'-controlled women's press but had not bargained for physical ejection from women's centres like A Woman's Place, which, being funded by the GLC, was not supposed to discriminate on grounds of sexual orientation. Any sense of isolation, however, quickly disappeared when the censoring of letters to the women's press, the appearance of WAVAW 'snatch squads' raiding bookshops, and further physical attacks on Dykes at various lesbian discos began to polarize opinion. WAVAW's thuggish behaviour, unknown in the twee British women's movement, where everyone was supposed to behave like a therapist, undermined WAVAW credibility. Even WIRES, fearful of losing influence, had to relent and publish letters about censorship. But far from reconsider their position, WAVAW launched a major 'offensive' and attempted to have SM Dykes barred from London's new Gay Centre.

In 1985, the GLC had advanced some £1 million to help fund a Gay Centre for its citizens. Separatists, whose public funding was drying up as rate-capping hit the tokenistic London Boroughs, looked at the centre with an envious eye. Despite being granted a 'wimmin only' floor, WAVAW also demanded a ban on the SM Dykes meeting there on the incredible grounds that the Dykes' leather jackets and skirts were Nazi uniforms and promoted men's freedom to be violent against women. Sheila Jeffreys, the separatist ideologue, penned their justification:

We recognise that many expressions of male violence current amongst sado-masochists include symbols and activities that are directly fascist and racist. Sadomasochism does not exist in a cultural vacuum; as the name suggests, it comes from a male, violent view of sexuality that goes back centuries. There are clear links between sado-masochism in Berlin in the 1930's and the rise of fascism; the same events are beginning in Britain today.

In reality, these 'links' only existed in Sheila Jeffreys' fantasies. Jeffreys, who was already incensed by the Dykes' 'effrontery' in joining in that year's Lesbian Strength march, had distributed a polemic against the SM sex among London's women's groups. According to her tacky missive, SM sex, like waxing, replicated Nazi SS torture techniques, and was a direct threat to female sexuality. It was bad enough, Jeffreys reasoned, that *all* little girls were socialized to be submissive by aggressive boys at school pulling their knickers down and adult men sexually abusing them. But if the Dykes were allowed to flourish, all women, including the lesbian vanguard, would have their masochistic tendencies 'triggered', by SM/Nazi symbolism, be turned on by the idea of being powerless or humiliated, and succumb to the total victory of the abusive, cruel and arbitrary power of males.

The first time I read this, I couldn't believe my eyes; the language was so inflamed it sounded like someone who understood masochistic eroticism; surely Jeffreys was not admitting that WAVAW crusaders held a dark secret. The answer is yes. Six years later in an obscure American book, Jeffreys admitted that:

Those of us involved in the British feminist movement against pornography often sat around in groups and admitted, though not at first since it was not easy, that even the most anti-women material which we were dealing could cause us to be turned on. ... What I think happened is that as feminists started putting out slide shows ... and as women started having reactions to these slides – at times becoming turned on by those slides themselves – there were two choices that women could make. They could say: 'I am turned on by these slides. Isn't it absolutely horrifying how my subordination as a woman has been eroticised and gotten into what is the most intimate and personal part of me –

the middle of my heart and my body – and appears to be what is most personal and most mine?'

They could say that, and become absolutely furious about the extent to which women's oppression can actually enter into our hearts and minds. *That is the choice I have made and other feminists have made. And therefore it motivates us even more* to fight pornography and male violence.

Alternatively, women who had been turned on by such slides could think: 'I am aroused by this material. Therefore, I am angry with the feminists who are showing it to me. I am angry because they are making me feel guilty and ashamed. Therefore, I will fight them.' I think this is why some feminists are fighting the anti-pornography activists, are fighting us.

There are, of course, many other things women could say; these options only reflect the typical simplistic dualist thinking of anti-pornography activists. However, Jeffreys, who led the anti-pornography movement before Dr Itzin, has clearly admitted that numerous activists were actually turned on by what they sought to eradicate; and that means that when WAVAW claimed that such an assertion was an evil male fantasy, they were lying. Which makes their crusade, like Caton's, a huge exercise in the projection of their sex guilt on to others. Further proof that motivations are often tangential to their justification came in WIRES #144 when a woman called 'Sky' admitted destroying the Sisterwrite bookshops' copies of SAMOIS's *Coming to Power* because she believed it promoted and condoned violence against women. She also admitted that her annoyance at the shop's sensible attitude to controversial ideas was motivated by having suffered a *physically abusive lesbian relationship*. Whereas this had apparently undermined her 'self-love', she could now regain her self-respect by destroying copies of the book.

WAVAW, of course, were hardly likely to alter course and face up to the reality of such motivations, they were too busy hiding the hypocritical desires of 'wimmin-identified wimmin' from the public, by redoubling their attack on the SM Dykes. Jeffreys not only denounced them as porn apologists but insisted that they were 'agents of the Thatcher Government', who deliberately sought meeting places in a coordinated campaign to spread confusion and disunity among lesbians. By insisting that the Dykes' leather clothes were an insult to disabled, black, Jewish lesbians in London, Jeffreys believed all women would rally against the Dykes. But whereas this emotional appeal might go down well in women's 'I am more oppressed than you' circles, the gay centre's membership, despite being boosted by a sudden influx of WAVAW supporters, rejected the proposition after several heated meetings.

Clashes with WAVAW were not a new experience within the feminist movement; but their major opponents, the Marxist English Collective of Prostitutes, known as the ECP, had been somewhat marginalized in the past. The new dispute, however, meant that more women began to consider the ECP alternatives. Based at the Women's Centre in King's Cross, London, the ECP and allied groups like Women Against Rape (which helped secure the legal precedent of rape within marriage) championed the cause of sex industry workers, and had always thought the anti-porn line was counterproductive.

Like that of the SM Dykes, the ECP's very existence undermined WAVAW's exclusive perspective on pornography, but to make matters worse, the ECP spent a lot of their time lobbying patriarchal councils, Government departments and the Criminal Law Revision Committee to change the laws discriminating against prostitutes. As far as the ECP were concerned, anti-pornography campaigns increased patriarchy's power, and were anti-women; and they did not shirk from telling everybody so either:

> It is no accident that most of the countries hardest on pornography, also trample the hardest on women's rights. It is, therefore, extremely dangerous for all women that the attack on pornography and the call for censorship is spearheaded by so-called 'feminists.'

> Anti-porn campaigners have also been so busy discussing the effects of pornography that they sometimes forget to discuss the effects of censorship. They have been so concerned with the imagery that they have forgotten all about reality. With rising unemployment, increasing numbers of women are turning to the sex industry to provide a living for themselves and their families.

Have the anti-porn campaigners considered what effects greater censorship and forcing the sex industry underground would have on the working conditions and the safety of women in the sex industry? We cannot be concerned only with the safety of *some* women in 'approved' occupations.

This was not what the middle-class members of WAVAW wanted to hear; and though many feminists had other disputes with the ECP, it was hard to ignore their arguments for prioritizing issues like economic inequality. Apart from providing a more detailed and consistent Marxist position than MacKinnon's, what really riled WAVAW was that the ECP insisted that if anyone was going to speak for women in the sex industry and offer advice to the women's movement it should be sex workers and not WAVAW. It was obvious what those women would say: porn crackdowns led to worsening work conditions, police harassment, and inhibited collective organization, thereby increasing the rate of exploitation in the industry, furthering the possibility of robbery, rape, and violence at the same time.

If the ECP's arguments embarrassed WAVAW, WAR theorists made them wince by pointing out WAVAW's crass simplicity and even questioning their personal motivations by drawing an analogy between prohibition and contemporary anti-porn crusades whereby:

The prohibition movement, mostly women, had a point when they said that men got drunk and then came home and beat their wives. It was true, and it still is true. But is the solution to ban the sale of alcohol or to fight for wives to be in a position where we no longer have to put up with being beaten?

The source of the problem – and of the images – is real-life power relations, which is why *WAR has preferred to focus most of our energy on actual violence and on the way that the Court, the law, the women's financial dependence makes us vulnerable to this*. [emphasis added]

The ECP and WAR, unlike most other feminists, had always been wary of the British movement's puritanical tradition, which in one way or another still divided women into the polluted and the pure; and their knowledge of content also challenged Dworkinite claims about soft-core violence:

> From what WAVAW have written, it is clear that for some women any depiction of heterosexual sex is violence in itself. WAVAW have frequently stated that they are against all porn, whether or not it portrays violence, because they don't like the kind of sex it shows. For others, nude and masturbating women are violently offensive. There is no reason why any woman should be forced to look at any pornographic images she finds offensive, but nor is there any reason why a particular view of sex, or particular sexual morality, should be imposed on all women by forbidding the sale of pornography to those who want to buy it.
>
> Part of the market for pornography is both lesbian and straight women who enjoy pictures of nude women and enjoy an open display of female sexuality. Women in small towns who have no access to a public lesbian movement have found in this kind of pornography some confirmation of women's enjoyment of our own and other women's bodies. Some sex-shops are now introducing women-only hours, and while their interest is purely commercial, any move which enables women to talk more openly and frankly about our sexuality, and not to feel ashamed of our enjoyment of sex, including through the use of mechanical aids like vibrators, has to be to women's advantage.
>
> To clamp down on this kind of pornography is to clamp down on sex and sexual expression in a way which can only be to the detriment of women generally and lesbian women in particular. We cannot ignore the fact that anti-sex crusaders like Mary Whitehouse think that all lesbianism, homosexuality, and even all heterosexual sex outside marriage, is pornographic and should not be allowed. It cannot be the purpose of the women's movement to dictate any women's sexual expression when what we should be campaigning for is more choices for women.

Though similar critiques have since emerged in the women's movement, for many years the ECP and WAR were the only feminists who would publicly say so; and for this the women's movement owes them a debt.

The split between ECP and WAVAW can be traced back to the Reclaim the Night marches, when WAR were involved in the 1981 organizing committee, before withdrawing after several disputes. WAR would have preferred to avoid Soho; it was hardly an unsafe part of London, and if the demonstration wished to target sexual imagery it should stop at violent pornography. WAVAW supporters refused to make distinctions, and also rejected WAR's insistence that no one should intimidate prostitutes or sex workers. WAR withdrew, and warned that the failure to draw a clear distinction between the small amount of material glorifying violence and soft core would ensure that feminists would be seen as opposing what is sexual, rather than what is violence. To try to avoid this, the ECP released an *Open Letter to All Women* which argued that by not helping sex workers to unionize, feminist crusades had merely played into the hands of 'moralists' like Labour MP Frank Dobson, and the police, who were already harassing women on the grounds that eliminating prostitution was part of the feminist agenda to make streets safe. Prostitutes, of course, were also easier to catch than rapists.

Given that serious research reveals that most women enter the sex industry for economic reasons, that they are introduced by other women, and wish to work in it temporarily, the ECP's perspective made a lot of sense. If ECP had a failing, it was that their loyalty to women as a class blinded them to the fact that WAVAW were not simply mistaken in providing the police with good excuses, but that WAVAW welcomed the persecution of sex workers. During the mid-1980s, when a group of peep-show dancers attempted to extricate themselves from Soho's slimy operators, established a cooperative of their own and ran a show from 28 Wardour Street, they were vehemently opposed by WAVAW and the politically correct GLC's Women's Committee. To allow women to run voluntarily any aspect of the sex industry would, of course, negate most feminist justifications for attacking it; but by attacking the women's peep-show separatists proved once and for all that they were opposed to sexual display, not male power.

Nevertheless, as far back as 1983, the ECP posed four prophetic questions for the women's movement:

1. Is the women's movement going to fight for more power for women, *including women in the sex industry* (for example the abolition of the prostitution laws) or more power for the police?
2. Will the starting point be more sexual choices for all women or the imposition of sexual 'standards'?
3. Are the demands going to be made which bring women more choices, or are the women in the sex industry to be blamed for violence against women, and hounded out of making a living?
4. Will the actions women propose bring women together or drive them apart? In other words, are they going to build a movement or a backlash?

WAVAW's answer came in the *City Limits* special issue on International Women's Day the same year. Having claimed it was not the sex, but the violence innate to pornographic images that she objected to, Jeffreys lost her dictionary and asserted that there were 'two' options for women. One was the long-term plan to abandon 'compulsory heterosexuality'. The second was 'the short term' picket of sex shops to raise women's consciousness, which would increase the speed at which women would arrive at the long term. This *single* option did not stand a chance, because by 1985 the tide had turned. Activists laughed when the *London Women's Liberation Newsletter #375* accused ECP of being a CIA plot, and were not going to be told what to do.

Faced with the threat of open debate with other feminists about soft core, WAVAW were in real trouble, as their skills stopped short at intimidation; so they desperately tried to regain some initiative through symbolic actions. In 1985, for example, they badgered Haringey Council and the dying GLC to refuse a small Asian-owned cinema club called the Curzon a new licence. The public justification was that the Curzon's choice of films, including the '15' certificate *Choose Me*, broke GLC regulation 116(d). This regulation, which effectively meant any 'sexist' films were to be denied a showing in London, had been added to the licensing regulations by the Women's Committee, but had never been used before. In reality, this move was pure spite following the imprisonment of two supporters for non-payment of fines following convictions for criminal acts committed in a previous anti-Curzon demonstration. The GLC hearing, with the male crusaders Branagan and Cassidy sitting on the panel, was the first in living memory to remove a club licence when the police had made no complaint, the local residents were in favour of renewal, and the licence holder had kept exemplary records. The owner did not even wish to continue to show such films; he had merely inherited a play list and was desperately trying to interest the council in turning it into a local arts centre. But why worry about losing the opportunity to create a real local resource, when you can strike a blow against patriarchy? Quite rightly, the decision was overturned by a Crown Court a couple of months later, because the films in question had *all* been exhibited by the major cinema chains, which were not being penalized, and because the four GLC female barristers had to admit to the judge that the mighty GLC Women's Committee had not even been competent enough to brief them!

WAVAW's other attempt to win back credibility and maintain membership morale was another round of sex shop pickets in 1986. As these shops were all going to close anyway, these pickets were pointless. In Portsmouth, for example WAVAW supporters, calling themselves Women Against Pornography, suddenly appeared as the only remaining shop, owned by the Private chain, was about to lose its battle with the Council in the High Court. Though there was an eight-year-old precedent for anti-'pornography' feminism in the city – the local polytechnic Women's Action Group had slapped 'Sexist Crap' stickers on posters, spray-canned walls with the odd symbol, and picketed the screening of *Monster/ When a Stranger Calls*, WAP were trying to ride on the back of PACs' fifteen years' hard work. During WAVAW's week of action in February 1986, WAP daubed slogans and feminist symbols on the windows and door of the shop. During the spring, they attempted to hold a picket but the best they could muster was half a dozen students. As so often happens on such occasions, people with no intention of using the premises otherwise entered the shop in protest against the blocked pavement! Then, on Saturday 12 April, two of the pickets entered the shop and snatched a petition. WAP threatened to 'expose' the customers on it to their families and neighbours 'as people likely to commit degrading and humiliating acts against women and children', by placing posters near their homes. They also promised to write to the men concerned 'to tell them what we think of them' before declaring that court action against the raiders would not stop their campaign to close the shop.

The police announced they would do nothing about the threats as long as none of the letters sent constituted a demand with 'menaces'; but they thought that the public would be interested to know that sex attacks in Portsmouth had *not* increased because of the shop. The shop owner laughed off the protest.

This damning indifference was not the only surprise for the group; for many of the signatories turned out to be women, several of whom wrote to the local papers defending the shop's existence, and their right to use it. Even women who sympathized with the group disagreed with the tactics. This response merely confirmed the fact WAP locally, like WAVAW nationally, were making no impression at all.

The real reason for the raid was to pre-empt adverse publicity expected after the following Friday's court case. On 17 April, two pickets pleaded guilty in the local Magistrates' Court to causing £400 worth of damage to the shop a month earlier. If, as their solicitor reasoned, these two 'lesbian-feminists' were making a 'political statement', it was not by attacking the shop, but walking into the police station ten minutes later and demanding that they should be arrested! The bemused police officers had to go to the shop to confirm that a crime had occurred. Now in court, the women claimed they had been 'subject to abuse and ridicule' in a Southampton public house – twenty-two miles distant from the shop! No reference was made to the national WAVAW campaign; but their aim, to gain self-publicity and martyrdom, had been achieved.

By 1988, WAVAW had all but disappeared. Stuck with the Christian rhetoric of degradation and humiliation, all they were doing was opening the door for those attacking feminist 'freedoms' and 'rights' such as abortion on demand, lesbian custody of children, and gay sex education. Even their belated attempt to ride the child abuse bandwagon, which secured several of their leaders cosy jobs, did not win their credibility back.

The decision by the Conservative Government to back the Party's Christian-inspired Family Group's Section 28, which outlawed gay sex education material in schools, clearly spelt out the threat censorship posed to the lesbian and gay community. Then during the summer of 1988, rows over the American lesbian film *She Must Be Seeing Things* at a lesbian summer school where WAVAW members tried to stop extracts being shown, and the Joan Nestle tour in which the author completely debunked the puritanical streak British feminism had come to stand for, even led to former supporters denouncing WAVAW. Nestle, being a Jewish, working-class, lesbian feminist, had more politically correct points than WAVAW's membership put together. When the WAVAW rump then pulled out of a debate on SM politics in front of several hundred women, rather than put their argument to the test, the anti-porn position had even lost its base among lesbian feminists.

WAVAW's final response? The second *option* Jeffreys forgot to mention in that *City Limits* article: an embarrassing capitulation to the contemporary Christian crusade against newsagent soft core, and an appeal to the patriarchal state to impose sexual standards upon the women who did not agree with them.

Summary

The separatist feminists' theories about women's sexuality were so bizarre they would be rejected by anyone without a self-interest. Initially this did not matter, because WAVAW foolishly thought that once women 'as a class' heard the word they would see the crusade was in their interest too, and made no attempt to justify their rationales in public.

As their crusade was really an attempt to prove their theories about the meaning of heterosexual sex, when the 'patriarchal ruling class' they so despised initiated numerous controls between 1977 and 1984 at the behest of the Christian crusaders, WAVAW's public rationales, which made far less sense than the Christian critique, were redundant anyway.

By proclaiming from 1987 that there were now 'new' reasons for opposing soft core, WAVAW supporters hoped for a revival. They could simultaneously put their disastrous past behind them, mobilize old friends who had no idea about the current debates, emotionally intimidate the rising politically correct, who had let them get away with it in the student unions. In doing so, WAVAW proved that the ECP had been correct all along.

The means by which the separatists and Christians got together will be taken up in Chapter 7; but before then, it is time to take a look at all this 'accumulating evidence' and soft-core content they keep talking about.

Chapter four

Pornography Effects Studies

THE media reports denouncing soft core which appeared between 1987 and 1992 were based upon interviews with several former WAVAW supporters who had joined CAP, and along with Dr Itzin, Clare Short MP asserted that there was accumulating evidence of a causal connection between soft-core magazines and videos and violent sex crimes.

Over the last twenty-five years a large number of pornography effects studies have taken place; a review of the methods used and the results obtained, however, not only fails to support CAP's claims, but demonstrates that those who quote from them do not have the intellectual capacity to understand the methodology, and are woefully ignorant about the actual results.

Quoting studies

The reports and TV programmes which referred to several results that supposedly proved evidence of a link only served to demonstrate that the reporter's informant invariably had no knowledge about physiological arousal, less than an inkling about the historical development of the studies, and no awareness of the major problem areas in that research. Ironically by treating effects studies like a 'pick 'n' mix' display where one can select what one likes and ignore the rest, CAP ended up quoting studies which contained numerous other results that contradicted their beliefs.

Effects research is a minefield where researchers have preferred methodology or theories, and unless one is able to assess critically the methodology used, whether or not it has been applied successfully or whether the results have a bearing on alternative theories must remain a mystery. In order to avoid 'top-lining' results, and puffing up unwarranted extrapolations as did CAP, one needs to be aware of some fundamental drawbacks in this area, and the way they may affect the highlighted results.

The Buss box

The most common method used is known as the Buss Paradigm. The participants (known as 'subjects') enter university campus laboratories often without being aware of the real purpose of the study. They will be exposed to arousing material, in our case pornography, and then placed in a position where they are encouraged to deliver 'rewards' or 'punishments' to someone they think is another participant, but who is really a research assistant (known as a 'confederate'). This confederate is not passive, and helps the researcher manipulate the experimental conditions. In the case of pornography studies, this is done by insulting or injuring the subject in order to make them angry and aggressive *before* the exposure to pornography occurs, during a pre-exposure task. This provocation ranges from making derogatory comments about the subjects to their face, up to and including giving subjects *real* electric shocks.

Once the subjects have seen the material, they are given the opportunity to show aggression towards the same confederate who angered them in a post-exposure task. They may, for example, be asked to deliver a form of punishment for an incorrect answer in a test. In reality they do not; in Buss box experiments, the juice is not turned on second time around.

The purpose of this procedure is to measure the 'effect' of the arousal *stimulus* of the pornography upon the subjects' existing level of aggression, *compared* to that of another set of volunteers who have not been exposed to the same stimulus (known as the 'control group'). The difference between the two groups' behaviour towards the confederate is then used to measure the effect of the arousing stimulus as opposed to the non-arousing stimulus on existing aggression.

There are two major justifications for making the subjects angry before seeing the material. First, some researchers believe subjects need to be provoked in order to overcome social inhibitions. The second is that researchers are often looking for the effect of pornography on individuals who are predisposed, ready, or 'primed' to behave aggressively. Angering the subjects, however, means that it cannot be stated with certainty that the aggressive behaviour which follows is solely the result of exposure. As a result, the laboratory tests cannot be used to suggest that normal consumers, in normal conditions, would react in the same way; the alleged effects would apply only to those with an immediate predisposition to aggression and who have the opportunity to carry this out.

As we shall see, pornography rarely leads to aggression in non-angered subjects, and even when the exposure material is highly explicit soft core it invariably still fails to increase aggression; on the contrary, soft core reduces subjects' aggression levels. As this decrease in aggression is very common, when aggression is recorded it is vital to take careful note of what else was happening, and remember that when Fisher gave his subjects the free choice to leave or to continue with the experiment, the vast majority took the option to leave despite having suffered aggression from the confederate and having their arousal enhanced.

Even if this were not the case, as the 1990 Reading Group Report demonstrated at length, no one would call the subjects' retaliation 'aggression' if instead of a physical act, their reprisal towards the confederate was measured post-task by adding to or subtracting from a pool of counters, and their frustration was given a non-violent channel.

Arousal and aggression

Most crusaders do not even realize that the arousal referred to in studies is not necessarily sexual arousal, and that the 'aggression' that follows reflects the methodology employed and not the content of the material.

Everybody's level of aggression is determined by both the amount of anger held against the target, and their physiological arousal at the time. The Buss tests are premised upon the belief that when an external arousing stimulus is added to a subject's anger this will enhance that anger, encouraging the subject to aggress against the target of their anger; but what the crusaders do not realize is that *any* arousing stimulus will have the same effect.

The reverse is also true. If the subject is not pre-angered, the arousal stimulus will *not* enhance the aggression, let alone 'cause' aggression. It is the pre-anger and not the exposure which is the cause. The test really measures the level of enhancement. As non-angered subjects, even when exposed to pornography, do not show aggression, it is not possible to assert that pornography could evoke aggressive acts like sex crimes. Even where pornography may play a role in enhancing aggression, there would have to be another cause.

Soft core is good for you

The vital, but ignored, role of prior reason, anger, or other predispositions in the cause of aggression is demonstrated by parallel 'pro-social' effect studies, which crusaders do not even know exist.

A person's level of pro-social behaviour (being nice to people), like aggression, is caused by two major factors: their predisposition to be pro-social towards a target, and their level of arousal. As with aggression, a subject's level of pro-social behaviour can be enhanced by the amount of arousal stimulus; and subjects who feel pro-social before their exposure to pornography invariably demonstrate a marked increase in their pro-social behaviour afterwards, especially towards a member of the opposite sex. Researchers at New York University at Albany found that, when given an opportunity that they *could* ignore, subjects exposed to pornography reacted faster, more often, and for longer in aiding females with problems than the control group. The results were replicated more frequently and consistently than the results obtained by those seeking aggressive effects.

Taken together, the two kinds of effects studies establish that the subject's predisposition is the most important factor, and that the outcome of a test tends to reflect the design and purpose of the experiment. The major difference is that in adverse effects studies subjects have to be encouraged to take an aggressive opportunity, before a minority do so; whereas in pro-social experiments you merely have to create an opportunity to be pro-social for the majority of subjects readily to take it.

People with attitude

Another kind of experiment designed to test the effect of viewing pornography is the 'effect' upon subjects' attitudes. These usually involve completing questionnaires, or being asked to assign a sentence to the 'rapist' in a mock trial. Yet the 'change' in the subjects' attitudes is not usually measured in the form of before and after answers, but in comparing their attitudes with those of a control group, or with other subjects who have seen different material. The difference in attitudes expressed by the different groups is then assumed to be a function of exposure.

Before one extrapolates from these experiments, therefore, it must be realized that where attitudinal change appears to occur, it does not do so in reality. The attitudes recorded are merely measured by comparison. This means that the stimulus could just as easily have uncovered a pre-existing attitude as 'caused' it.

In any event, a measure of a difference in attitude does not mean, of course, that the subject will act upon it. As well as eighty years of psychological research suggesting that subjects do not act solely upon their attitudes, there is another reason why they probably would not in pornography 'effects' research. In most cases the behavioural scientists, whose training is based upon making rats run around a maze, have failed to realize that they have ascribed a meaning to the 'attitudes' recorded which may not be shared by the subjects. A subject's rationale for, and connotation of, an answer may be completely different from the researchers' assumptions about the answer. But as rats do not talk, these researchers have never developed the habit of talking to subjects.

As we shall see, these caveats are vital when considering the outcome of mock rape trials where the pornography viewers' assignment of a lower sentence for the 'rapist' than the control group's is hailed as 'proving' that the material promotes callous attitudes towards rape victims.

What exactly did they do?

The researchers' presentation of their experiments and results makes it very difficult for other researchers, let alone lay readers, to assess what has really happened. The most common source of information comes in major reviews written by the researchers themselves. Most people stop there without realizing the dangers.

If you track down the original reports in an academic journal, they tend to refer to a 'study'. This 'study', however, may have included several sets of numerous experiments; and that makes it difficult to review all the work, and to compare all the experimental results. Worse still, some articles, let alone the reviews, frequently discuss a conflation of several sets of studies. The details required to check the validity of any particular experiment among the dozens that took place, such as the title of the material used, the number of participants, and so on, are rarely recorded. While they may mention which attitudinal questionnaires were used, you never get a full breakdown of the answers. The most infuriating omission is the frequent failure to publish tables of results, especially including the women who have been tested. Researchers also have a habit of only referring to 'positive' results, unless they have a very special reason. Despite these serious problems, crusaders' résumés always boldly state that X result proves Y effect, when they do not know what the other half dozen experiments threw up, then assert that this also proves that men have innately different attitudes and reactions to pornography as compared with women, when they could not know this.

A decade of research reports, from Baron (1979) to Zillmann (1989), tends to suggest the opposite. Far from exhibiting a 'different' reaction to pornography, when women are given an equal opportunity to show aggression, research indicates that their arousal and aggression are similar to those of men. In many studies, the reaction is the same irrespective of the target, but some suggest that when females view soft-core pornography their aggression level remains higher than the males'. In Baron, for example, pre-angered females viewing pin-ups demonstrated reduced aggression levels, those viewing simulated sex demonstrated no change, but those viewing copulating couples demonstrated increased aggression. Those not pre-angered demonstrated no aggression. In Zillmann's later study women produced scores that would make them more callous towards women than the men! Incidentally, when Krafka (1985) tested women's reactions to material that feminists defined as dehumanizing and degrading, it was discovered that the subjects did not exhibit greater sex-role stereotyping, lower self-esteem, or inferiority regarding their looks.

By omitting female scores, researchers effectively overemphasize male reactions to exposure; and in doing so they imply that there is something special about males which makes them behave that way.

Even single experiments have their problems. The subjects' scores will invariably be averaged, so no one can know which subgroup or individual's very high scores bumped up the average – a fact that has clearly been missed by crusaders and CAP members who like to infer uniform effects.

Many of the experiments' original résumés that they quote cannot be taken at face value either, because the study occurred before researchers realized the importance of attitudinal predispositions which ensure that some subjects are far more likely to record aggressive scores than others, and bump up the average. It is vital to note the date of any 'study' anyway, because all results are subject to reinterpretation in the light of later discoveries.

Consequently, picking out and highlighting the result of a single experiment among a 'study', and failing to take account of averaging, is the act of a fool or of an ideologically motivated person, or both.

Motives

As we saw, unlike all other forms of social science, 'effects' study researchers rarely take account of their human subjects' motives, let alone cognitive processes, and this leads to many problems. In the early studies the human subjects were treated like rats, and it was assumed that the stimulus input was the only difference between the exposure and control groups; yet there were always good reasons to believe that this is not the case, especially when dealing with students, who make up most of the subjects.

Student subjects can be very compliant, as Milgram's original 1963 experiment demonstrated. His subjects, thinking they were taking part in a 'memory experiment', willingly 'zapped' a confederate using a fake control panel with switches ranging from 15 to 450 volts with labels from 'Slight Shock' to 'Danger – Severe Shock'. At 75 volts the confederates would grunt; at 120 volts they would complain verbally; at 150 volts they would demand to be released; and on 285 volts they would let out an agonized scream. Yet twenty-six out of the forty subjects continued to give what they thought were severe shocks, either because of the promise of payment if they completed the experiment, or, as Milgram believed, because they were simply used to obeying orders. And there was no pornography in sight.

As with behaviour, so with ideas. Manson University lecturers gave undergraduates a dummy survey asking them to approve of research into the most effective means to eliminate the 'mentally and emotionally unfit' whose birth rate was increasing faster than that of the 'emotionally fit and intelligent', who were thereby endangered: the important issue is not that two-thirds were in favour of the research, but that not one student questioned the ethics of the question.

Proof that this factor even overcomes a student's morality can be seen in a Princeton University study on theology students, which demonstrated the dilemma all subjects can face between a moral ideal and the compelling demands of an authority figure. Having just been given a short impromptu talk on the Good Samaritan or 'How to be a good Minister', the students were asked to cross the campus to complete a task. Half of the students were asked to hurry over, the others were not. On the way, they all passed a confederate posing as a 'victim', sitting slumped in a doorway, coughing and groaning, whose own task was to note which students stopped to help and which ones 'passed by on the other side'. The main factor determining whether or not they offered help was not which talk they had been given, but whether they had been told to hurry. Which goes to show that there is a huge gap between what people, including Christians, profess to believe, and their subsequent actions; and we should not forget it.

There are, however, even more important reasons why students are not the best subjects.

Most people will realize that the laboratory does not reflect real life; but it can be important to spell out how in the case of effects studies. Laboratory research presents the material in a more concentrated form than one may experience in real life; and it decontextualizes it. The absence of research on the wider population not only prevents us from knowing how most people would react, it takes the subject matter out of its usage patterns, and keeps us ignorant of real-life thoughts and reactions; and, as we are talking about sex, of all the social processes which lead to the viewer's choice. As a result, a vast amount of research is wasting its time.

The biggest problem, however, is that students, especially from the middle class, will tend to have a less formulated sense of self than adults. Their self-esteem rises and falls very easily. They suffer identity confusion. They can be insecure but egocentric. As they frequently do not yet know their own minds, and are quite uncertain about many of their values, preferences and emotions, they may over-identify with what they *think* their peers believe because they seek approval. As, at the very least, their attitudinal dispositions will be based upon poor information and little direct experience (especially when it comes to sex), there will obviously be a much larger gap between their attitudes and behaviour than in a more general population.

Bunging this lot into a laboratory when they may compensate for their insecurity by picking up on the external cues rather than introspection would be a risky guide at the best of times. Yet crusaders are asking us to believe that the 'adverse scores' recorded in some experiments have nothing to do with these adolescents' virginal, first-year, low self-esteem; or their egocentric preoccupation with perceived needs and desires which are now being encouraged by a heightened state of emotional arousal, not to mention annoyance at being attacked in the pre-test phase! That is just plain stupid. Likewise, crusaders want us to accept that some of these males' attitudinal statements have nothing to do with an opportunity to display their bravado or machismo – a standard trait among inexperienced adolescents. As we shall see, there are good reasons for considering students' reactions with some care.

In short, simplistic readings of experiments in aggression do not consider the questions of situational effects, motives, and the role of authority in the experiments.

What does it mean?

Gaining quantifiable results is one thing, working out what they mean is another. The kind of problems data throw up, even at the best of times, can be seen in the male students' answers to a questionnaire covering coercive sexual fantasies issued by Greendlinger and Byrne, used to suggest possible links between fantasies and aggressive tendencies.

The separatists no doubt would jump upon the 'facts' that 53.9 per cent fantasized about 'forcing' a woman to have sex; 39.1 per cent were sometimes violent towards women in fantasies; and 63.5 per cent got excited when a woman struggles over sex. These results would then invariably be used to prove American campuses are full of violent rapists 'date raping' freshers, and the Dean should outlaw gender contact. The politically correct would then sadly nod their heads at the score of 82.6 per cent who found the *Story of O* exciting; and let the separatists do as they please.

Apart from the fact that no sensible social scientist would accept these figures without question, especially the incredibly high number claiming to have read the book, unless it was prescribed reading – which would recontextualize the answer – suppose we take the rest of the questionnaire at face value. The 'real life' section found that 76.5 per cent of these 'rapists' would report a roommate who raped a woman, and 89.6 per cent could not understand why a man could possibly rape a woman. How can one make sense of this apparent contradiction? By also noting that 80 per cent not only found sexually aggressive women to be a turn-on, but wanted to be tied up and forced to have sex by a woman. These 'rapists' probably want to be 'raped' because they are not talking about rape, but about having exciting sex; and as 80.9 per cent apparently believed that women thought about them as sex objects, and 70 per cent that women would want their bodies, it looks as though any opportunity to have sex will do; for these are precisely the kind of scores one would expect from the sexually inexperienced.

As for the connection between the fantasies and aggression 'found' in this study, the researchers invented it by defining as 'a coercive act' every occasion a male said something to a female he did not really mean, and this grossly inflated the miserly real 1.6 per cent of real coercive acts the sample really uncovered. If the same definition was applied to women, most men on this planet have been 'raped' too.

Once one has seen how straightforward answers can be reinterpreted by politically correct research, it is easy to see how misleading impressions could follow from their interpretation of answers to attitudinal questionnaires where the meanings are far less straightforward; and why one needs to see the questions as well as the answers before accepting anything.

Similar questionable assumptions appear in researchers' labelling of the material used. Zillmann, for example, is not averse to reversing the definition to suit his case. Like his co-workers, Bryant and Weaver, he seems oblivious to the simple facts that while pornography promotes different messages at different times, it does not do so at his convenience, and that the same material could be interpreted by subjects in a way completely different from his own interpretation. When Zillmann and Bryant announce that an 8 mm 'stag film' shows females being 'sexual objects for exploitation by men', they are claiming that even within the context of the 'plot', as opposed to the actual conditions of production, the female can never be considered to have derived any pleasure from the experience. This is propaganda, not science.

The myth of the rape myth

The most damning consequence of this manipulation is that researchers assume too much in the very area they cannot afford to: movies alleged to promote 'rape myths'.

In these cases, researchers do not show unambiguous scenes in which a man commits a brutal rape upon a woman who then gets up and says, 'Gee that was great, when can we do it again?' They do not, because such films do not exist. They cannot use the very small number of simulated 'torture' movies (torture movies are no longer made but a few are, unfortunately, in underground circulation) because the women are not shown enjoying the experience. No; researchers have a habit of picking clips from potentially ambiguous movies, such as consenting SM 'scenes', or where a female's simulated initial reticence turns into pleasure with persistent male attention. The clips are then designated as 'positive' or 'negative' outcomes, i.e. whether the victim was seen to be enjoying or disliking the experience. 'Positive' outcome movies are deemed to be promoting 'rape myths' on the grounds that no woman could or would enjoy the experience. But to do so is to adopt a ridiculous assertion that no women could possibly enjoy an SM experience, and to mislabel a 'let's try something new' scene as 'rape'. Separatists may appreciate this tokenism, but it is not scientific.

A film which suggests that *all* women feel they have to say 'no', but they will enjoy it if you proceed, or that if you force a woman to do something she thinks she will not like, she will come to enjoy it, is obviously promoting an erroneous message; but as researchers frequently fail to name the movies used, readers cannot always judge which type of film has been shown, and extrapolating from such a study can be dangerous. The consequence should be as obvious, and it is ironic that many researchers as well as crusaders have failed to see why. By failing to take account of the different kinds of film, on top of failing to record a subject's interpretation, the researcher could attribute an adverse effect to a 'rape myth' message when the subject thought they were merely watching an 'exciting sex' movie. As the subject would not deem the scene a 'rape', the researcher could be underestimating the negative effects from explicit soft-core movies and ascribing it to a 'rape myth' message which was not perceived by the subject. Unless one records the variation in the subject's reading of the material, uniform attitudinal results could also mask the very different reasons for what follows.

The reason that many researchers are oblivious to this problem is a damning one: far from looking for adverse effects from 'rape myth' movies, they were really seeking a justification for damning movies containing sex acts they personally disliked. Yet it is a fact, whether researchers or crusaders approve or not, that many people not only enjoy 'kinky sex', they often come to do so after, and in spite of, initial hesitation or reticence. Indeed, devotees of various minority sexual practices will often talk at length about how much time they wasted worrying about whether they would enjoy it. Likewise, most people have no problem distinguishing between devotees of such practices, models who are paid to do things, and the many women who may not; that, it may surprise crusaders, is one reason why models are revered. Decontextualized extracts from full-length movies depicting someone's initiation, without coercion, into a different sexual practice that the researchers do not like the idea of women doing, are not 'rape myth' movies.

To claim that when subjects perceive movies as proof that women *may* enjoy such practices, or that they then overestimate the number who do (an impossibility when researchers fail to provide, let alone justify, their own base figure), they have succumbed to a 'rape myth' is absurd. While it may suit simplistic research designs to claim it has, it can tell us nothing about the reality of 'rape myths' or their effects. To justify the claim that any movie has encouraged a subject's belief in 'rape myths', one requires that person's interpretation of the movie; but even objective researchers are very reluctant to talk to their subjects, because it confuses things and complicates experiments. Researchers would also have to accept that a subject so inclined could also turn any consenting extract into a 'rape scene' and vice versa, thereby undermining the ability to blame the content. Given these Catch-22s in rape myth studies, their results must be treated with care.*

---

* Male readers should realize that it is inequitable even to induce a woman to engage in a minority sexual practice without a very clear indication that it is her wish to experiment. All readers should be aware that pornographic scenes can mislead the ignorant. When they show an anal sex scene, for example, the lubricant that may be required may not have been shown, for aesthetic reasons, thereby giving the impression that anal sex is an easy act, when really it takes some very careful practice. If you should ever feel so inclined, remember that it is in your own interest to discover all you can about any minority sexual practice before you undertake it. Do not leave it to a partner, especially if they exhibit any compulsive behaviourism; their desires may be greater than their knowledge, and an injury or unnecessary upset may result. Remember too that several minority sexual practices are illegal or are restricted in law. The best readily accessible source of necessary practical sexual knowledge is *Forum* magazine.

Is it science?

Crusaders who like to think that the case against pornography is 'scientific' have a serious problem. While researchers may be using the best methodologies available, to claim that something is 'scientific' requires much more than a laboratory, the title Professor, and results published in a friendly journal which rejects results it does not like. Some of the procedures used would embarrass a real scientist; and so would many of the theories on which they are based. Zillmann, for example, is convinced that he could find a link between aggression and pornography because a link between aggression and sex has been 'found' in rats! (1984). Most behavioural psychologists show no understanding of social construction of beliefs and actions whatsoever.

To be 'scientific', results must be able to be replicated at will, and the theories that follow from them need the power of prediction; these two basic requirements divide science from ideology, and have given it credibility over the last four hundred years. The results of a single experiment without replication cannot give rise to a proven scientific fact.

Fisher and Grenier (1988) clearly demonstrated, by their failure to obtain the same results in a series of experiments replicating the most frequently quoted 'path-breaking' studies, that pornography–aggression research has yet to reach the scientific standard. Despite painstaking efforts to use the same types of subjects, materials, patterns of exposure, questionnaires and tests, they obtained completely opposite results. Given that the demand for further controls of pornography is premised upon the idea that the material has an innate quality, and the same effect upon *all* males, at *all* times, leading to aggression against *all* women, this study undermines the crusaders' cause.

While the need for replication suggests that no study's results can be taken as the final word on the subject, you cannot even take some experiments as the first word either. A typical example of the manipulations of subjects and their attitudes which take place in the name of science is Malamuth's (1984) famous discovery of the existence of the male's Likelihood to Rape tendency (hereafter abbreviated LR score). Like other researchers

Malamuth wanted to see how 'aggressive pornography' may affect men's attitudes and subsequent behaviour towards women. Unlike many, he also wanted to see what mediating effects individual personal differences might have on the subjects' results; and for various reasons he chose a 'propensity to rape'. Obviously, in order to do this he had to establish whether or not men had an LR factor; so subjects filled in a self-assessment questionnaire containing five options in an LR scale: one recording 'no likelihood', and the others ranging from (i) 'not at all likely to rape' to (iv) 'very likely to rape' – all, it must be noted, with the pre-condition that they would not be caught and punished. This raised immediate difficulties of validity.

The scale is what is known as 'constraining': four of the five scale points measure an increasing LR, but there is no opportunity to express a differentiation in the 'No Likelihood to Rape' option. The wording also presented an interpretative problem, as the connotations of the word 'rape' and its meaning for subjects was assumed to be obvious, when it is precisely the lack of agreement in society over what 'rape' is that aggrieves feminist theorists. The public tend to believe it should be judged and defined from a situational perspective – how far both parties were culpable in what occurred, with physical coercion treated as a major indicator of male intent (Amendolia and Thompson, 1991). While this reasoning can be unfair, such as when a woman is too frightened to resist, many alternatives are worse. Judges think it has something to do with short skirts. Some feminists, if the date rape crusade is anything to go by, want us to believe a woman is raped if she changes her mind afterwards. Separatists demands that we should automatically accept every rape charge even if the man was not there at the time. So how on earth do we know what Malamuth's subjects' definition of rape was? Were they using a version of the legal definition, situational culpability, or the radical feminist position? Whichever definition they were using, as it was premised on the idea 'if I am not caught and punished' it did not denote an LR score anyway. The LR scale, therefore, is merely a methodological tool: it does not by itself indicate these males' likelihood to rape.

Even if we ignore these subjective questions, Malamuth ruined everything, because despite dividing the subjects into three groups and exposing one to a video interview with a rape victim, another to a textual account of what Malamuth calls a 'pornographic description of rape', and the third doing nothing, Malamuth did not differentiate the scores by these three groups. All three scores were conflated to produce one set of figures, justified by reference to 'a great deal of consistency' across these conditions. To make matters worse, once Malamuth found that even the conflated scores revealed that only 35 per cent recorded any LR 'if guaranteed to avoid detection and punishment' at (ii) or above on the scale. As that meant that 65 per cent of all subjects recorded *no* LR, because rape had no appeal even with guaranteed avoidance of detection and punishment, Malamuth blithely recoded the scores to overcome the problem that the remaining sample size would cause. The 35 per cent were now designated as having a HIGH LR irrespective of the initial gradation, and the 'innocent' 65 per cent were designated as having a LOW LR.

This manipulation of subjects' scores for the convenience of the experiment may be viable for the purposes of the single experiment, but is unscientific, and the implications of this recoding for the untrained eye are obvious: it implies that all men have a 'scientifically' proven LR score, and that 35 per cent of men have a very high potential to rape (which is exactly what CAP members asserted at the Liberty meetings in 1989 and 1990) when this was not the case.

The most common misapprehension, however, occurs in studies alleging a correlation between pornography sales and rape rates. Despite the fact that a correlation merely demonstrates an association between two variables, and does not demonstrate 'cause', crusaders act as if it does. Yet most social scientific studies which use correlation do so as an aid to further inquiry, not as the end point, because the association may disappear if you add a third variable, such as consumption of alcohol. Serious correlational studies will run numerous potential correlations before making claims concerning 'possible' cause. This was not a feature exhibited in the most widely quoted study; but when the authors introduced associated factors in later extensions (research which is rarely quoted), the supposed correlation between sex crime and geographical consumption of pornography disappears completely.

Those quoting correlation studies also tend to highlight supposed trends that suit their ideological perspective. Feminists, for example, for some reason never explore the potential correlation between the sale of feminist literature and the rise in sex crime; and you will never hear the anti-tobacco lobby cite the correlation between the decline in tobacco sales and the rise in juvenile crime.

When American researchers use 'soft core' or 'non-violent explicit material' in studies, this can range from *Playboy* to *Swedish Erotica* and *Colour Climax*, which would be deemed 'hard core' in Britain. Unless one pays careful attention to the material used, the suggestion that an effect for British top-shelf material can be inferred from the study is erroneous.

During the last decade, it has become very popular for lazy academics to try to pass off a humble review of others' research as a new 'study'. Although many journalists are too stupid to tell the difference, in most cases they are being deliberately misled by the claim they are being offered 'meta-analysis'. This would be true if the review clearly stated the methodological difficulties involved, and spelt out the basis of its selection; but I have only seen Cumberbatch and Howitt do that in Britain. What follows here is not 'meta-analysis'; it is merely an example of how to apply the necessary qualifications to the studies most commonly quoted by the crusaders, and to show what emerges as a result.

Sex offenders

Crusaders frequently point to sex offenders' claims that pornography was to blame for their crimes, the most obvious example being the serial killer Ted Bundy. Systematic research like Marshall's (1989) *does* suggest that up to one-third of all sex offenders in American studies utilize pornography directly prior to and/or during their crime; but these figures are inflated by child sex offenders, who invariably use material made by themselves. Marshall (1986) found that paedophiles were almost twice as likely as incestuous offenders to prefer pictures of children to those of adults, but a review by Abel found no direct relationship between the consumption level of pornography and the frequency of sex crime or degree of violence among child sex offenders.

What crusaders ignore is that sex offenders' pattern of consumption is different from that of the general population. Even the

Meese Commission realized that sex offenders tend to have less exposure to the material than control groups. It has also been suggested (Walker, 1970) that when sex offenders deliberately consume pornography, the material chosen is more likely to include *hard core* featuring less common sexual practices, for which they may have already developed a compulsion. Several studies, most notably those by Abel and associates (1977, 1978), found that sex offenders appear to be more aroused by coercive imagery involving non-consenting females, when compared to control groups. But others like Baxter (1986) claim that bigger samples do not find such differences. Marshall (1986) has also discovered cases where rapists were inhibited by non-consenting imagery. The major problem with most of these studies, however, is that Wydra (1983) discovered that rapists can become adept at controlling their arousal to exposure – the major means of testing their reaction to pornography. Other researchers, especially Dietz (1986), who have worked in asylums for the criminally insane have suggested that the sadistic rapist is more drawn to the imagery of crime and detective magazines like *True Detective* rather than mainstream pornography.

Not surprisingly, crusaders never allude to the fact that while there is no clear relationship between consumption of pornography and sex crimes, there is a *clear relationship between family background and sex crimes*. Studies from Kant and Goldstein (1978) to Check and Malamuth (1986) have all noted the tendency for sex offenders to come from households where sex was rarely discussed, but which promoted 'traditional' or 'conservative' sexual values in the form of proscriptions instead of basic sex education. Several studies, including Rada (1978) and Langevin (1985), also found stronger correlations with the rapists' family background experience of high alcohol consumption, violence, and sexual abuse, than with their pornography consumption. Goldstein's sampling (1973) discovered that all rapists who had been found reading pornography in their teens were severely punished, while only 7 per cent of a cohort sample (same age, background, etc.) caught with this material were punished. Marshall (1986) found a similar pattern among child sex offenders.

In short, the claim that there is a link between pornography and sex offences masks the fact that convicted rapists tend to suffer from a lack of sexual knowledge within a rigid, authoritarian, and sex-negating family background, and thereby seek out *hard core* as part of the pathology that follows: a perfect description of Ted Bundy.

Soft core

While crusaders like to dismiss early research which found no link between soft core and aggression, they are stuck with the embarrassing fact that every major researcher since 1971 has found that soft core, especially explicit kinds, actually reduces subjects' aggression levels, even when they are angered. Baron's 1974 studies even found that subjects exposed to pin-ups demonstrated *lower* levels of aggression than the control group! As Donnerstein (1987) reminds us, these findings conform to media effects models which suggest that anger can be reduced by material a subject finds engrossing.

Consequently, anyone who asserts there is 'accumulating evidence' to prove a link between soft-core consumption and aggression is misleading the public.

Correlations

Despite the amount of attention crusaders give them, only a couple of correlation studies have ever examined associations between availability of pornography and rape rates. John Court has written a series of articles which have argued that a correlation exists not only between pornography and rape rates in various countries, but also between the rape rate and the content of material (1976, 1981, 1982). Court insists that: countries which liberalize their pornography laws see a corresponding rise in rape rates; countries that have stricter controls against pornography have lower rape rates; and that where pornography laws have become strict, as in Japan, there has been a corresponding decrease in rape rate.

West Germany, however, demonstrates that the first suggestion is not always the case; and Britain – whose sex offences have risen dramatically since 500 sex shops were closed, and strict limits were placed upon video film content and upon public displays of nudity – suggests that the opposite can also be true. While the second suggestion may hold true for Singapore, Stockholm – which next to Los Angeles has probably the highest pornography output in the world – has had a lower increase in rape rate than Singapore, which incidentally boasts a vast underground network of prostitution, and whose authorities can be very unpleasant to rapists. The third observation is disingenuous; it deliberately ignores the exact nature of the law involved. Controls are strict, but not only is the material freely available in controlled outlets, Japan produces the most violent pornography in the world. Bondage, domination, and torture make up the mainstream. The only thing you must not do is show pubic hair, as the makers of the sex education video *The Lovers' Guide* discovered. These contradictory examples demonstrate the weakness of simplistic correlations offered by the likes of Court: they do not have universal application.

The most glaring problem with Court's 'correlations', however, is that they are too general. Attempting to link a country's laws with rape rates makes far less sense than comparing consumption and content to rape, and Court has never offered meaningful data involving these variables.

Baron and Straus did. In a series of studies they looked at detailed statistical correlations between soft core sales and rape rates in the USA (1984, 1985, 1986). The first study is widely believed to have found a direct per capita correlation between the various states' sales and rape rates; but it never really did. Missouri, for example, had a higher rape rate per capita than Kansas, but Kansas sold almost twice as many soft-core magazines per capita than Missouri. Mississippi had the lowest per capita sales figures but a rape rate higher than that of 17 other states! Such a 'link' would be meaningless without a corresponding check on the state's hard-core sales, anyway. Such a check by Scott (1985) unearthed Court's weaknesses. If Court was correct there would be a higher correlation between rape rates and the number of hard-core sex theatres and bookstores, yet Scott found no link whatsoever. Those who like to imply that correlation is cause are therefore faced with the embarrassing situation of explaining why rape rates can be higher when there is a lack of hard core around.

Being serious academics, Baron and Straus of course did not stop at the first study anyway, and looked for other variables too. When they tested the apparent link with a state by state 'Violent Approval Index' – using indicators such as use of guns – they found that simple correlation between soft-core sales and rape rates disappeared!

The obvious problem with all these studies is that the people committing the sex crimes may not be those buying the material anyway; and when it comes to the United States there is good reason to believe this is the case. In a special session at the American Society of Criminology a couple of years ago, participants were taken through the Government's own sex crime statistics. These revealed – much to the horror of the politically correct – that the greatest percentage of most individual states' rapes occur in the inner-city areas of the individual states' major cities; and that the vast majority are committed by social groups not known for purchasing the leading 'men's magazines'. In order that these groups would not be identified publicly, participants were asked to return the data they had been given before leaving the room; the researchers did not want to be responsible for causing a race riot. They also stressed that they did not believe their data 'proved' these social groups had a particularly high proclivity to rape compared to other social groups; for the statistics could just as easily highlight the social circumstances these groups find themselves in, the nature of policing and so on. They are correct to insist this; but they had also revealed that it was not the soft-core magazine buyers who were committing the rapes.

Given that correlational studies are still in their infancy, frequently failing to take account of other obvious variables, they cannot be used to prove anything – a point amply proven by Scott (1985), who when running a series of different magazine sales against the various states' rape rate found a correlation between the latter and sales of 'country sports' magazines! Perhaps Court would be better employed taking on the US gun lobby.

American soft core

Once we start considering the effects of American soft core featuring explicit acts of intercourse, the situation becomes more complicated.

Donnerstein's early studies (1978) involved numerous experiments to test whether or not the subjects' post-exposure level of aggression depended upon how arousing the material was. When three groups of subjects were shown three different types of photographs – non-sexually-orientated adverts; soft-core 'pin-ups', and explicit acts of intercourse – non-angered subjects displayed no aggression. Once angered, those exposed to the pin-ups demonstrated *lower* aggression levels, and those exposed to explicit material exhibited *no* increase in aggression. In other words, material deemed hard core in Britain failed to increase subjects' aggression levels.

Donnerstein's next experiments attempted to test the effect of altering the levels of anger and arousal in subjects in order to overcome what he believed was male 'reticence' to express aggression against females. In the first experiment with Barrett (1978), Donnerstein had subjects shown extremely explicit material. They demonstrated more aggression than a control group; but the gender of the confederate made no difference to the aggression levels. The pre-angered subjects responded as they would to any stimulus, and so their actions could not be considered to be violence against women induced by pornography. Failing to find the result Donnerstein expected, he and Hallam (1978) then attempted to dis-inhibit male subjects and deliberately encouraged their aggression against women by getting them to watch another male apparently aggress against a female confederate first. Contrary to all expectations, one group of pre-angered males shown extremely explicit films, despite displaying the highest level of physiological arousal, recorded higher levels of aggression against the male confederates in the post-test! Once again the soft-core pornography reduced aggression levels; and despite perfect laboratory conditions, pre-angered subjects exposed to what in Britain would be called hard core did not demonstrate higher levels of aggression against women, even when deliberately encouraged to do so.

In order to get a higher level of aggression against a female than a male, Donnerstein and Hallam had *personally* to encourage the subjects to show aggression towards females. Five years later, Leonard and Taylor (1983) also got male subjects to record higher levels of aggression against females than males by getting the female confederate to imply continually that she wished to act out the scenes seen, while simultaneously giving the subject higher and higher levels of electric shocks! In other words, the first experiment ever to record an aggressive response did so only after the subjects were told to 'try again' by the researchers, and the second only after the young subject, who despite suffering the kind of torture that would have led to an Amnesty International protest if he had been a political prisoner, retaliated only when he could not stand it any longer. Despite being the real victim, his desperation was hailed as proof that he had developed a sexually callous attitude towards women after being exposed to pornography! Whatever the theoretical justifications for these methods, it is hard to see how this young man, with a tolerance level beyond that of most people, can be 'scientific proof' of pornography's role in promoting callous and aggressive attitudes towards women. Given these extraordinary circumstances it is highly debatable that the aggression against women had anything to do with the material.

Meanwhile, Zillmann had made a startling discovery. Explicitness had nothing to do with it anyway; the subjects' subsequent actions to exposure were determined both by their anger having been provoked and their personal attitude to the material. Any kind of stimulus that the subjects found displeasing or revolting enhanced their level of aggression (1981). No wonder soft core tended to reduce aggression levels. The implications for porn study interpretation was dramatic: reaction would *not* depend upon the sexual content *per se*, or even the themes displayed, but the subjects' personal feelings about the material, especially an *adverse* reaction.

Support for this theory came from Kelley, the only woman publishing in this field. Her research, at New York State University, Albany, was designed to explore the relationship between sexual attitudes and sexual fantasy provoked by viewing various forms of pornography. In the short term, effects were more dependent upon the subjects' sexual attitudes than the content (1985). When Kelley then tested a subject group's reaction to four films differing in aggressive content, male subjects who did not condemn the material or practices depicted demonstrated the least antisocial effects. The most important factor in promoting antisocial acts appeared to be feelings of 'sex-guilt'. In another set of experiments with Musialowski (1986), Kelley found that these subjects were also more likely to recommend censorship; and, if female, were more likely to develop negative attitudes towards males. The implications of this research for other studies which did not seek the subjects' attitudes towards sexuality *prior* to the tests are obvious. Adverse reactions as well as the increases in aggression were related to the subjects' core sexual attitudes. Those receiving a traditional sexual socialization and experiencing guilt or disgust at what they saw could be responsible for aggressive scores. Any study that had averaged scores and assumed that the content alone was responsible would be invalid.

No wonder crusaders never refer to these studies: it was people (like themselves) who found the material objectionable, because of negative attitudes towards sexual material and/or various practices, and felt guilty about being turned on by what they saw, who then demonstrated increased aggression! People who really enjoyed pornography would be far less likely to do so.

The crusaders try to deflect attention away from this implication by frequently citing Zillmann and Bryant's 'massive exposure' studies, which are alleged to prove a link between consumption and aggression. So let us put the record straight. The three subject groups – viewing neutral films, a mix of neutral and sexual films, and sexual films respectively, over a six-week period – revealed that the group exposed exclusively to sexual films exhibited *less* aggression than those exposed to the neutral films! The mixed group demonstrated a slight decrease in aggression. The results were the same for both females and males. By using physiological tests and self-report responses, Zillmann also discovered that repeated exposure to pornography, of all forms, reduced both physiological arousal and negative feelings regarding content, compared to a control group. This was especially true for the explicit soft-core subjects. This would therefore, reduce the effects of the stimulus and weaken aggressive reactions. Once again, soft core gained a behavioural clean bill of health.

Violent pornography

With results coming from tests using explicit material, deemed hard core in Britain, pointing to a non-guilty verdict, attention began to switch to 'violent' material.

As far back as 1978 Malamuth found that subjects presented with a story in *Penthouse* in which the woman 'enjoyed' what Malamuth thought was really 'rape' produced a higher level of aggression than did a group exposed to a non-aggressive sexual scenario, and the control group; all three were pre-angered and encouraged to show aggression. A Donnerstein experiment produced similar results: pre-angered subjects exposed to non-aggressive but highly explicit films showed no increase in aggression; while those exposed to a Donnerstein-defined 'rape film' did. What was more worrying was that the latter group also scored higher aggression levels when they were not angered! Worse still, another Donnerstein and Berkowitz study (1981) demonstrated the same effect with pre-angered subjects exposed to both 'positive' and 'negative' outcomes, i.e. whether the victim was seen to be enjoying the experience or not. Non-angered subjects only demonstrated an increase in aggression level following the positive-outcome film. Everyone then got into the 'rape myth' phase of research.

Yet when Malamuth and Ceniti (1986) undertook a similar, but longer, study they found no difference in the aggression levels of subject groups watching material labelled violent 'rape myth', explicit material, and a control group.

Whether or not it increases aggression level, Malamuth (1980) began to claim that later experiments suggested that violent material led to adverse male attitudes towards women with regard to rape victims' culpability. Careful attention, however, must be paid to all the results. Male subjects exposed to a positive-outcome rape story, when asked to read a second story with a negative outcome demonstrated a greater tendency to assign less suffering to the woman in the second version, and exhibited more sexual arousal than those who had only read a sexually explicit story at the first stage. Yet when the subjects assigned sentences to the rapist depicted, it was the 'rape myth' story group who recorded the heaviest sentence! Far from leading to adverse action, those who believed rape less traumatic for the woman punished the rapist more severely – the reverse of what one might have expected. Even more intriguing was why, when they were asked how likely they were to behave like the rapist in the second story if they were guaranteed not to be caught, the 'rape myth' story group recorded exactly the same score as the other group: 51 per cent said they might.

Unlike most previous studies, however, all the subjects had been through pre-exposure attitude testing, and there was a clear link between those who now suggested they might rape if they got away with it, and those demonstrating a callous attitude on their pre-test score. The exposure to 'rape myth' stories made no difference to the subjects' pre- and post-exposure scores. Subjects unlikely to rape did not have their minds changed by the exposure. Similar prior testing in another study, by Malamuth and Check (1980), revealed the same link too. Likewise, subjects with a high LR score, having seen a 'positive outcome' movie, were also more likely to believe that women enjoyed rape and engaging in forceful sex (1985). Those who suggested they would not rape even if guaranteed not to be caught did not share these attitudes. The rape-myth movies had little effect on subjects who find rape abhorrent; only those demonstrating prior attitudes exhibited callous attitudes. Even so-called 'rape-myth' movies did not change subjects' attitudes.

These results finally encouraged Donnerstein and others to consider the possibility that the effects of violent pornography may not be the engendering of callous attitudes, but the strengthening and reinforcing of attitudes that already existed: especially as males with an LR score demonstrated a propensity to be aroused to rape depictions irrespective of the females' response. And once Malamuth and Donnerstein altered the direction of their effects research, the results threw light on some previous ambiguities and confusions. Adverse effects to exposure may follow a callous attitude towards women, as well as sex guilt.

With studies finally beginning to distinguish between the inevitable arousal which would follow from any stimulating material, including 'heavy sex', and the subject's attitude-determined reactions, attention focused on the possibility of clearly demarcating the stimulating effects of the 'action' and the sex.

Malamuth and Check (1981) looked at non-sexually explicit 'violence' in general release movies like *The Getaway* and *Swept Away*, and found these increased male, but not female, subjects' acceptance of researcher-designated 'rape myths'. Donnerstein (1986) found that aggression-only scenes produced greater increases in aggression than non-violent but very explicit sex scenes. He did this by manipulating scenes so that the original sexually explicit and aggressive scene was now offered to three subject groups in different versions: the whole sequence, the violent sections, the sexually explicit sections. While only 11 per cent of those viewing the sex-only sequence recorded a *post-exposure* LR score, and 25 per cent of whole-sequence viewers, the violence-only sequence group hit a 50 per cent LR score. Whatever the validity of the LR test, it was clear that viewing non-sexually explicit *violence* provoked four times the reaction of soft-core material.

This finding, and later studies showing the importance of prior callous attitudes, led Donnerstein (1987) to argue that aggression against women in 'R' rated movies with no sexually explicit scenes was far more worrying than pornographic material. In other words the violence in *Friday 13th* was more likely to invoke an aggressive response than the sex in *Loose Ends*, and more likely to reinforce any violent attitudes towards women. This suggestion was, however, challenged by Fisher and Grenier (1988), who replicated several studies. Their subjects, even after viewing violent material, did *not* produce any difference in attitudes towards women, acceptance of violence, 'rape myths' and so on.

Separatists were not pleased with this turn of events. Christian crusaders, if they knew, ignored it completely. But what they both have to face up to is that another of their pet theories, namely that being 'desensitized' to sexual material and needing harder 'kicks' inevitably leads from perusing *Penthouse* to purchasing snuff movies, also received a blow at the same time.

This silly theory, based upon the belief that one sin leads to a bigger one, and used by all crusaders, whatever their target, never made any sense when it came to pornography, because it is scientifically flawed. While constant exposure may decrease subjects' response level, it simultaneously reduces the physiological arousal required to turn anger into physical aggression. One could have discovered this by reviewing the 1970s studies into TV violence which were deemed proof of the theory in the first place. As Cline discovered, the children who became most physiologically aroused when exposed to violent imagery were those who watched the least TV. They did so because the stimulus was unusual. The same may apply to adult subjects viewing violent hard-core movies for the first time too. On the other hand, although adults exhibit a high correlation between viewing television violence and self-reports of aggressive behaviour, and laboratory subjects exposed to highly aggressive TV shows exhibited marginally higher aggression than lower arousal levels to further exposure, Eron and Huesmann found that the most aggressive group of subjects were those exposed to an exciting but non-violent film!

If crusaders wish to persist with their desensitization theory, they will have to accept that many of the effects they like to quote may be following selective, concentrated, and initial exposure; they will also have to accept that as a subject's arousal rate falls with familiarity, anyone committing an adverse act in real life will have deliberately and consciously chosen to increase their arousal rate beforehand.

Sexual callousness

A more durable theory suggests that heavy viewers, while not provoked to violence themselves, may become desensitized to violence in others. This idea is based upon Thomas's (1977) famous experiments demonstrating that children who were heavy viewers of TV violence were less likely to report a 'mock' fight between other children in the laboratory to the researcher. When it comes to pornography, Donnerstein (1987) has argued that viewers may perceive rape victims as less harmed. We have seen that several studies suggest that this may be the case. The conundrum here, however, is that those who have high LR scores or high 'rape myth' acceptance scores, despite exhibiting more post-exposure aggression and less sensitivity to the victim's harm, simultaneously are more punitive towards rapists in their sentencing policy.

To discover what effect violent movies, as opposed to sex movies, had on desensitization and passive callousness, Linz and Donnerstein undertook experiments substituting 'video nasties' for explicit sexual material. In one test, Linz (1984) screened subjects for high psychoticism first: the tendency towards being a solitary, hostile person, incapable of empathy, and with a disregard to danger – the type of person who Eysenck also found to prefer impersonal, non-caring sex, and with just the kind of characteristics likely to produce a predisposition towards violence and callousness giving a high LR score. Linz then excluded them from the study, and exposed the rest to five 'R' rated films over five days: *Texas Chainsaw Massacre*, *Maniac*, *I Spit on Your Grave*, *Vice Squad*, and *Toolbox Murders*. As one would expect, by day five these 'normal' subjects were rating the film scenes less violent and less sexual, irrespective of the order in which they saw them. If such a measure is 'desensitization', as opposed to expanding knowledge of such films' conventions and a means of comparison, then such films desensitize 'normal' viewers. The same subjects, however, recorded *more* examples concering the portrayal of violence towards women set in a sexual context, and they increased their scores when coding scenes they designated as a sexual assault upon or rape of a woman. Contrary to what would be expected from desensitization theories, subjects' perceptions of sexual violence against women actually increased! What is intriguing, however, is that when the subjects took part in a rape trial simulation, it was those judging the films as *less* offensive or violent who were more lenient towards the defendant. A second study produced similar results.

Completely forgetting that these are not pornographic movies, and that subjects were exhibiting ambiguous signs, the crusaders began jumping with glee; but they failed to notice that when female subjects are used, they not only become 'desensitized', they appear even more reluctant to sympathize with the victim – effectively scoring a greater degree of 'male callousness' toward women than men do! Thankfully, Krafka's studies, referred to earlier, offer us a clue to what is happening here. Female ratings, unlike male ratings, of violent scenes did not decrease; but like the males, the women became less anxious as they became used to the material. Numerous explanations for this effect were offered. Krafka favoured the idea that the women were developing a defence strategy to reduce the stress. Donnerstein (1987) reasoned that women steeled themselves against the inevitable belief they could not control negative events. These are sexist explanations.

To make sense of what is happening, we need to transcend the limited stimulus–response theories of aggression research; because, despite their reputations and credentials, those involved in this research seem totally incapable of doing so. They are surprised when their 'callous males' are the most punitive, when a first-year social psychology student could have told them that was inevitable.

The major drawback of the 'video nasty' studies, like those which preceded it, is the naive failure to consider the multitude of viewers' *interpretations* of the content offered to them. The five films chosen have their own characteristics. *Texas Chainsaw Massacre*, for example, is a truly horrifying film, especially for the uninitiated. The desperation of the flight through the woods could give viewers a very close taste of what it is really like to come face to face with psychotic killers. *I Spit on Your Grave*, despite deliberately showing the callousness of gang rape, is something else: the victim takes it upon herself to exact revenge, successfully. And the manner in which it is done tells us something more about rape too; she skilfully exploits the male characters' 'rape myth' acceptance to make them vulnerable. Likewise, the rape scenes are not exploitative, as the camera concentrates on the males' callous facial expressions, but the acts of revenge are very explicit. The study would have been more useful if it had utilized five similar movies.

Be that as it may, the nature of the films can easily explain why subjects tend to suggest lower sentences. The films seen will have provoked reflection in the subjects, enabling them to put the mock trial events into a perspective, and a continuum of possible harm and the extent to which it should be punished. The control group would have nothing to judge the mock trial events against. As the subjects were screened for psychoticism, which invariably produces higher sentencing, these 'normal' subjects would record a lower punitive score anyway. The real question to ask is whether the scores recorded in mock trials are less than those in real life. Invariably they are still higher. The real question to ask, therefore, is why controls give higher sentences than juries in real life.

The failure of the researchers to offer a satisfactory reason for what occurred led to two studies at Reading University. In the first (Amendolia and Thompson, 1991), we discovered that university students did not utilize ideologically absolute standards of culpability, but applied a situational one relating to the amount of force and deviousness of the male, and the 'foolishness' exhibited by the female; so that while rapists were always held to be ultimately responsible, the victim was also perceived as culpable to varying extents. The indication that this may occur in real life too came from a second study covering attitudes towards rape among undergraduate and non-student populations (Carr and Thompson, 1993). We found that despite identifying all the scenarios as rape, women were more likely to apportion some blame to the female victims than males were! Having a situational assessment, rather than an absolute standard, subjects may be trying to allow for this in the sentencing policy. One thing, however, was clear. The content of the scenarios has an important bearing upon sentencing.

Similar problems arise in another, far more potentially damning set of studies. In contrast to Malamuth and Donnerstein's move away from sexually explicit material, Zillmann and Bryant, having failed to find a soft-core sex–aggression link, began to test for callous reactions in soft core. As they continued their 'massive exposure' studies, male and female subjects were exposed to material deemed 'demeaning and debasing to women', such as a male ejaculating upon a female's face. After six weeks of this, Zillmann asserted that *both* genders became more tolerant of what he deemed 'bizarre and violent' pornography, became less supportive of 'sexual equality', and more lenient in assigning punishment to rapists. Unfortunately, for those wishing to claim that here was the elusive proof that soft core was promoting callous attitudes, the study had several crippling drawbacks.

Despite knowing how important it was, Zillmann failed to test for psychoticism, prior attitudes or even LR scores – a serious weakness given what everyone else was now doing, and so he had no way of knowing if the males' higher 'callousness' scores followed from their sex-negative attitudes, as Kelley suggested, or Malamuth's theories about LR. The subjects' supposed 'appetite for stronger material' was solely based upon observing them flicking through a choice of magazines in an ante-room, and thereby merely showing a preference for looking at something different having spent four weeks looking at nothing but soft core. When tested for aggression, these subjects also demonstrated less than the control group.

These weaknesses would be bad enough; but there are far more compelling reasons why quoting this study demonstrates a crusader's ignorance. First, even Zillmann heavily qualified his findings, because he had to:

> The withdrawal rate upon the revelation of the nature of the research was substantial ... as a result, the findings on non-students cannot be considered representative. . . . (1989)

Almost half of the original exposure group dropped out because they were morally offended by what they were to be exposed to. As a result, the scores for the exposure group were based upon the younger subjects who stayed, but the scores for the controls still included the older more conservative subjects and were not weighted. No wonder there was a difference in post-exposure scores.

Second, the 'adverse' attitudes recorded rested upon the researchers' personal interpretation of the subjects' answers to a 'value of marriage' survey and the 'Indiana Inventory of Personal Happiness' questionnaires. Being demographically younger and socially more liberal in attitude than the controls, the 'exposure' subjects recorded scores showing less regard for the institution of marriage, and a different set of values about happiness. As Zillmann and Bryant were committed to the values of the controls, they interpreted the different scores by the subjects as 'adverse attitudes' towards women, when subjects merely disagreed with the researchers' concept of family values. Zillmann was particularly upset because the females did not live up to his stereotypical expectations; the modern young woman was as instrumental as the man.

The results of more reliable studies which specifically concentrated on the issues of behaviour and attitude towards partners and potential partners, changes in sexual practice, and attitudes towards sex, are far more ambiguous.

Kenrick (quoted in Donnerstein *et al.*, 1987) demonstrated lower scores on a 'caring, needing, trust, and tolerance of partners' scale among subjects exposed to *Playboy* and *Penthouse*. Thomas (1986), however, has demonstrated that this material is favoured by middle-class readers, while the pictorial imagery available in working-class magazines like *Hustler*, which is similar to the most popular British titles, may not have the same effect, because their models have a much wider age, body figure, and ethnic range. This contention is supported by Dermer and Pyszczynski (1978, quoted in Donnerstein, 1986), who found that subjects reading passages from sexually explicit magazines (where images would rely upon imagination) had their attachment, caring, and intimacy ratings for their partners increased!

As Zillmann and Bryant had blown the chance to conduct a useful test for non-violent material, Check (1985) filled in the gap. Having pre-tested his subjects, and recorded differential reactions between those exposed to violent, dehumanizing (Zillmann's 'demeaning'), and erotic soft core, Check discovered a clear association between the subjects' psychoticism, age, scores on numerous tests for propensity to rape and propensity to use force (knowing they would not be punished). Check concluded:

> Exposure to non-violent erotic materials did not have any demonstrated antisocial impact on any of the other independent variables. This was in contrast to sexually violent and dehumanising material.

Once again, soft core had been cleared, and subjects exhibiting high psychoticism in pre-tests were twice as likely to report a potential to engage in rape and forceful acts as a control group after viewing 'dehumanizing' pornography. Prior attitude was vital to subjects' reactions.

Check also uncovered two other interesting results, which have serious consequences for all research, if not his own politics. Having included non-students in his sample, Check found that students recorded a higher incidence of psychoticism and a higher LR than the general public. Could this mean that studies with student subjects will record more adverse effects than the general population would? The second finding was that subjects with low psychoticism scores in pre-tests who were then exposed to violent material recorded lower LR scores than *all* the other groups involved! Could it be that even violent pornography has no adverse effects for low psychotics and liberal subjects? Whatever these findings meant, a furious and acrimonious 'debate' broke out among the researchers regarding Check's use of material – he only ever showed decontextualized 'dehumanizing' scenes, destroying the wider context and motivation in the film. Everyone had a go.

When Linz (1985) used complete films, such as *Debbie Does Dallas*, to place the scenes back in context, subjects' scores on callous attitude, sexism, rapist non-culpability, and rape victim's own culpability did not increase. Similar results were reported by Krafka (1985) and Malamuth and Ceniti (1986). Buchman (1989) then found that while his explicit films led to subjects suggesting lower sentences for non-violent or non-coercive sex crimes, there was no change when it came to accounts of violent sex crimes. After Weaver (1987) gave four groups of male and female subjects different film extracts – 'explicit lovers', 'nymphomania behaviour', 'rape', and non-sexual threats against women – and compared their sentencing policy in two rape cases, he found no differential sentencing in the cohabitant scenario, but subjects exposed to the 'nymphomania' extracts passed much lower sentences in a 'stranger' rape case. While context clearly has its part to play, especially in invoking pre-existing high psychotics to be aroused and articulate their callous attitudes, doubts about the labelling of the films' content by the researchers must also be raised.

The only clear conclusions we can draw, therefore, are that the 'callous' sentencing policy may follow from the types of extracts and rape scenarios used, and that without a clear demarcation of the subjects' prior attitudes we cannot extrapolate from such studies.

The real problem is not the contradictory results but the manipulation of the experiments by the researchers. Until a rigorous and uniform standard is imposed so that the discoveries of the past are utilized whatever is being tested, we cannot transcend these self-imposed problems. Until researchers agree on a common standard, the claim that there is accumulating evidence of a porn–aggression link is merely a testimony to prejudice.

Check's claim that full-length film exposure would prevent a researcher's ability to differentiate between the reactions to different types of non-violence is debatable. Donnerstein's rebuttal – that complete films would mitigate the effects of 'demeaning scenes' – is more likely to be true. On the other hand, there is nothing, given modern technology, to stop those so inclined from taking any scenes out of context through freeze framing or making collations of selected scenes. This, of course, raises the question of what kind of person would want to do that.

The answer is: a psychotic, with a predisposition caused by a twisted sexual socialization, who thinks that non-'missionary' sex is somehow 'demeaning' and 'degrading', and that women who enjoy doing such things deserve anything they have coming to them. Now where on earth do people acquire that kind of attitude? It certainly is not from pornography.

Summary

There *is* long-established evidence which demonstrates that explicit soft-core pornography, much of which is illegal in Britain, causes no behavioural harm at all. On the contrary, it reduces aggression levels in pre-angered subjects. There is no evidence that sex offenders universally utilize soft core in the preparation and commission of their crimes. Correlational studies do not demonstrate a relationship between soft-core pornography consumption and rape rates. While non-sexual violent material encourages aggression in pre-angered subjects, it does so because of their illiberal sexual attitudes. Studies concerning rape myths are ambiguous and confusing, and have nothing to do with soft core anyway. Studies which draw attention to sex callousness induced by pornography, even allowing for the manipulation of the content's meaning, have yet to explain why women appear to be more callous than men. In any event, more recent studies suggest that these results are related to the tests' methods rather than the material used. Long-term exposure to pornography appears to reduce the subjects' arousal, and thereby potential to exhibit aggression. Many more factors than content are involved, and these need to be studied in greater depth to explain laboratory aggression against women.

A person's beliefs and socialization are far more important than pornography when considering the origin of sex crimes. People with liberal attitudes do not demonstrate an increase in aggression even after watching violent hard-core sex movies. People who do demonstrate aggressive and callous attitudes after exposure to this material appear to believe, like the crusaders, that several very common sexual practices are demeaning and degrading. Prior attitude is vital.

Pornography effects research, therefore, disproves the separatist slogan that 'Pornography is the theory: rape the practice', and undermines the Christian crusaders' attempt to scapegoat soft core. There is also accumulating evidence that the stereotypical values these groups promote is a major factor in the promotion of laboratory aggression.

No one claims that hard-core movies and magazines have no part to play in sex crimes. Those with a tendency to commit sexual offences can and do utilize pornographic material to justify their actions to themselves. It is quite possible, for example, that Gifford Titre, who had already been sent to a juvenile detention centre in 1980 for rape and robbery, and who received 14 years for raping two teenage girls from Surrey, may have been encouraged, like the other two men involved, by a copy of *Color Climax* found in the flat used for the rape. This does not justify Jill Knight's assertion that the magazine 'triggered' the crime, let alone an appeal for further controls on newsagents' soft-core stocks. The fact that thousands of other readers of the same magazine did *not* go out and rape teenagers suggests that 'the obvious truth that pornography distorts the balance of the mind' is a falsehood. On the contrary, it looks as if unbalanced minds distort pornography.

Chapter five

British and European Pornographic Magazine Content

APART from the bogus assertions about accumulating evidence about links between soft core and sex crime, the media attack on soft core between 1987 and 1992 also claimed that soft core content had become more violent, and more demeaning towards women. There was nothing new in this claim: groups like WAVAW had been saying as much back in 1983, although they usually referred to hard-core material. Having demonstrated, back in 1986, that hard core was actually becoming less violent, I was keen to see the evidence that this 'new' charge relied upon. There was none.

Dr Itzin constantly referred to 'a survey ' of top-shelf soft core, and CAP delegates at the 1989 Liberty conference declared that 50 per cent of newsagent magazines consisted of violent imagery, but the obvious fallacy of the charge was that without any historical data for comparison, no 'survey' could prove the contents had become *more* violent or demeaning. Bemused by such silly statements, I undertook a historical content analysis of soft core to test Dr Itzin's belief. The final results were presented at two international conferences, and incorporated in the third version of the Reading Group's report, *Soft-core*. The following year, I was interviewed about the results by a film crew for a TV documentary. When the programme was broadcast, my figures had been pulled; but there was Dr Itzin with a pile of magazines on a desk, claiming that she had just undertaken a study. So I waited with great anticipation for the publication of Dr Itzin's book *Pornography: Women, Violence, and Civil Liberties*, only to find no results, merely two and a half pages of 'extracts' of peculiar jottings made as she flipped through the material. Get this lot:

> Women's liberation harnessed: 'on the move' (i.e. driving cars, flying planes) naked. ...
> More specialist magazines. Particularly shocked by the 'big boobs' magazines (discovered that 50+ meant breast size not age). Women with large breasts posed in clothes and positions which squeeze, contort and often painfully distort their breasts to appear even larger. One feature was entitled 'Mammary masochism'.

Her other references to 'violence' include: the 'sadistic' appearance of a pair of scissors used by a model from *Shaven Ravers*, models wearing uniforms, a line or two of text from a spanking magazine, and the existence of a magazine called *Miss Sadie Stern*, the title of which Dr Itzin believes is a plot to convince males that women really edit these magazines and find their content acceptable. Not a lot to go on really; but yet another indication of the lack of historical data required to prove that soft core had become more violent.

Content studies

The two problems a serious study of content faces are the lack of previous work and standard assessment codes. As each author has tended to rely upon their own subjective standard, this would raise serious doubts about anyone's claims that content is becoming more violent. When the Reading Group looked at the results of existing studies, they found very little to go on.

Smith (1976) found that the contents of 'adults only' paperback story books had become more explicit after 1969, but thereafter remained constant until 1974, the end of the study. In the latter period, depictions of rapes doubled, and one-third of stories involved scenes of forced sex. Slade's (1984) historical study of stag films between 1915 and 1972 found that 5 per cent contained a rape scene, but that violence of any kind never exceeded 10 per cent of total output. Palys's (1984, 1986) selection of videos produced between 1979 and 1983 found that the Triple X (explicit and graphic sexual content) videos were far less violent than the 'Adult' R-rated (nudity and simulated sex) videos. Triple X videos also contained an equal number of dominant or initiative-taking acts by men and women. Men were far more dominant in R-rated videos, which also contained more acts of graphic aggression. There was no increase, however, in the number of violent images over the four years, and the number of violent scenes in Triple X actually fell.

Dietz and Evans's (1982) study of hard-core magazine covers of 1760 magazines selected from four 42nd Street shops, covering the period 1970 to 1981, found that 17 per cent of their sample involved themes of bondage and domination, and some 2.3 per cent involved violence, such as spanking. Yet when Winick (1985) examined a similar pool of 430 magazines found in Times Square bookstores, 63.2 per cent of the material merely involved nude women, simulated sexual activity, and explicit sexual activity between couples. Sadomasochistic material – where one person appeared to be using forceful acts for the purpose of mutual sexual gratification – amounted to only 1.2 per cent of the sample, and even then the representation of force was very stylized and posed. Had Dietz used specialist stores? Even if he did not, his latter review (1986) of detective magazine covers places the previous findings in some context. Freely available, 76 per cent of their covers involved domination of one kind or another; 38 per cent including bondage.

None of this material, of course, is soft core. In an attempt to accuse this of violence, crusaders used to quote Malamuth and Spinner's (1980) review of violent imagery in *Playboy* and *Penthouse* illustrations and photographs, which claimed that violent pictorial imagery increased from 5 to 10 per cent between 1973 and 1977; but as they included cartoons depicting satirical comment regarding sadomasochism this would obviously raise doubts about their conclusion that soft core would add to 'a cultural climate of sanctioned violence against women' especially when many of those cartoons were of the Fem-Dom variety! What crusaders never mention was that Scott and Cuvelier's extensive follow-up of *Playboy* ten years later (1987), which extended the analysis from 1954 to 1983, came to a different conclusion. They discovered not only that a 'violent' image appear in only 1 page out of 3000, and 4 out of every 1000 pictures, but that since 1977, this violent imagery had actually decreased.

These studies, however, have little bearing upon the British debate. They either cover material not legally available here or are hopelessly out of date. The same applies to the list of titles contained in the Meese Report, many of which would be deemed hard core and indecent by British Customs officers, and hard core and obscene in British courts. As American soft core is far more sexually explicit than British soft core, it would have to circulate illegally. Those materials which do circulate illegally in Britain are more likely to come from the European continent than the United States. Material which is in illegal circulation from America tends to be pirated video versions of Triple X features, shown in sex cinemas, and rarely violent. Any attempt to determine trends in illegal violent material, therefore, should be based upon a European sample.

The European sample the Reading Group used came from a previous 1986 study covering an almost complete set of mail order catalogues from Europe's major distributors between 1972–1983. The catalogue imagery was subdivided into three periods: from the first American President's Commission in 1971 to the Williams Committee; the duration of the Williams Committee and Report, 1978–1979; and the period from Williams to 1983, when the claim that pornography had become more violent was first made. The purpose was to determine whether European material content had developed in the way that separatist feminist groups, utilizing Ms Dworkin's theories, alleged it had.

The British sample collected and analysed between 1989 and 1990 took longer. The Reading Group had to purchase material from private collections, and find the largest selection of contemporary material at a newsagent on the South Coast in February 1990. The material was divided into three periods: 1965–1975 to represent the pre-Williams period; 1978–1983 to represent the rise of Sullivan's empire and the change in content which did take place; and 1990 to represent the material that according to the feminist crusaders' claims had a violence content of 50 per cent.

A cursory glance at the two collections showed that complementary coding would be difficult; Continental material began where British material stopped. To overcome this, the Reading Group adopted a two-step procedure in coding: first, it codified the predominant theme of the imagery itself; second, it regrouped the material by superimposing the definitions used by the Meese Commission (see Chapter 6) to separate different classes of material. Although Meese's categories are open to criticism, as the Report is widely quoted by crusaders it was an obvious choice for a universal standard. Meese used four categories:

Class 1. Sexually Violent Material:
Material featuring actual or unmistakably simulated or unmistakably threatened violence presented in a sexually explicit fashion with a predominant focus on the sexually explicit violence. Sadomasochistic themes, with the standard accoutrements of the genre, including whips, chains, devices of torture, and so on. A man making some sort of advance to a woman, being rebuffed, and then raping the woman or in some other way violently forcing himself on the woman. Sexually active or suggestive nudity coupled with extreme violence, such as disfigurement or murder. (Meese, pp. 323–4, e.g. slasher movies and SM.)

Class 2. Non-violent Materials Depicting Degradation, Domination, Subordination, or Humiliation:
The depiction of people solely for the sexual satisfaction of others. The depiction of people in decidedly subordinate roles in their sexual relations with others. The depiction of people engaged in sexual practices that would to most people be considered humiliating. (Meese, p. 331, e.g. oral sex, anal sex, more than two people.)

Class 3. Non-violent and Non-degrading Materials:
Materials in which the participants appear fully willing participants occupying substantially equal roles in a setting devoid of actual or apparent violence or pain. (Meese, p. 335, e.g. a couple's explicit copulation.)

Class 4. Nudity:
Depictions of nudity from the least explicit to that with a definite provocative element. (Meese, p. 347, e.g. British-style soft-core magazines.)

Soft-core magazine content in newsagents 1965–1990

A 'random sample' (i.e. representative) of British material was selected for each period from the magazine stock, the imagery coded, and scored. When coding 'violence', the Reading Group went much further than Meese and rated *any* imagery that involved *any* act of force or restraint, whether or not those on the receiving end were motivated to avoid this 'violence', and also recorded *any* 'paraphernalia' that could possibly be associated with an act of force or restraint, whether or not it was being utilized, or could be construed as inviting such activity, or could be regarded as an 'unnatural object' for the purpose of a sexual act. By choosing these extremely wide definitions the Reading Group's categorization could only lead to dispute over the issue of depilation. Dr Itzin for some strange reason believes depilation is a violent act, whereas the Reading Group know that it is undertaken to ensure public decency or as part of sex play.

The photographic imagery codes which emerged from the material itself we labelled as follows:

Topless: models with nude breasts wearing an item of clothing below the waist, or where the picture did not reveal the body below the waistline.

Nude sans pubic hair: models who were nude, or partially clothed, but where the picture angle did not reveal pubic hair. Most of these pictures would reveal the breasts.

Pubic hair: models whose pubic hair was partially or totally visible. The majority, but not all, of these pictures would feature exposed breasts.

Crutch: models posed in such a manner, or the camera angle so directed, that the tip of the vulva is visible. Inevitably, owing to anatomical differences, the degree of visibility is not uniform.

Open crutch: models who are so posed, or the camera angle

so directed, that the majority or whole of the genital region is visible. The largest single style was a model whose legs were apart.

Open crutch held: models who are so posed that they are deliberately parting their labia lips with their hands.

Couples: male and female models, or two female models, appearing in the same photograph. In the majority of cases they would be in various stages of undress, and so posed that they were in bodily contact. In several cases they were simulating sexual acts.

Violence: models so posed that they were engaged in an act of force or restrained, whether another model was depicted or not.

Paraphernalia: a model appearing in a photograph which also includes an item that may be associated with force and or restraint in sexual activity, whether or not the model is interacting with the item.

Strip: a model appearing in a series of photographs where she is in a progressive state of undress.

Rear: a model so posed that, in the majority of cases, the back of the body is exposed. Any model so posed that her pubic hair or genital region is exposed will be included in that appropriate category.

Miscellaneous: included model's faces or legs, or models who are fully clothed, or wearing wet T-shirts, and male models.

Shaven: a model whose pubic hair has been shaven, thereby revealing, depending upon anatomical differences, the genital region in some detail.

Masturbation: models who are posed so that the pose may be interpreted as the model engaging in an act of masturbation.

Group: three or more models of either sex appearing in the same photograph.

Sample A

The magazines from the pre-Williams period covered both popular titles such as *Club International, Fiesta, Men Only, Mayfair, Penthouse,* and *Knave,* and ten miscellaneous titles. They tended to contain clearly demarcated photo sets of young women, wearing panties or in the nude but masking their pubic hair. Similar photographs would appear among the editorial pages, but were generally unconnected with the article or feature. Over the sample period, the short stories changed from spy and private eye adventure themes to sexual encounters and experiences. In the early days only one of the features would be related to sex, such as a prurient exposé of the vice dens of Istanbul or call girl confessions, but they were soon joined by satirical pieces, such as 'How to Marry a Rich Girl', and pseudo-sexology. The early features were illustrated with line drawings, but quickly began to include photographs. This caused coding difficulties.

What does one do with stills from a feature on the *Rocky Horror Picture Show*? Some found their way into the miscellaneous category. An exception to this rule are pictures which could be designated paraphernalia or violence, and unambiguously sexually orientated photographs such as a nude picture of Linda Lovelace illustrating a feature on her early life.

Letters pages expanded steadily over the sample period, as did their themes to include sexual anecdotes and adventures. The adverts were mainly non-sex-related: tobacco, alcohol, clothing and electronic equipment – all by leading manufacturers. There was, however, an increasing trend towards advertising sex-related products, and by the end of the sample these had become a major element of the magazines. Throughout this period these advertisements were dominated by a single mail order company, though escort/massage services and the cinema clubs that sprang up in the London area were also advertising towards the end. Small pictures of nude models enhancing these advertisements were not included in our tabulation, as their features were often indistinguishable.

The average number of photo-sets was 4.5, with a range of 1

to 7. One magazine, *Fiesta*, regularly featured a strip-tease sequence, but this was unusual. The 'miscellaneous' photo-set pictures recorded consist of the model fully clothed or a close-up of the face, at the beginning of the photo feature, underwater poses, displaying speciality underwear, etc.

Towards the mid-point of the sample, pubic hair made its appearance at the expense of purely topless pictures. Most models were shown in affluent surroundings, such as the bedroom of large town, or country, houses. Couples, which would be required by Meese's definition in order to make an act or scene 'demeaning', were rare.

Subjectively, apart from in the one magazine which clearly prided itself on using 'working-class girl next door' models, and two cheap 'pin-up' magazines, the models had an appearance of being 'untouchable', or 'not affordable', being reserved for those who enjoyed the standard of living depicted by the advertisements; in short, a cross between a *Playboy* centrefold and a soft-focused 'artistic' pose. Perhaps this was in keeping with the image these magazines wished to portray at the time.

There was no hint of violence, or any sign of paraphernalia whatsoever, in the photo-sets. The only violence to appear does so in feature illustrations, such as the humorous article on *Orgy of the Dead*, a low-budget horror movie, which included several stills in which a couple were bound to posts during a 'Satanic' ritual!

Sample B

Sample B included a much larger range of titles, many being undated to prolong their shelf life, but whose month of issue was discernible by the volume and issue numbers. The Group's selection process enabled them to include the most popular titles from Sample A which were still in print, while making space for magazines representing the new titles, especially those from the Sullivan empire, and the path-breaking *Escort*, thereby ensuring that the sample reflected the most popular magazines available during this period.

Covering the period from the rise of the sex shops to the height of the sex industry in Soho, the sample presented a dramatic contrast to the previous one. The average number of photo-sets, across a range of 2 to 13, was 6.2. There was a reduction in the number of editorial page photographs, but a marked increase in couples and women revealing their labia lips, which in one publisher's magazines were frequently held apart.

Sexually themed stories of an explicit nature took over from features, and those which remained became more sex-related. Advertisements, with the exception of the market leaders, were almost exclusively sex-related, and most magazines now boasted a large classified section offering more material, sex aids, or services. Some magazines also ran contact sections. The Group deliberately excluded the photographs of the 'swingers' in these sections as they would grossly inflate the figures for topless and nude categories. Otherwise, faces and clothing still account for most of the miscellaneous pictures.

More and more models began to wear suspenders, stockings and high heels; and a few wore fetish garments like PVC. The vast majority of violent imagery recorded was to be found in the photo-features, such as 'Sorry I'm All Tied Up', which contained 11 stills from old movies like *King Kong*, to demonstrate bondage themes in general-release movies. Photo-set 'violence', however, did appear in the form of simulated spanking, two models in a boxing ring, and another two wrestling. Otherwise, although crusaders may have found such themes, there are no 'demeaning' pictures as defined within the Meese guidelines. In most cases, those models revealing their crutch did so owing to a change in camera angles and the model's pelvic region, rather than overtly drawing attention to it. The exceptions were to be found in David Sullivan's magazines. The activities of couples will be covered separately below.

Forced to make a subjective assessment, the Group suggested that this sample clearly saw the demise of the so-called 'double standard': Madonna–Magdalen or housewife–whore dichotomy. All categories were collapsed into one, epitomized by the success of *Escort*. The paid models were posed, and the growing number of amateurs appeared to wish to pose, anywhere and everywhere, from the kitchen to outside the local Town Hall! The major exceptions all emanated from one publisher, who clearly wished readers to see the models as sexually obsessed; though unlike in the American descriptions the Group reviewed, a great deal of effort is made in the accompanying text to convince readers they were initiating *their* pleasure.

Sample C

This sample was also selected using a pool system: popular titles and those representing the new titles, after purchasing one copy of every item available from a flabbergasted newsagent with the largest selection in a major South Coast city.

Within the larger 124 item sample the Group discovered: 10 gay magazines (8 per cent), 15 contact magazines (12 per cent), 7 magazines covering fetish material, such as rubber clothing, including 1 transvestite-orientated magazine (5.6 per cent), and 6 magazines covering corporal punishment (4.8 per cent). The last six magazines would fit Meese's Class 1 category of violent material; and the fetish magazines would fit the definition of paraphernalia. Therefore, although this material by no stretch of the imagination parallels the violence available in some US hard-core material, the Group record that *4.8 per cent of magazines available in their 1990 newsagents' sample involved the depiction of violence*. It should be noted, however, that these magazines carried only a score or less photographs, so that *the figure for violent material as a percentage of total pictorial content in the 1990 newsagent sample is less than 4.8 per cent*. Furthermore, as the majority of this material covered the theme of *female* dominance of men, it could hardly constitute violence against women!

The Group then removed these magazines from the new material pool for three reasons. The thesis the Group were supposed to be testing was that soft-core magazine content had become more violent; not that corporal punishment magazines had become more violent. Second, to include specialist material that has always been recognized as a sub-genre would be to misrepresent the content of the typical and average soft-core magazine. The Group had no way of knowing how many titles from this sub-genre were stocked on the top shelf prior to the demise of the sex shops. Third, and most important, *to have included this material would have 'proved' that far from increasing depictions of violence towards women, over 80 per cent of top-shelf violence consisted of violence towards men!* Gay magazines were then removed, because the claim that men in such material are really symbolic women is not only stupid, it is a stereotypical slight against gay sexuality; and the Group made a conscious decision not to discriminate against any minority group.

Once the magazines designed specifically for contact services were removed this left 69.4 per cent of the total sample from which the Group made their selection to test the thesis that widely available soft core pornographic magazines found in newsagents have become more violent.

Overall, the final sample was showing more genital flesh than the first two. Open-crutch photographs were again in evidence, and a sizable minority of these involve models deliberately holding their labia lips; though once again these were mainly found in one publisher's titles. On the other hand, topless and pubic hair photographs were making a come-back, at the expense of couples. The range of photosets was 0 to 11, with an average of 6.95. Features had all but disappeared, except in the market leaders. The latter were the only magazines in which the advertisements were not restricted to sexually orientated products and services.

The themes, contrary to the crusaders' claims, were milder and less 'exploitative' than those of the previous decade. The accent was clearly upon an extremely pluralistic form of beauty, decorated in brightly coloured underwear. In a phrase: everyone was 'out for a laugh'. Though such an idea may appear 'demeaning' to many, the material did not fit any of the first three Meese classes.

Violent imagery

The Reading study found there was an almost complete lack of violent imagery between 1960 and 1990 in British soft-core material displayed upon the top shelf of newsagents.

No imagery in British soft core met the Meese classification standard of violent material. The examples of 'violent imagery' and paraphernalia that did appear were not representations of 'sexually explicit violence'. That appearing in Sample B, for example, included five *simulated spanking* photographs, four pictures from a photo-feature of bondage scenes in BBFC-certificated general-release films, and two females in a simulated boxing match. Two of

Table 1: Soft-core Material: Totals and Mean Scores per Issue

Format	Sample A Total	Mean	Sample B Total	Mean	Sample C Total	Mean
Topless	222	11.10	113	05.65	312	15.60
Nude sans pubic hair	164	08.20	074	03.70	125	06.25
Pubic hair	228	11.40	276	13.80	340	17.00
Crutch	066	03.30	201	10.05	437	21.85
Open crutch	000	00.00	021	01.05	068	03.40
Open crutch held	000	00.00	003	00.15	064	03.20
Couples	041	02.05	229	11.45	139	06.95
Violence	000	00.00	009	00.45	000	00.00
+ features	013	00.65	021	01.05	000	00.00
Paraphernalia	000	00.00	016	00.80	010	00.50
+ features	002	00.10	027	01.35	010	00.50
Strip	115	05.75	059	02.95	023	01.15
Rear	040	02.00	094	04.70	131	06.55
Miscellaneous	086	04.30	076	03.80	176	08.80
+ features	169	08.45	212	10.60	176	08.80
Shaven	000	00.00	000	00.00	029	01.45
Masturbation	009	00.45	005	00.25	005	00.25
Group	016	00.80	075	03.75	035	01.75

Mean = number of pictures per magazine.

those pictures merely involved the clothed models sitting in their respective corners.

There was an almost total lack of paraphernalia which could be used to produce a violent effect. Sample B paraphernalia included several photographs of a model holding an ornamental bull-whip, of the kind proletarians bring back from Spanish holidays as a prop; and two representations of the same photograph of a model wearing a pair of handcuffs, illustrating a fantasy story which did not involve a male. Even if the group were to define this material as 'violent imagery', it was clearly becoming less, not more, prevalent!

Demeaning imagery

The suggestion that British soft core is demeaning to women, while so easy to assert, it difficult to prove. It is impossible

Table 2: Soft-core Magazines: Totals and Frequency per 1000 Pictures

Format	Sample A Total	Per 1000	Sample B Total	Per 1000	Sample C Total	Per 1000
Topless	222	205	113	080	312	165
Nude sans pubic hair	164	151	074	052	125	066
Pubic hair	228	210	276	196	340	180
Crutch	066	061	201	143	437	231
Open crutch	000	000	021	015	068	036
Open crutch held	000	000	003	002	064	034
Couples	041	038	229	162	139	073
Violence	000	000	009	006	000	000
+ features	013	012	021	015	000	000
Paraphernalia	000	000	016	011	010	005
+ features	002	002	027	019	010	005
Strip	115	106	059	042	023	012
Rear	040	037	094	067	131	069
Miscellaneous	086	079	076	054	176	093
+ features	169	156	212	150	176	093
Shaven	000	000	000	000	029	015
Masturbation	009	008	005	004	005	003
Group	016	015	075	053	035	010
Sample size:	1085		1410		1894	pictures

Table 3: Soft-core Magazine Violent Imagery: Total and Averages

Format	Sample A Total	Average	Sample B Total	Average	Sample C Total	Average
Violence	000	00.00	009	00.45	000	00.00
+ features	013	00.65	021	01.05	000	00.00
Paraphernalia	000	00.00	016	00.80	010	00.50
+ features	002	00.10	027	01.35	010	00.50

to find an unambiguous depiction of models who fit Meese's Class 2 definition: people 'solely' for the sexual satisfaction of others, or people in 'decidedly subordinate roles' in their sexual relations with others, or people 'engaged in sexual practices'. The British magazines are simply not explicit enough for any of these definitions to be applied to them. One would also be pushing one's sanity to infer that the models are degraded by being portrayed as 'masochistic, subservient, socially non-discriminating nymphomaniac' (p. 330) solely from the increase in genital-orientated material seen between Samples B and C.

Even if a picture of a model holding her genitals open can be designated a depiction 'solely' for the sexual satisfaction of others (p. 331), by denying any possibility that the model gained any satisfaction from, or that she might enjoy the attention given to her by, holding that pose, one creates a contradiction. For how could the model be depicted as a presumably self-satisfaction-orientated 'nymphomaniac' while simultaneously be there 'solely' for the benefit of others? She cannot; because that inference was originally based upon the context of US movies or highly explicit photo-sets, not 'pin-up' magazines.

Table 4: Images That May Be Considered Degrading by Social Groups Using a Subjective Standard

Format	Sample A		Sample B		Sample C	
	Total	Average	Total	Average	Total	Average
Open crutch	000	00.00	021	01.05	068	03.40
Open crutch held	000	00.00	003	00.15	064	03.20
Shaven	000	00.00	000	00.00	029	01.45

Couples, groups, and masturbation

The same problem presents itself when considering couples and groups. The depictions were simply not explicit enough to fit either Class 2 or Class 3 material. As a result, its designation as 'degrading' would rest solely upon a subjective or ideological viewpoint. Simulated 'masturbation' is another case in point. The Group were at a loss to see how depicting masturbation, let alone simulated masturbation, could be seen as innately demeaning, as the pictures would clearly imply that the models represented were enjoying themselves. Even if they were to 'be used' afterwards, they would not exist 'solely' for others. Once again this would require one to accept that models in particular, and people in general, can never obtain pleasure by concentrating on giving pleasure to others. Those who hold such views must be very selfish lovers. In any event, as the poses published never became more explicit than the hand in close proximity to the genital region, or holding a penis, they all fell into Meese's Class 4: 'nudity'.

Table 5: Soft-core Magazines: Depictions of Couples, Groups, Masturbation, etc.

Format	Sample A		Sample B		Sample C	
	Total	Average	Total	Average	Total	Average
Couples	041	02.05	229	11.45	139	06.95
Masturbation	009	00.45	005	00.25	005	00.25
Group	016	00.80	075	03.75	035	01.75
Miscellaneous	086	04.30	076	03.80	176	08.80
+ features	169	08.45	212	10.60	176	08.80

An impression, however, is not accurate enough. In order to charge the changes in these and other areas, Jason Annetts devised a Sexual Simulation Imagery Scale to produce 'SSIS scores' in order that the Reading Group could assess photographs involving couples, and as a first stage in creating a more objective means to assess content. The scale categories were defined as follows:

> *High-level sex simulation*: anatomical areas of the body considered sexual in contact with another person's genital region: e.g. penis touching mouth, lips or tongue touching anal passage, and sucking nipples.

> *Medium-level sex simulation*: anatomical areas of the body considered sexual in contact with another person's anatomical areas in close proximity to genital areas, i.e. the picture *implied* that sexual contact was imminent, e.g. an extended tongue touching pubic hair, buttocks, or tips of breasts.

> *Low-level sex simulation*: any physical contact with another person's body, but excluding the above; and anatomical

areas considered sexual in close proximity with another person's genital region or breasts, e.g. kissing, naked embrace, an extended tongue near breast.

Non-sex simulation: no contact of anatomical areas regarded as sexual, e.g. hugging when clothed, undressing, two naked people not touching each other.

When the couple depicted in the samples were analysed using the SSIS code the results shown in Table 6 were obtained.

Table 6: Soft-core Magazines:
Sexual Activity Simulation Scale
Scores

SSIS scores: mean per magazine:		
Sample A	Sample B	Sample C
H 00.00	H 00.10	H 00.00
M 00.15	M 03.60	M 02.10
L 01.90	L 10.25	L 03.75
N 02.45	N 04.00	N 03.25

In other words, only two photographs in the three samples scored high enough to be considered *simulated* sexual activity. This suggested that British pornography is more than one step away from its American or Continental rivals. The vast majority of material involving couples scored 'low' on the SSIS scale; over twice as much as material that scored medium. Bear in mind that the Group were finding a medium to low level of sexual simulation imagery; although it has become more explicit over the last 25 years, the trend is downwards from around 1982. Using the Meese definitions, widely recommended by crusaders, and Dr Itzin in particular, this imagery has certainly not become more demeaning.

Even if this material had been explicit enough, a substantial amount of the imagery clearly depicted models who appeared to be 'fully willing participants' and 'occupying substantially equal roles' in a setting devoid of actual or apparent violence or pain, and that would place them in Meese's class 3 material: non-degrading.

Nudity

The vast majority of British soft-core magazine imagery depicts no more than what Meese called 'nudity': from the 'least explicit to that with a definite provocative element'.

Table 7: Soft-core Magazines: Nude Imagery

Format	Sample A		Sample B		Sample C	
	Total	Average	Total	Average	Total	Average
Topless	222	11.10	113	05.65	312	15.60
Nude sans pubic hair	164	08.20	074	03.70	125	06.25
Pubic hair	228	11.40	276	13.80	340	17.00
Crutch	066	03.30	201	10.05	437	21.85
Strip	115	05.75	059	02.95	023	01.15
Rear	040	02.00	094	04.70	131	06.55

Magazine covers

Covers had hardly changed at all over the period. They had rarely exhibited any more nudity than topless imagery, and this has declined in recent years. The most common pose was a clothed model.

Summary

The major development in British soft-core material concerns the nude imagery; since the late 1960s there has been an increase in the display of pubic hair and the female genitals. Most imagery involving couples and groups also fits into the 'nudity' category, because the individuals are merely posing together in a state of undress. There has, however, been a contemporaneous

Table 8: Soft-core Magazines: Cover Imagery

	Sample A	Sample B	Sample C
Clothed	04	04	14*
Nude sans pubic hair	06	05	01
Rear	01	03	01
Topless covered breast	06	01	05
Topless	01	04	01
Pubic hair	00	00	00
Other	02	03	02†

* Includes more than one model per cover.
† For example, a model wearing a wet T-shirt.

three-fold increase in the number of photographs taken from the rear and the steady return of the topless pose. Group photographs are on the decline.

The Reading Group, therefore, concluded that their samples not only demonstrate that there is no evidence for the proposition that soft-core magazines bought from newsagents had increased their violent imagery, contradict those who assert that violent imagery has increased. The claim that newsagents' stocks of soft-core material consist of 50 per cent violent imagery, and that the level of violence is becoming more explicit, is not only exaggerated, it is wildly inaccurate, and possibly a perverse fantasy. This material does not carry any demeaning material, as defined by the Meese Commission. Those who find all pornography degrading will find British material degrading, but it is impossible to suggest that it has become more 'degrading' or 'demeaning' in the last decade. British soft-core magazine production continues in the long tradition of the pin-up.

On what basis, therefore, did so many MPs sign the Early Day Motion asserting that British material had become more violent and demeaning?

Utilizing an ideological reading

Despite their findings, the Reading Group did not stop there. Suppose, they asked themselves, that the crusaders, having discovered the consequences, now wanted to change their minds and pretend they had never promoted the Meese definitions, and continued to insist that soft-core couples, masturbation, open crutch, open crutch held, and shaven models were 'demeaning'; how would this affect the Group's findings? In order to test this, the Group redesignated the categories, utilizing the same standard statistical methods as before, shown in the following manner.

Table 9: Ideological Definitions of Demeaning Material
(a) Violence:

Format	Sample A		Sample B		Sample C	
	Total	Per 1000	Total	Per 1000	Total	Per 1000
Violence + features	013	012	021	015	000	000
Paraphernalia + features	002	002	027	019	010	005
Violence:	0015	0014	0048	0034	0010	0005

(b) Demeaning:

Format	Sample A		Sample B		Sample C	
	Total	Per 1000	Total	Per 1000	Total	Per 1000
Open crutch	000	000	021	015	068	036
Open crutch held	000	000	003	002	064	034
Shaven	000	000	000	000	029	015
Masturbation	009	008	005	004	005	003
Group	016	015	075	053	035	018
Couples	041	038	229	162	139	073
Strip	115	106	059	042	023	012
Demeaning:	0181	0167	0392	0278	0363	0192

(c) Nudity:

Format	Sample A		Sample B		Sample C	
	Total	Per 1000	Total	Per 1000	Total	Per 1000
Topless	222	205	113	080	312	165
Nude sans pubic hair	164	151	074	052	125	066
Pubic hair	228	210	276	196	340	180
Crutch	066	061	201	143	437	231
Rear	040	037	094	067	131	069
Miscellaneous + features	169	156	212	150	176	093
Nudity:	0889	0819	0970	0688	1521	0803

Given that the violence category was so small, the group multiplied each category to obtain a rate per 1000 pictures. When this was tested statistically, the group established a one-in-a-hundred chance that the data's trend could have occurred by chance: a high level of significance. They could, therefore, proceed to test the following two questions: Has the rate of violent imagery increased between our samples; and if so, to what extent? Has the rate of demeaning – determined by the widest possible definition – imagery increased between our samples, and if so at what rate?

Subjecting every calculation to the appropriate statistical test, the Group discovered that:

1. Between Sample A and Sample B, 1965–1975 and 1978–1983, violent imagery increased; but that between Sample B and Sample C, 1978–1983 to 1990, it decreased. The trend in violence between Sample A and Sample C demonstrates that *there has been a net decline in violent imagery in the thirty-year period covered.*

2. Between 1965–1975 and 1978–1983, the trend in demeaning material, using the crusaders' definition, dramatically increased by 66 per cent; but then dramatically declined by 31 per cent from 1978–1983 to 1990. This meant that the overall trend, comparing sample A with sample C was that *'demeaning' imagery slightly increased (by 15 per cent) between 1965–1975 and 1990.* This trend, however, did not meet the statistical significance test, and could therefore have occurred by accident of sample. Whatever the reason, despite the increase over the period, *the current trend is downwards.*

In other words, even when one adopts the widest possible definitions of violence and demeaning imagery, British soft core is 'not guilty' as charged by the crusaders.

European pornographic imagery

Hard-core pornography coding presents greater problems than soft core; not least its cost, and the illegality of importing such

material into Britain. So the Group used a series of hard-core illustrated catalogues displaying the covers of the then current magazines, conveniently subdivided by genre indicating the meanings
given to the material by the industry. As the Meese Commission
and several other surveys used covers, there was a precedent for
their use. The Reading Group, however, wished to determine
whether or not one could infer content from cover, so I took a trip
to the Netherlands, purchased a representative selection of the
actual material from Rotterdam sex shops which held extensive
collections of back issues, and discovered that although the contents tended to contain a wider selection of activities than that
depicted on the cover, the genre theme depicted on the cover *was*
the predominant theme presented in the magazine. The cover cannot, however, be taken as a complete guide to the total contents of
the magazine, but merely shows the major theme. Theming the
covers makes sense, anyway, because a picture set contains pictures
which build up to the central activity. I then disposed of the material.

The Reading Group's method of coding now had two
advantages over previous attempts to describe what hard-core material was available. By publishing the listings in full, the group
enabled those who wished to do so to test their conclusions with
their own typology; other researchers could easily place their categories within any larger or smaller generic group. second, while
the Group's survey categories were value neutral and industry
defined, it enabled both readers wishing to make judgements about
the material, and those who are more concerned with ethnographic
interpretations, to utilize the same data.

The range of imagery in European magazines was far more
extensive than British material. Over the period covered, the group
found depictions of: anal sex, animals, 'big boobs' (breasts), big
penises, bondage, (underage) boys (male child pornography), coloured women, coloured men, corporal punishment (spanking),
domination (by one means or another), faces, fat women, Fem-
Dom (women dominating men), 'fifteen' (implying virginal status),
'fist fucking' (by one woman of another), 'gang bang' (four or more
males to one female), group sex (four participants of any gender
combination), he/she (pre-transsexual), homosexual, incest
(implied), 'irreligion' (imagery involving religious paraphernalia),

leather (person/s engaging in sexual activities wearing leather clothing), 'lesbians', 'lolitas' (female child pornography), masturbation, mixed (several categories), normal sex, nudes, 'nude cunts' (shaved models), nymphomaniacs (implying a sexual orientation), old men/young women, older women, orgies (four-plus, equal gender), oral sex, oriental women, pregnant women, rape (implied), rubberwear (person/s engaging in sexual activities dressed in rubber clothing), 'schoolgirls' (women dressed in school uniform), sadomasochism, 'spunk' (ejaculation), teenage (young women), torture (simulated scenarios), transsexuals (post op.), trios (of either combination), transvestites (men who dress as women), 'twat' (close-ups of female genitalia), 'vampirism' (implying blood letting, not drinking), virgins, 'water sports' (urolagnia), and unclassified (reproduction of imagery too poor to determine a dominant theme).

The meaning of each category could be easily inferred from its title, with the exceptions of trios, orgies, group sex and gang bangs. The catalogue copy-writers tend to describe the first three as 'orgies', and the group needed to distinguish between them because of the potential interpretations that can be made regarding the level of 'mutual enjoyment' implied. The group used the term 'gang bang' to cover an imbalance of male to female participants, or where the theme was reflected in the title. Appropriate material was coded 'lesbian' irrespective of the assumed predominant proclivities of the female models.

The European sample

Every magazine in the sample was coded on the basis of the dominant genre imagery, or qualified according to the caveats, and a score recorded. The group then reclassified following the Meese guidelines by total number of images and frequency per catalogue.

The reclassification in Meese's categories demonstrated the huge gap between British soft core and European material. Whereas the former slotted into Class 4, most European imagery could easily be placed into one of Meese's first three classes. On the other hand, the Group had several reservations.

Meese failed to provide a much-needed fifth class enabling

Table 10: *European Magazines: Violent Imagery*

Imagery:	Years					
	1972–1977		1978–1979		1980–1983	
	Total	FPC	Total	FPC	Total	FPC
Bondage	06	0.32	03	0.38	05	0.42
Corporal punishment	08	0.42	00	0.00	00	0.00
Domination	00	0.00	01	0.13	00	0.00
Leather	00	0.00	01	0.13	02	0.17
Rape	02	0.11	00	0.00	00	0.00
Rubberwear	22	1.16	09	1.13	05	0.42
SM	30	1.58	00	0.00	01	0.08
Torture	11	0.58	02	0.25	10	0.83

designation of illegal acts such as incest and pornography involving children. The Group, reluctantly, had to add this imagery to Class 2, as the imagery was not violent, whereas the act in real life may have been. The fact that crusaders back Meese when it failed to address such issues is appalling.

Likewise, Meese makes numerous 'sexist' assumptions regarding sexual minorities such as transsexuals, and often infers too much. It is highly debatable, for example, whether bondage pictures by themselves should be classified as violent *per se*; the thrill of bondage resides in its passive helplessness, completely mitigating any need for force.

Given the numerous inferences contained in Meese's text, the group also included imagery such as oral sex in the Non-violent Demeaning category, although the Group were not convinced it should be placed there. They took the decision that neither 'teenage' nor 'fifteen' imagery necessarily implies 'decidedly subordinate roles', and included these categories within the Non-violent and Non-degrading category, and were able to place close-ups of genitalia where it really belongs.

As a result, the Group did not claim that their application of the Meese categories was necessarily correct or watertight; it was obvious that separatist feminists are likely to disagree with Meese's guidelines for depilation – the early appearance of which clearly demonstrates that this practice has nothing to do with being a substitute for child pornography, and its declining frequency after

Table 11: *European Magazines: 'Demeaning' Imagery*

	1972–1977		1978–1979		1980–1983	
	Total	FPC	Total	FPC	Total	FPC
Anal sex	20	1.05	16	2.00	37	3.08
Animals	34	1.79	08	1.00	18	1.50
Boy	12	0.63	00	0.00	00	0.00
Fat women	03	0.16	02	0.25	00	0.00
Fem-Dom	05	0.26	07	0.88	25	2.08
Incest	04	0.21	01	0.13	01	0.08
Fist fucking	01	0.05	01	0.13	00	0.00
Gang bang	01	0.05	01	0.13	02	0.17
Group sex	22	1.16	02	0.25	02	0.17
He/she	00	0.00	00	0.00	09	0.75
Lesbians	35	1.84	15	1.88	15	1.25
Lolitas	88	4.63	45	5.75	07	0.53
Nymphomaniacs	00	0.00	01	0.13	06	0.50
Old men/young women	00	0.00	01	0.13	01	0.08
Oral sex	49	2.58	23	2.88	31	2.58
Oriental	04	0.21	02	0.25	03	0.25
Orgies	17	0.89	10	1.25	04	0.33
Schoolgirls	06	0.32	01	0.13	01	0.08
Spunk	08	0.42	04	0.50	07	0.53
Transsexual	04	0.21	00	0.00	03	0.25
Trios	91	4.78	34	4.25	25	2.08
Transvestites	04	0.21	00	0.00	06	0.50
Vampire	01	0.05	00	0.00	00	0.00
Virgins	04	0.21	00	0.00	03	0.25
Water sports	10	0.53	08	1.00	20	1.67

the mid- to late 1970s clearly disproves the thesis. The following findings, therefore, demonstrate trends.

As with the soft-core data, when the Group applied statistical 'significance' tests, the score was highly significant, which suggests that the data were reliable. Further statistical tests, all outlined in detail in their Report, revealed that:

1. Violent imagery in European pornography declined from 1972–1977 to 1978–1979, by 42 per cent; it then possibly declined from 1978–1979 to 1980–1983 by 7 per cent (though because the Group had to use the rate per 1000, as the figures were small, it could be random vari-

Table 12: *European Magazines: Non-Demeaning Imagery*

	1972–1977		1978–1979		1980–1983	
	Total	FPC	Total	FPC	Total	FPC
Coloured girls	11	0.58	02	0.25	01	0.08
Coloured men	06	0.32	00	0.00	00	0.00
'Fifteen'	06	0.32	00	0.00	02	0.17
Homosexual	18	0.95	00	0.00	07	0.53
'Irreligion'	05	0.26	00	0.00	00	0.00
Masturbation	10	0.53	12	1.50	17	1.42
'Normal'	52	2.74	24	3.00	36	3.00
Older women	03	0.16	00	0.00	00	0.00
Teenage	05	0.26	04	0.50	27	2.25

Table 13: *European Magazines: Nudity*

	1972–1977		1978–1979		1980–1983	
	Total	FPC	Total	FPC	Total	FPC
Big boobs	19	1.00	13	1.63	08	0.67
Big penis	00	0.00	00	0.00	01	0.08
Face	06	0.32	00	0.00	00	0.00
Nudes	52	2.74	10	1.25	53	4.42
Nude cunts	06	0.32	04	0.50	03	0.25
Twat	10	0.53	03	0.38	12	1.00

Table 14: *European Magazines: Miscellaneous*

	1972–1977		1978–1979		1980–1983	
	Total	FPC	Total	FPC	Total	FPC
Mixed	22	1.16	1	01.3	2	0.17
Unclassified	40	2.10	0	0.00	0	0.00

ation). There was, however a definite decline in violent imagery in European pornography between 1972–1977 and 1980–1983, by some 54 per cent.

The Group therefore concluded that violent imagery in European pornography had dramatically declined. As a result, the claim that

Table 15: European Magazines: Trends in Imagery

	Sample A		Sample B		Sample C	
	1972–1977		1978–1979		1980–1983	
	Total	Per 1000	Total	Per 1000	Total	Per 1000
1 Violent material	079	102	016	059	023	055
2 Non-violent, demeaning	423	547	182	672	266	541
3 Non-violent, non-demeaning	116	150	042	155	090	215
4 Nudity	093	120	030	111	077	184
5 Miscellaneous	062	080	001	004	002	005

violent pornographic imagery, of the kind most likely to circulate in Britain during the last decade, has dramatically increased is not only unfounded, it is untrue.

> 2. Non-violent but demeaning imagery in European pornography rose from 1972–1977 to 1978–1979, by 23 per cent; it then declined from 1978–1979 to 1980–1983 by 19 per cent. The figures between 1972–1977 and 1980–1983 remained constant, but the change was too slight to be statistically significant.

The Group therefore concluded that the claim that degrading pornographic imagery has dramatically increased is erroneous, as the change over the period is literally insignificant.

> 3. Non-violent and non-demeaning imagery in European pornography appeared to rise between 1972–1977 and 1978–1979, by 3.3 per cent, but the change is too small to establish statistical significance; it then rose from 1978–1979 to 1980–1983 by 39 per cent; and when a comparison between the periods 1972–1977 and 1980–1983 is made, the group find it has increased by 43 per cent.

The Group therefore concluded that there has been a dramatic increase in non-violent and non-demeaning imagery in European material. Far from decreasing, as crusaders imply, this type of imagery appears to be making a resurgence.

> 4. Nudity in European pornography appeared to decline between 1972–1977 to 1978–1979, by 7 per cent, though the figure is not statistically significant; it then rose between 1978–1979 and 1980–1983, by 66 per cent; and between 1972–1977 and 1980–1983, it rose by 53 per cent.

The Group therefore concluded that simple nude imagery in European pornography greatly increased.

In short, violent imagery in European pornography had not increased, but had declined from a high point in 1972–1977. Likewise, it would be difficult to demonstrate that degrading imagery had increased. Both non-violent non-demeaning and nude imagery appeared to be making a resurgence. This means that the claim, made by several anti-pornography organizations during 1983, that pornography was becoming increasingly violent and degrading was not only unfounded, it was the complete opposite of the truth.

Although ten years have passed since the data were collected, and eight since the study was conducted, these conclusions are still reasonable for two reasons. First, the contemporary claims do not originate from any content study, but a repetition of assertions that first surfaced in 1983; and secondly, anyone conversant with *all* European material today (as opposed to the unrepresentative samples shown to parliamentarians) will tell you that the major growth area among violent material is SM and rubberwear devotee material clearly involving mutual satisfaction for the parties concerned, while French companies like Video Marc Dorcel, with their glossy ninety-minute non-violent movies, are literally 'cleaning up' the rest of the market.

Summary

Given the high standard of statistical significance obtained in the Reading Study, it can be said with a high degree of certainty that to assert that British soft-core and illegal European magazines circulating in Britain have increased their violent imagery is to promote a falsehood. Given that there is no accumulating evidence to demonstrate a link between explicit soft-core pornography and sex crime either, the two major justifications for imposing further controls upon British soft core have been shown to be totally unfounded misrepresentations of the truth. And the reason is not surprising; for the crusaders' and separatists recent claims rest upon one of the most ideological reviews of the evidence ever: the Meese Commission, which claimed without foundation that violent and demeaning imagery had dramatically increased between the years 1971 and 1985.

Chapter six

Ideological Evidence

AS the media justifications for new controls on soft core concerning this 'new', 'gathering', 'conclusive' or 'overwhelming' evidence of a link between soft-core pornography and sex crimes was bogus, the crusaders had to get it from somewhere. Although individual research studies and the 'anecdotal evidence' from Minneapolis Ordinance hearings were sometimes referred to, the ultimate source was the American Attorney General's Commission on Pornography, known as the Meese Commission. It was released on 9 July 1986, a matter of months before separatists began proclaiming that there was new evidence.

In reality, the Report *did not* demonstrate a link. Precisely because it could not find any evidence, it actually consists of bizarre justifications for asserting that soft core is still 'harmful' *by redefining what 'harm' is*. It pulled together every secular reason it could think of to suggest that, as soft core shows pre- and non-marital sexual acts, it promotes promiscuity, and then insisted that promiscuity was socially harmful. The continued attempt to convince those who have never seen it that Meese proved soft core was harmful, by playing off the public's assumption that the 'harm' refers to violent sex crimes, tells one far more about the crusaders' attitude to truth than the effects of soft core.

Reading Meese, however, quickly exposes this obfuscation, and explains the Report's poor reception in the United States. Far from there being the result of a deliberate conspiracy to discredit the Report, as Dr Itzin has asserted, Meese discredited itself. Its most damning feature was the unresolved contradiction between its two core rationales for controlling material.

Towards Meese

Unlike in Britain, the American liberalization of pornography between 1960 and 1978 extended far beyond pin-up magazines. While obscenity does not have First Amendment protection, after the 1970 Pornography Commission which recommended decriminalization, the Supreme Court, by redefining what obscenity was not, dramatically increased the types of materials that were protected. As long as the material did not have direct harmful consequences or did not offend community standards, it was protected. On the other hand, few states repealed their obscenity statutes; they simply did not enforce them because the convicted would win on appeal. The Christian community set about finding a new reason to reverse the 1970 Johnson Report, which claimed there was no evidence of direct harm, and to instigate new legislation or get prosecutors to reinforce existing statutes.

For twenty years numerous groups – the National Federation for Decency, Interdenominational Citizens Council for Decency, National Coalition Against Pornography, American Family Association, National Christian Association, Religious Alliance Against Pornography, and Morality in Media – tried in dozens of ways to reverse the situation. They failed. During the 1980s, however, the rise of the 'Moral Majority' put pornography back on the political agenda; but while Ronald Reagan wanted their votes, he knew he would never be able to pass their political demands, like the Families Act and the outlawing of homosexuality, without severely disrupting the economy and throwing America into social turmoil; so tossing them the Meese Commission was the answer.

The Christians claimed, with some justification, that the 1970 Commission had been packed with liberals. Yet having $2 million, hiring a staff of 22 and pioneering five huge volumes of original research, they had taken their task seriously, and decriminalization was premised on the simultaneous recommendation for systematic sex education to inhibit the sexual difficulties and beliefs which encourage sex crimes. This humanistic approach was challenged by a minority report penned by Morton Hill of Morality in Media, and the Methodist Revd Link, who believed that governments should regulate against moral corruption. Another dissenter was Charles Keating, Jr, who had spent millions ever since trying to discredit the majority report through the group Citizens for Decency Through Law; it was Keating who helped convince Reagan that America needed a new Commission, and he got one in May 1985.

Unfortunately, Reagan did not put the Government's money where his mouth was. This Commission had only 12 months and less than half a million dollars to spend; half the time and only 10 per cent, in real terms, of its predecessor's budget. A lot of time, however, was spent vetting both Commission and staff members.

The Chairman was 'hang-'em-high' Henry Hudson, an Arlington County, Virginia, attorney who gained his nickname from a personal crusade against adult bookstores and prostitutes. The Executive Director was Alan Sears, a Federal prosecutor from Louisville, Kentucky, who had never given up trying obscenity cases. Being a Southern Baptist and opponent of sex education, Sears believed that pornographers must have kidnapped their models. Tex Lezar, an ex-deputy sheriff who dreamed of becoming an attorney, was signed up as the vice-chair.

The Commission members were also highly morally motivated. Father Bruce Ritter, a Franciscan priest, had made his name as an expert on child abuse, prostitution, and pornography, through his horror stories about Times Square runaways which he placed in his Justice Department-funded Covenant House. Just as Britain's Ray Wyre justifies his claims by citing his anonymous charges at Gracewell, Ritter, a veteran of the 1977 child pornography panic, peddled his 'expertise' for moral causes on what the runaways allegedly told him. Ritter was obsessed with conspiracies concerning paedophile rings, which was not surprising as it turned out *he* was using them as his private sex slaves, and is now in disgrace as a result.

Dr James Dobson, founder of Focus on the Family, a Christian counselling and crusading body, had already served on a National Advisory Commission for the Juvenile Justice and Delinquency Prevention. His personal obsession was white slavery, and he hoped that the Commission would consider the threat posed by a Hispanic ring who were apparently drugging nice middle-class girls in shopping malls before shipping them to Tijuana. They were backed by Diane Cusack, whose only qualification appeared to be her religious fanaticism and friendship with Keating; and Deanne Tilton, head of the California Consortium of Child Abuse Councils, whose horror stories during the White House Task Force on Family Violence had impressed Mrs Ursula Meese. Tilton, like Ritter, was obsessed with child pornography.

Science was represented by Dr Park Elliot Dietz and Dr Judith Becker. Dietz, a University of Virginia psychiatrist, and an FBI consultant, specialized in pathological sex criminals, who he believed got their ideas from *True Detective*-type magazines. Becker, the Director of the Sexual Behavior Clinic at the New York State Psychiatric Institute, was a recognized expert on the treatment of sex offenders. The law was represented by Frederick Schauer, a University of Michigan Law School Professor, known for his opposition to pornography's Constitutional protection, and Edward Garcia, a Reagan-appointed Federal judge, who had made his name thirty years before as a DA prosecuting obscenity cases when everything was illegal and the result was a foregone conclusion. The final member, Eileen Levine, the Decorating and Food Editor of *Cosmopolitan*, who had written the well-known classic *Planning Your Wedding*, was supposed to represent media interests. The media were not impressed; but they would be.

The means by which the panellists were selected is illustrated by the experience of Lois Lee, the dynamic Director of Children of the Night, a Los Angeles prostitutes' counselling service, who unlike Ritter really did some good, and may have had a real contribution to make. But while she was more than willing to accept an appointment, she was very unhappy about supplying 'victims of pornography' for staff member Ed Chapman, who insisted that she find teenagers 'who started turning tricks after their fathers showed them *Playboy* or *Penthouse*'. When Lee informed him that young prostitutes did not start out that way, she was told 'I don't think we are going to want your kids'; or Lee either! The Revd Donald Wildmon, then running the National Federation for Decency, was asked to find some 'victims' instead.

Fixing the result did not stop there. Determined to prove a causal link, the vast majority of the more than two hundred witnesses were selected to justify the anti-pornography measures drawn up by Tex Lezar *before* the Commission's members even started their discussions! Staff members kept such a tight reign on the agenda that the Commissioners had to demand the ten days they spent discussing the issues raised. Even Dr Dobson could not believe his ears when at the first of the business meetings, held after the public hearings, Hudson suggested they need not waste time because the evidence already existed. The staff also picked the subject areas of the hearings.

The hearings

Far from collecting evidence, the hearings were Justice Department publicity stunts; and the origin of many unsubstantiated one-liners that British crusaders have been repeating ever since.

The first in Washington, for example, featured Lois Herrington's assertion that 29 out of 36 serial killers were 'attracted' to pornography. Mr Hames, head of Britain's Obscene Publications Squad, has been stunning audiences with this 'fact' ever since. What Hames fails to mention, however, was that Herrington was a Meese aide, whose appearance was engineered to promote the Justice Department's own rationales for a clamp-down. Apart from Herrington, the WAP founder Dorchen Leidholdt turned up with her WAVAW-type slide show along with six Senators who disliked pornography, and a dozen 'victims' of the 'adult survivors' type who had just recovered their memories of 'porn abuse' in time to collect their expenses.

In the business meeting which followed, even Ritter denounced their claims as ridiculous. Typical was the professional 'victim' Mary Steinman, whose horror stories of sexual abuse from the age of three secure her fees on the anti-porn circuit of churches, radio and television shows, and public hearings like Indianapolis. Ironically, Mary's story, given her age, actually proves that sexual abuse existed long before pornography was freely available!

Law enforcement was the theme in the Chicago hearings, where Christian policemen queued up to offer their ideas about pornographic crimes. What they proved was something else. LAPD sergeant Don Smith, by raising his concern about Los Angeles' 49 adult bookstores, 49 hotels with pornography on cable, 38 book-stores, 25 adult arcades and 27 massage parlours, actually revealed how few businesses it takes to become 'the porn capital ofithe world'. Most other witnesses were vice cops and government law-yers praising their own efforts.

Given Dr Itzin's high regard for the Commission, one wonders why she does not broadcast the real evidence offered that day. By demonstrating that 80 per cent of all America's porn output comes from Los Angeles, but only makes $550 million annually, the LAPD actually exposed the separatists' ludicrous estimates about pornography being an eight billion dollar industry. And why do Christian crusaders never remind us that Sam Currin, who was proud that almost 90 per cent of North Carolinians were church-going folks with traditional values, then let it slip that it also has the largest number of pornography outlets in the USA!

The highlight in Chicago was a set-piece battle between MacKinnon, then WAP's lawyer, and Nan Hunter, the New York attorney and member of the Feminist Anti-Censorship Task Force, formed after the Indianapolis Ordinance. Hunter dismissed porno-graphy as the major validator and channel of women's oppression; there were many more powerful means and institutions doing that. She also raised the awkward question that if Meese was so interested in violence against women, why was he cutting the funds to clinics for battered women? MacKinnon spent so long waffling through her neo-Marxist justifications that she had to be cut short; the panel were completely lost.

The star witness, however, was Brenda MacKillop, a former *Playboy* Bunny from 1976, who claimed that Hugh Hefner was a pimp. Her evidence: some men at Bunny Clubs offered her trips and money to go to bed with them, 'but, although I never accepted, others *may* have'. This born-again Christian then contradicted her-self: 'I got on casting couches in the attempt to become a movie star. Although I received small parts in *Godfather II* and *Funny Lady*, had sex with movie stars and producers, I felt worthless and empty'; and obviously in need of something to blame instead of herself. This ex-Bunny now does very well on the Christian anti-pornography circuit.

Commissioners then fell out with the staff over the publicity being released in their name. Dr Dietz was particularly incensed that people like David Alexander Scott were having an input when they were neither panellists or staff members; and so he might. What panellists did not know was exactly how much Meese relied upon Scott.

Scott, a Toronto Christian therapist, had written a review *Pornography: Its Effect on the Family, Community and Culture*, published by the Child and Family Protection Institute, Washington, DC, backed by the Republican Free Congress Foundation, and distributed by the Christian broadcasters' Contact America. The content is enlightening, not for what it says, but because it bears a remarkable similarity to the Meese Report published twelve months later. Everything one finds in Meese appeared in Scott first; from the effects studies quoted, through the legal and moral rationales, to the references about 800 magazines and 2000 feature videos. Scott's solutions all appear in the final Report too; the only difference is that Meese is fatter.

Scott, like Meese, went after soft core, which he credited with four evil messages: sexual repression is unhealthy; promiscuity is healthy; sexual 'deviance' including homosexuality is not deviant'; and 'mature love' is not sophisticated. It had caused the rise of promiscuous, homosexual, drug-enhanced, sadomasochistic child-molesting white slavers who now threatened the American way of life. Meese did not go quite that far; they forgot about the drugs.

The Commission heard about the social scientific evidence in Houston, though those who appeared read like a Who's Who from the Christian and feminist crusades.

Dr Court was flown in to repeat his correlations before denouncing pornography as 'psychological AIDS', claiming that his work (which does not actually require him to view the material) had affected his own marriage, and then asserted that everyone with anorexia nervosa was really a 'porn victim'. It was a hard act to follow; but Dr Victor Cline managed it with his theory that there would be no pre- or extra-marital sex, group sex, partner switching, voyeurism, exhibitionism and fetishism without pornography. WAVAW's Dr Diana Russell then went over her dubious 1978 San Francisco survey which found that 44 per cent of females were upset by pornography, and peddled the usual inferences. Russell, however, did not make a good witness. Panellists' questions forced her to admit that the reasons for such 'upsets' were not what she or separatists like to imply at all. One woman, for example, was 'upset' about her boyfriend's idea 'of putting objects in my vagina *until I learned it is not as deviant as I used to think*'. Likewise, Russell had to admit that contrary to her inflated claims about her sample, it had only really turned up 1.6 per cent who had suffered from any pornography-related rape or attempted rape. Trying to explain this away by suggesting that 'although it may sound low, it represents 16,000 rapes per 1 million people' only made it worse. While Russell is a good separatist, Dr Dietz is a better mathematician, and knowing his official rape statistics, he embarrassed the separatist movement by pointing out that it would take up to 20 years of all reported rapes to get to that many given the USA's population. When he then asked her to distinguish between a reasonable and a 'degenerate request' by a male partner, Russell was forced to back down, admitting that her study had never differentiated between them.

If Russell had blown her chance to puff her separatist bluff to the world at large, Dr Diane Scully, the sociologist from Virginia Commonwealth University, did not live up to Hudson's expectations either. On the basis of a naive, but worthwhile, study of incarcerated rapists, Scully is erroneously regarded as an expert of rape myths. Her own published evidence actually demonstrates that high-psychotic factors are more important than the rape myths she was looking for; but, although Scully was unaware of the value of her data, she had clearly demonstrated that there was no evidence of a direct causal relationship between rape and even violent pornography in her sample, and, to her credit, was not afraid to say so either. Worse was to follow.

Psychologist Dr Wendy Stock was a disaster. This fan of Brownmiller, by running through her study on female undergraduates' attitudes to rape myths, came up with the wrong answer. The students were offered three variations on the theme of: a woman meets a man in a bar, he takes her into the men's room, pulls off her clothes, ties her up and has sex, and then the woman, who climaxes repeatedly, looks forward to her next encounter with her attacker. In the first version, the woman initially resists, has to be dragged there, is forcefully tied up, but says 'yes with her body' (yes, a feminist dreamed up this filth!); in the second, she goes voluntarily and has sex without coercion; in the last, she resists all the way, is fearful, and suffers pain. It turned out that the students were highly aroused by the first, 'rape myth', version; less by the second, pleasant sex, account; and not at all by the third. Exciting sex, vehemently denounced as a male 'rape myth' by separatists and researchers alike, turned out to be very exciting for women. Stock's ideology, of course, left her without an explanation; though the answer is obvious, and both feminists and men should listen: women enjoy rape *fantasies* but not the real thing.

Once the Christians and feminists had missed with their best shots, the real researchers took the stand. Yale's Dr Baron put the panellists straight about his correlational study. He was followed by several eminent sex educators including Mary Calderone MD, who testified that America's sex education programmes left a lot to be desired but was America's best hope to avoid the sexual pathology that *leads* some people to become obsessed with pornography, and sex crime. Dr Donnerstein, the University of Wisconsin's Professor in both Communications and Women's Studies, keen to absolve himself after the Ordinances, admitted he now knew the difference between the effects of sex, and the effects of violence in provoking aggression. It was all falling away long before Dr Richard Green, founder of the International Academy of Sex Research, former President of the Society for the Scientific Study of Sex, and editor of *The Archives of Sexual Behaviour*, treated the panel to an overview of what science knows about sexually orientated material and its effects. He brought Court up to date by pointing out that Germany with its extensive public pornography experienced a decline in sex crimes by 11 per cent between 1972 and 1980, while non-sexual violent offences rose 125 per cent. He provided a critique of the laboratory studies and prison research, pointing to the need to be conversant with the nation's real sexual habits before listing pornography's educational and therapeutic value, demonstrated by its use in over 40,000 institutions and 8000 individual practices dealing with clients' sexual difficulties. Hudson was horrified; they had deliberately avoided the issue of sex therapy; but for every one of his victims, Green was offering a dozen beneficiaries, demonstrating it is not the material but what people do with it that counts.

Dr Donald Mosher finally finished Hudson off. If, he

emphasized, by modern standards the 1970 Commission's research studies were less sophisticated, the present batch presented a bigger problem: members of the scientific community were promoting convictions based more upon their beliefs than the evidence they had gathered. When the religious panellists attempted to bamboozle Mosher and deflect attention back onto alleged harms by demanding to know how he could justify claiming that sadomasochism or bestiality would not be harmful, Mosher's simple answer destroyed every crusader's secular justifications for controls: even if bestiality and sadomasochism appeared every night on TV, it wouldn't make people engage in such acts, because it simply doesn't appeal to many people.

It got tougher in Los Angeles, where the porn industry fought back through Beverly Hills lawyer John Weston, representing the Adult Film Association. Weston had done a little research of his own: why, he wanted to know, was the Commission worried about pornography when most serial killers in the United States actually come from rural, right-wing, fundamentalist protestant backgrounds, where their reading matter would have been mainly limited to the Bible in their formative years; 'Would one literally extrapolate from that undeniable fact that somehow the Bible or formal fundamentalist protestant theology inculcates within its adherents the desire or necessity of serial killing? I think not.' The rest of the two-hour polemic dismissed many of the myths surrounding the industry.

Bill Margold – actor, agent, critic and now director – then pointed out that the blue movie was undergoing a natural change anyway. Today's industry was nothing like the past; the only thing that would encourage objectionable material was the attempt to drive it back underground.

Staff members thought they had an answer in Ms Garcia, the January 1973 Playmate, who was once Hefner's Promotions Coordinator, but was now denouncing indiscriminate drug use, prostitution rings, and her rape at the hands of a celebrity during her employment. But no one bought this once it emerged she was seeking a publisher for her 'kiss and tell' memoirs. *Playboy* laughed the accusations off, having defended itself back in Chicago. *Penthouse* made its defence in New York, where it hired Harvard law professor Alan Dershowitz to raise an obvious rebuttal:

Let's assume that every rapist in America in 1984 was exposed to *Playboy* and *Penthouse*. We would still have to determine what proportion of their readers went out and committed rape. Even if we were to assume that each rape was committed by a different person, certainly not the case, approximately 99.97% of readers did not commit rapes. That makes *Playboy* and *Penthouse* purer than Ivory Snow.

Before then, however, the constant disputes between Commission members and the staff came to a head in Los Angeles, when Tex Lezar presented the Report's law enforcement proposals. How, the panellists asked, could they set prison sentences and fines for promoting harm when they had yet to discuss the issue of harm, let alone determine whether or not pornography led to harm? Sears attempted a fob-off; that all depended on how one interpreted the Attorney-General's Charter. It was the final straw. Levine wanted to know just how representative all those slide shows they had sat through were; and what did the endless examples of bizarre sexual practices and old copies of child pornography have to do with soft core? And when were the staff going to produce at least one witness who claimed that pornography had been beneficial? Dr Dobson suggested contacting the Lutheran Social Services. Father Ritter suggested Dr Ruth. They were wasting their time.

Next stop Miami; the Justice Department's last shot: surely a non-stop focus on child pornography would regain public sympathy. No. The FBI Director told the Commission they didn't need any new laws; and as the Florida police seemed to have little difficulty in securing prosecutions, they could not have too many problems either. The major problem, however, here was that the witnesses would not stop contradicting themselves, and their inflated estimates about the evil trade and its alleged link with the soft-core industry collapsed as the media pressed for verification.

Hudson was banking on Dr Reisman's $734,000 study of soft core cartoons, funded by the Justice Department's Office of Delinquency Prevention which hoped to demonstrate that *Playboy*, *Penthouse* and *Hustler* were child pornography, negating their First Amendment protection.

Apart from writing children's songs, Reisman's major claim to fame until getting the grant had been an article in a WAVAW book which compared Hefner to Hitler. Her lack of a university affiliation, necessary for a grant, was solved by a professorship at the American University in Washington, which just happened to have Meese's wife on the Board. Reisman then blew her mega bucks poring over soft-core magazines' cartoons, and, having failed to note what was satire or irony, alleged that the magazines contained child pornography in 2016 cartoons and 3988 photographs. Unfortunately the claim that these images featured exaggerated sexual parts, including ample cleavages, gave away Reisman's definition of children: those under the age of 20! A typical charge against cartoons was a skit on the *Wizard of Oz* in a 1979 issue of *Playboy* in which a just-ravaged 'Dorothy' is turning over the Tin Man, Lion, and Scarecrow to a cop, while saying: 'That's them, officer'. This, according to Reisman, positively promoted the gang rape of children by surrogate protectors. Other silly claims included the WAVAW standard that adult models with shaved genitalia were a 'troublesome new phenomenon' and 'a substitute for child pornography'. In fact, depilation is an age-old practice undertaken by 'show-girls', which spread with trimming 'bikini lines' in general and backless, micro-front beach thongs in particular.

Ironically, the study's validity was somewhat undermined by her slide show. One picture which clearly showed a young woman in her late teens was passed off by Reisman as 'really a six- or seven-year-old', and she had a Georgetown paediatrician's opinion to prove it! Rather than make a fool of herself, however, Reisman passed the job over to staff member Edna Einsiedel, who had the embarrassment of clicking through a series of satirical cartoons, in which the children portrayed were simply making ironic, naive, but telling and amusing comments about sex.

Dr Judith Becker could not believe anyone could be so ridiculous. Nor could Dobson; and the business meeting took up the issue of sex education. Panel members surprised the staff by thinking there should be more of it, and that accusations that it was 'pornography' were absurd. Even Tilton had had enough. Child abuse was one thing, but thanks to the silly Satanic abuse allegations, constantly referred to by the 'victims' in Miami, pre-schools were depriving children by firing male workers and forbidding natural touching.

The road show finally came to an end in New York with its

emphasis upon organized crime. The religious witnesses, organized by Father Bruce Ritter, had some important issues to raise about moral decline, but not pornography. Mrs Griffin, an officer of the Cumberland Missionary Society from Tennessee, didn't think pornography had anything to do with it; it started the day Hollywood made its first film.

Bedlam ensued when Hudson called lunch recess on the opening day. WAP's Dorchen Leidholdt rushed the witness table, grabbed the microphone, and began blurting out twelve 'non-negotiable' demands, as the panellists looked on open-mouthed:

> We demand that the Commission acknowledge that the eight billion dollar a year pornography industry is built on the sexual enslavement and exploitation of women and that the Commission acknowledge that pornography targets *all women* for rape, battery, sexual harassment, prostitution, incest and murder.

Non-negotiable? Who was holding whom to ransom? It certainly was not organized crime. The NYPD sent over a single sergeant, Jerry Piazza, who assured the Commission that the police had received only two complaints about Times Square in the last two years. To save the day, Hudson brought in two ex-FBI agents: William Kelly, who served under Hoover; and a former colleague, Homer Young; neither of them represented the Bureau's current concerns. Both insisted that the whole porn business could be closed down in eight months if State Attorneys wished – the Justice Department's line. The problem, as Kelly saw it, was that State Attorneys these days were too young; things would be different if Hoover were still alive. Homer, momentarily forgetting he was not addressing a Full Gospel Businessmen's Fellowship meeting, announced he had been Called since 1955 to defeat pornography, and that he thanked the Good Lord each day that he could continue the fight. Being a close friend of the 1970 dissenter Revd Hill, Homer than offered their conspiracy theory about the role of pornography in the downfall of Pearl Harbor, whereby the Imperial Japanese Navy had traded stag films depicting priests and nuns to American-born 'Japs' in return for the soundings in American harbours and the movements of the fleet!

OK, so this had nothing to do with organized crime, but the tape-recorded testimony of 'Jimmy the Weazel', Aladena Frattiano, from the Federal Witness Rehabilitation Programme would. Jimmy's tape swore that the pornography industry was full of unsavoury characters; and ... That was it.

Another taped witness revealed why. This anonymous interview with a Chicago Adult Bookstore owner admitted *paying protection money in order to stay in business*; and he saw no difference between the mobb and the Justice Department:

> I pay extortion to the Mob, and they piss my money away, sending their kids to Harvard Law School and making him a member of the Justice Department. ... The Federal Government extorts me every time I pay taxes and they piss the money away ... overseas.

Not only did the mob not control the industry, insisted American Civil Liberties Union attorney Jerry Meyer Guttman; if they were using it to launder their ill-gotten gains, why go after the porn industry when they were definitely laundering in the building trades, transportation, unions, casinos, and even the sale of avocados in New York City? The solution to all these problems, for Guttman, was simple: to enforce the law against criminal and protect legal activities from protection rackets; no disease was cured by killing the patients.

Never mind, the staff assured themselves, we still have Linda Marciano. Better known as Linda Lovelace. The now thirty-seven-year-old mother of two repeated her claim that she was forced to make *Deep Throat* under death threats; but she did not toe the staff line either: on the contrary, she believed the solution to the exploitation of girls like herself was early sex education. Over-protective parents made their daughters easy prey for the Chuck Trainers of this world. Hudson's gloom was temporarily lifted when Dietz took this opportunity to gain some insider knowledge of 'snuff movies'. Linda, unfortunately, could not help there either: 'the wife of a friend of my husband said she had seen one'.

But then came Andrea Dworkin. She knew all about 'snuff movies'. No; she had never seen one herself, but she had *heard* that you could buy them in Los Angeles for $3000, or pay $250 for a private screening.

She also 'knew' that such movies were also being used to encourage prostitutes, who were forced to watch them, and then submit to heavily sadomasochistic acts.

Where?

She did not know.

There was *no doubt* in her mind, though, that women were being murdered for men's entertainment, and that people who defended this form of 'freedom', like the Civil Liberties Union, were really a front for pimps.

Not only that. She had now discovered why the women were being murdered by men. It had all begun during Vietnam. The women were killed in films, so that every orifice in their head could be penetrated by men's penises. This was known as 'skull fucking'!

When the panellists finally recovered consciousness, and one brave soul asked for her evidence, Dworkin stared forward incredulously; could they doubt her word? This evil secret had been discovered by 'a woman' who had seen the films, but escaped.

At the business meeting after New York, the panellists were presented with Sears' recommendations for a Federal Task Force to destroy obscenity and to operate forfeiture procedures against stores which continued to sell 'the wrong magazines'. Hudson also wanted them to support North Carolina Senator Jesse Helms' Bill, which would restrict 'indecent' material on cable TV; but when Levine asked the staff members how many cable systems actually presented X-rated material, the staff had no idea. Levine was adamant: she wanted to hear facts and figures. The staff were adamant: she could not – probably because, at that point, only one cable system was offering X-rated movies as part of a regular cable package, and it was based in Bethlehem, Pennsylvania. It could only get worse.

Scotsdale and the Sears letter

Having failed to make any headway in the business sessions, the panellists demanded time to discuss the issues; and the staff finally relented, picking February 1986 in Scotsdale, Arizona, which just happened to be the national headquarters of Citizens for Decency Through Law, which had recently contributed several thousand dollars to Mrs Cusack's re-election as a town councillor. If this was not an embarrassment, two developments were.

The first problem began back in Los Angeles, when Donald Wildmon, the smartest anti-pornography campaigner on the planet, appeared. No quoting scripture; still less rants against filth and degradation. Don runs skilful campaigns. The year before he had organized consumer boycotts of several companies for selling *Penthouse* and *Playboy*. Chief among them was the 7-Eleven chain, which sold around 20 per cent of all *Playboys*. Others included National stores, K-Mart, and Circle K; CBS for distributing the Playboy Channel; Time Inc. for its cable outlet screening *Hollywood Hottubs*; and Ramada Inns for showing adult films to guests.

Playboy was already under pressure from Falwell's Moral Majority, which during 1985 led a demonstration outside the Southland Corporation, the parent company of 7-Eleven. The publishers were very wary, given Hudson's hints that the Meese Commission would legitimize the Moral Majority's campaign. Then Wildmon damned RCA, CBS, Ramada Inns, and Warner Communications as being no better than pornographers. Professor Schauer suggested sending letters to the companies named by Wildmon. Hudson thought it was a good idea, and Sears drafted the letters. It warned the companies that they had been identified as pornography distributors and that they would have thirty days to disprove the claims or be described as pornographers in the Commission's final report.

Sent out on 11 February, the Sears letters included Wildmon's testimony but not his name. Though most companies simply denied the charges, Southland panicked. On 10 April it stopped selling *Penthouse*, *Playboy* and *Forum* at its 4500 outlets on the grounds the Commission was claiming a link between soft core and sex crime. *Penthouse* and *Playboy* sued the Commission for a restraint of trade, because while courts had decided they were not obscene and were protected by the First Amendment, here was a Government department blackmailing retail outlets. Analogies with McCarthyism were rife; and contrary to Dr Itzin's conspiracy theory about the American Booksellers Association getting soft core off the hook, hundreds of newspaper editorials from coast to coast lambasted the Commission for its Star Chamber-like procedure.

In July, the Federal Court ordered the Commission to retract the Sears letter. Having had little to do with the letters, the Commissioners were shell-shocked, and Hudson was forced to make a public statement that no link between *Penthouse*, *Playboy* and sex crimes existed. Dr Dobson went on radio to clear the titles, and Dr Dietz gave them a clean bill of health too.

While this pandemonium raged around them, panel members tried to make some sense of the 'evidence' placed before them, and faced their second problem: before condemning material and recommending new laws, there was the thorny problem of what pornography was. They had already lost three business sessions trying to define it. Hudson wanted MacKinnon Ordinance definitions; but every Commissioner had one of their own. Levine wanted to know how a feminist definition could make no reference to sexual pleasure. Dietz preferred: 'any presentation of felonious or violent behaviour which is sexually arousing'. But what about arousal, the religious asked. Dietz thought a medical laboratory might help!

As discussions became more ridiculous, the debate went round and round; and ten days were down to four. They were not helped by the non-appearance of Dr Edna Einsiedel's review of the social scientific data. She had got a job at the University of Calgary shortly after joining the Commission, and simply did not have the time to cover all the data. So Meese stumped up another $50,000, to be matched by the Surgeon General's Office, to secure an overview; but that would take more time. Levine pointed out that to produce that review after their Report was published was lunacy. So Dr Einsiedel had to carry on.

Meanwhile, Dietz had been playing around with definitions and had produced the four inclusive classes of pornography that we saw in Chapter 5. Apart from Dr Dobson, who disliked the scientific-sounding neutrality of it all, and would have preferred a clearer statement about 'perversions', everyone seemed reasonably happy. Now to business.

With the deadline fast approaching, and with little time for deliberations, the only chance to establish anything was to link

Einsiedel's review of effects to Dietz's categories, and vote on harm! This might just have made sense if Einsiedel was objective; but given that her doctoral supervisor was none other than Professor Dolf Zillmann it was difficult.

As the Commission went through the four classes, they simply voted on whether or not they thought each class would promote harm. The first two gained adverse votes on the grounds they would promote violence against women, promote rape myths, and degrade women. How Fem-Dom magazines or gay sadomasochistic material could do this was never explained.

Class 3 material, American 'soft core', gained a not-harmful verdict. The panellists even decided that it did not degrade females *per se*. Class 4 material, which encompasses British soft-core magazines and video material, was unanimously cleared of any harmful consequences. Given the make-up of the Commission, these two votes are extremely significant.

Although they had lost their aim to 'get' soft core, staff members fared better when it came to the voting over the law enforcement initiatives, especially Justice Department pet projects. To justify these recommendations and in an attempt to split liberal opposition, Dr Dobson and the staff members decided to utilize the sexual politics of Andrea Dworkin rather than their own fundamentalist rationales. Dworkin was overjoyed when Sears told her the final report would endorse her views.

The report's concept of harm

Finally securing some kind of agreement was one thing; letting people know what had happened was another. Much of the above account would not have been possible without the Civil Liberties Union lawsuit forcing the Commission to release its documentation (a legal duty), and the ability of a couple of journalists to produce a concise summary. Controversy did not stop there.

The reason why it proved difficult to get hold of a copy is not, as Dr Itzin asserts, that there was a conspiracy to bury it by the book trade, because all one had to do was order it; copies were initially scarce because the panellists objected to the first version, with its religious biases, and it had to be rewritten in an attempt to maintain any public credibility. Be that as it may, the Meese Report, far from exonerating Dworkin's position, merely negates the findings of the Johnson Report by substituting a religious value system for the liberal one; and here is how the staff members did it.

The emphasis upon harm and the recommendations are there primarily because the Commission's terms of reference were to halt the spread of pornography, and review any research relating to a link with sex crime. Together with the individual Commissioners' preconceptions the Report could do nothing else.

Yet proof of harm rested upon pulling several fast ones. From the beginning, the Report declares that pornography is

> immoral, and to the extent that it encourages immoral behaviour, ... exerts a corrupting influence on the family and on the moral fabric of society ... [and] ... is both causal and symptomatic of immorality and corruption ... an offence against human dignity.

In other words, pornography causes harm because they define harm in terms of religious, not physical, definitions: the depiction and promotion of sex acts that panellists did not like or thought abnormal. Consequently, when the Report refers to anti-social behaviour it is not referring to sex crimes in law, but practices like masturbation, homosexuality, premarital sex, and oral sex! While Dr Itzin may swallow that definition, no real feminist would. The Minority Report penned by Dr Becker and Ms Levine vigorously objected to this con trick, denounced the use of religious inferences and beliefs, lamented the absence of satisfied customers asked to testify at the public hearings, and reasoned that samples used to discuss trends in imagery were not representative of the market.

That this religious justification appeared in the Report despite the fact that panellists cleared both Class 3 and Class 4 material of secular harm is a scandal; but they were desperately needed because beyond the voting there was no agreement; and as the published personal notes of the panellists reveal, the Report tended to reflect the views of the Justice Department rather than their own.

The core problems

Part 1 of the Report is devoted to establishing reasons to outlaw soft core despite the votes and Hudson's admission that they found *no evidence* linking explicit soft core to direct physical harm or even that it promoted adverse attitudes.

The Report offers three reasons. First, the pictures and actions depicted in Class 3 imply that women can be as hedonistic and promiscuous as men, and that this tends 'to distort the moral sensitivity of women and undermine values underlying the family unit'. Second, soft core does not refer to love, marriage, and pro-creation, but merely seeks to arouse sexual desire. Third, Baron and Straus's correlation study. In other words, despite admitting that it is not harmful, the Report wants us to believe that soft core is harmful on the basis of: an erroneous sexist belief that women do not like instrumental sex; defining non-marital sexual arousal as socially harmful; and quoting a finding that the study's own author does not agree with.

No wonder Dietz admitted that the moral 'evidence' utilized was more important than the social scientific evidence; and Ritter argued that *all* sexual imagery divorces sex from love and the sex act's 'necessary and essential ordering towards procreation' (not that these convictions prevented him from being convicted).

Far from resting upon social scientific or even the dubious anecdotal evidence, the Report's claims regarding harm rest solely upon religious definitions, which even Hudson admitted would not gain a public consensus. Such reliance upon religious 'insights' is tantamount to admitting defeat, that they could not prove soft core to be harmful.

Part 2 then offers arguments justifying greater controls on all pornography based upon very contentious assertions about what people learn from pornography, and the Commissioners' in-terpretation of the social scientific research.

Given their remit and belief about increased availability of violent material, the causal relationship between pornography and sex crime was presupposed from the outset; but once again, the Report admits that its recommendations are justified by opinions and beliefs beyond the evidence reviewed. Unlike the 'insights' in Part 1, however, those in Part 2 are dishonest as well as stupid.

Incredibly, the attempt to justify outlawing soft core by removing First Amendment protection actually negates the Commission's major finding – that pornography promotes harmful ideas! The Report argues that the First Amendment defence – that the law should not inhibit a free exchange of ideas – should not apply to pornography because it is not

> even remotely related to an exchange of views in a market place of ideas ... an attempt to articulate a point of view ... an attempt to persuade, or ... an attempt seriously to convey through literary or artistic means a different vision of humanity or of the word ... [and] ... What emerges is that much of what this material involves is not so much portrayal of sex or discussion of sex but simply sex itself.

But if pornography is not an exchange of ideas, how on earth can it possibly promote any messages, let alone adverse ones like 'rape myths', which are later used to claim Class 1 and Class 2 material are socially harmful?

While the crusaders may not like the fact, either pornography conveys ideas or it does not; and if it does, it is protected speech unless it causes direct harm. US law, of course, does not apply to Britain; but the Report's discussion of 'harm' can.

While it may be a good idea, as the Report suggests, to extend the concept of harm beyond direct physical harm, its suggestion that this should include *any potential* environmental, physical, cultural, moral, or aesthetic harm, could never work, given the lack of consensus in a pluralistic society. Apart from a Pharisee, only failed feminists could concur with the Report's assertion that the most significant 'harm' is the 'immorality' of pre-marital sex.

Given the simultaneous lament that 'we live in a society unquestionably pervaded by sexual explicitness', the offered rationale for singling out pornography for special attention, that it has a unique effect of undermining 'human decency', rings hollow; especially when Meese did not substantiate that it had become more explicit or contained 'degrading' material. The attempt to avoid that awkward fact by drawing a distinction between primary and secondary harms, and then recommending that if a primary physical harm does not occur, secondary harms like – wait for it – the fact 'some people think it will lead to promiscuity and these people find that idea offensive' should be activated is merely an appeal to prioritize the Christian view.

The Report could have saved itself dozens of pages if it had simply said: one, we believe, being Christians, that the law should reflect our religious belief that pornography undermines God's design, rather than reflect John Stuart Mill's definition of harm, and his justification for law; two, unlike the humanist Supreme Court, we, being Christians, think people who sell pornography should be locked up, along with anyone who looks at it.

The next section's emphasis upon organized crime in an attempt to illustrate harmful social effects fell down because it merely provided proof that the industry was really a victim of protection rackets. Readers were then invited to ignore that by considering the possibility that they were 'confused' by what 'organized crime' really means. 'Organization' need not be the Mafia or a similar group, merely a 'large and organized enterprise'; and 'criminal activity' need merely mean the existence of prostitution in the vicinity, even if not related to the business in question. Yes; they wanted the public to accept a definition which would make any corporate body whose employees parked on double yellow lines an 'organized crime' syndicate.

When it came to the social scientific evidence, the Report shamelessly admits that correlational evidence *cannot* establish a causal connection, and that one cannot extrapolate from a controlled laboratory to effects in the outside world; and then attempts to justify controls by referring to *theories* about effects, and more 'common sense'.

Controls upon Class 1 material, for example, are premised upon the erroneous claim that it was the most prevalent form. Yet this proof was achieved only by bumping up their own feeble 0.6 per cent sample figure by bundling in a Canadian sample, and then by adding the depictions of oral, anal, and group sex, from other classes, and redefining them as 'rape' on the basis that no woman would do this unless coerced – a move not 'plainly justified by our own commonsense'. They then skim like a Californian surfer over vital distinctions between sexually explicit films, slasher movies, and soft core noted in the studies, and completely ignore prior attitude. The Report simply degenerates from there.

Class 2 material is condemned because, having dumped all that 'rape' imagery back here, Class 2 is supposedly the most popular form of pornography! Readers are then treated to several moral arguments why sexual acts from blow jobs to multiple partners *should* be seen as degrading, subordinating, and 'embarrassing' to women. Very little is said about the alleged effects because, apart from Zillmann, they could not find any to stand up.

Knowing that readers were unlikely to be convinced, they then offer every possible adverse event that may in any obscure way be related to pornography consumption, from prostitution to the silly idea that if a child saw one of these pictures they would discover that 'sex can be divorced from any degree of affection, love, commitment or marriage', in the hope readers would accept one. None of these, of course, had anything to do with the social scientific 'evidence', and illustrated this whole section's weakness: preconceptions searching for proof. At one point, they even argue that pictures of blow jobs increase the 'likelihood' of aggression against women, because women should not 'disproportionately' satisfy the sexual needs of men.

Having failed to produce any evidence, justifying controls rests upon more appeals to readers' emotional sensibility; but in doing so Meese raises another contradiction. By dismissing deregulation on the grounds that 'the problems of sexual violence, sexual aggression short of actual violence, and sex discrimination, are serious societal problems' and then suggesting that 'dealing with the messages all around us seems an important way of dealing with the behavior' the Report had a problem explaining away why far more arousing and sexist material found in non-explicit films and magazines, prime-time TV shows, rock music lyrics, and blue jean adverts was going to be exempt. The excuses to single out soft core amounted to an assertion that pornography's images are 'a significant cause even when compared with all of the other likely causes', because it was immoral; and the fact that it would be unconstitutional to attack these other images!

Meese then promptly lamented that present laws were not

enforced because people did not perceive pornography as a serious threat, and so set out to try to justify changing the public mind, proposing a new piece of legislation to match. Prosecution of cable TV and of telephone messages were justified, for example, by the potential secondary 'harm' that minors would gain access. Yet in doing so the Report frequently undermined its core rationales; in this case, the recommendation for action does not rest upon the content *per se*, but the possible viewer's personal characteristics – minors. In other words, the adverse effects are situational – a point denied elsewhere in the Report.

There then followed the ninety-two recommendations for Federal and state legislatures and law enforcement agencies, which collectively reflected the Report's desire to use law enforcement to reverse America's '*laisser-faire* attitude' towards pornography.

Most amounted to a challenge to previous Supreme Court rulings in the hope that under Reagan it would prove more conservative. The Report even advocated the use of police action to provoke community intolerance. Individually, many recommendations set potentially dangerous precedents. Some were designed to reverse court judgments they did not like. Others sought to *create* the social harms they asserted already existed, but failed to demonstrate. Recommendations 3 and 4, for example, asked Congress to make it an unfair business and labour practice to hire models for sex performances, and by redefining pornographic modelling as prostitution, they would make it illegal, and turn their assertion that pornography had special social harms into a reality.

Other recommendations prioritized specific group interests over legal principles. Recommendation 11, which demanded that the Attorney-General direct local attorneys to examine 'the obscenity problem in their respective districts, identify offenders, initiate investigations, and begin prosecuting them without delay', was clearly aimed at New York and Los Angeles – and thereby constituted a direct attack upon the community standards principle when it did not work in the crusaders' favour. The closer one looks the more contradictions in the Report's justifications appear. In promoting recommendation 29, which sought more law enforcement agency personnel to be assigned to obscenity cases, the Report reveals that the figures for 'sex crimes' in 'pornstore' areas, used elsewhere to justify the idea that selling pornography leads to assaults on women, are really acts of 'indecent exposure' involving two or more gay men picking each other up!

The large number of the recommendations concerning child pornography, which were superfluous given numerous existing laws, were merely included to gain public sympathy, and to imply what the Report could not prove: that there has been a 'radical shift' in content since the last Commission in 1971.

Harm, harm and more harm

The reader's reward for struggling through the welter of poorly performed legal conjuring tricks of the last two sections, Part 4 presented wave after wave of anecdotal examples of pornography's 'harm' and the 'individuals'. By presenting an extremely depressing picture concerning callous coercion, and how pornography can be used in this way, it would strengthen the emotional appeal of the Commission's 'findings', and even back up separatist demands that readers' anecdotal evidence should not be dismissed, *except for three very good reasons*.

First, the majority of examples were so bizarre that even Meese cast doubt upon their truthfulness, kindly suggesting that some individuals appear to have suffered so much trauma in their lives that it was difficult to determine where, if at all, pornography was responsible. Second, 'witnesses' like Andrea Dworkin were not giving 'evidence', but offering ideology. Given her belief that all penetrative sex *is* rape, she has a theoretical reason for insisting that real rapes are filmed and sold, but also a practical one for never quoting a title; readers could check it out for themselves and find it wanting. Ditto her claims about 'force' and 'weapons', metaphors for oral sex and dildos. Like her sick 'skull fucking' fantasy story, this is not evidence, it is ideological trash, and fit only for the can.

The third, and most important, reason for not accepting most of the 'teeeeeestaments' relates to the Report's own disclaimer about credibility. They had to slip it in because they knew that one day they would be rumbled; and that day has come. A close inspection of the examples offered reveals that the Commission pulled two fast ones. They only utilized extracts from a very small pool of cases. Most did not come from their public hearings but were culled from the Ordinance hearings, WAP propaganda, 'Oklahomans Against Pornography', and WAVAW members! In their turn, the details were purloined from books like Lederer's *Take Back the Night* and the theoretical examples retold as a personal experience; or are of the 'adult survivor' type. It never happened. By presenting this twaddle, Meese is admitting that the junk heard at the public hearings was so bad even the staff members dare not attempt to put it before the American public.

By giving credence to these ideological examples rather than seriously considering real examples of potential causation, Meese not only lost an opportunity to test seriously the proposition that pornography leads to sex crimes, but *insults real victims, and undermines the important value of anecdotal evidence*. Social scientists take anecdotal evidence so seriously that they want real evidence, not crusaders' ideological exploitation of horror stories, or the separatists' desire to reinforce 'the authenticity of female voices' combating the 'silence' men have imposed upon them; they can get this elsewhere. As this pool of insults to evidence is then categorized to justify Meese's multifaceted list of pornography's 'harms', it is hardly surprising that the account given frequently fails to match the appropriate 'harm' referred to. Most of the authentic cases are taken from child-sex ring prosecutions where the 'pornography' concerned was made by the molester at the time of the crime, and was not commercial soft-core material, such as case 24.

The examples deemed to illustrate physical harm and rape are perfect examples of Meese's problem. Case 1 is an example of molestation, not 'rape'; case 3, supposedly concerning a child sex offender, is third-hand hearsay from Oklahomans Against Pornography. Three other examples are not rape at all, but allegations about *suggestions* made by a male partner of a separatist feminist (!) that they try a new sexual variation. Their sole purpose is a feeble attempt to extend the definition of 'rape'. Ironically, case 15 would clearly demonstrate that general violence and the role of drugs and alcohol in coercion are far more important than porn.

The section on 'forced sexual performances' again amounts to an attempt to label sexual *suggestions* as coercive acts. They range from the serious case 25, where a husband allegedly suggested bestiality, to the 'hearsay' of case 43's offer to participate in a very common slavery fantasy scenario, *with not even a hint that pornography was involved.*

Other examples relate to participation in sexual activities which did *not* involve force at all: case 26, for example, concerns prostitutes being hired to service a stag party where pornographic films were shown; the dubious case 51 makes a fuss of a prostitute's customer's request to pubic shave, and customers wishing to *submit* to spankings. Apart from obviously not constituting force against women, this theoretical 'case history' would actually prove that nothing adverse happens when such requests are declined; and even if such requests followed pornography consumption, that consumers prefer commercial services to coercing somebody. Case 36 has an anonymous (separatist or adult survivor) witness asserting that women are tortured and permanently disabled to satisfy the producers of sadomasochistic magazines. Not one title is named. The details are so incredible that even the Report notes that readers will be disbelieving. Others, like case 19, involve WAP ideologically exploiting an alleged child abuse case, apparently involving pornography, but it backfires. If it is authentic, it undermines the separatists' beliefs about soft core's content as the alleged offence took place in the 1950s!

The only 'evidence' offered under the 'murder' section is the ancient WAVAW delusion that there is a similarity between a photo-set in the December 1984 *Penthouse* and the murder of a Chinese woman some time after; and an assertion that a multiple child sex murderer once believed pornography made him lose his sense of decency and respect. The 'imprisonment' section draws heavily on case 54, Linda Lovelace's allegations regarding Mr Trainer. And proof that porn leads to STDs depends upon case 57, concerning an ex-Bunny, who 'heard' from another Bunny, about another Bunny, who supposedly had her reproductive organs removed owing to untreated VD – a classic occupational urban legend.

The further one goes down the list, the more feeble the examples become, such as citing pornography's availability in massage parlours as 'proof' that pornography leads to prostitution (case 64); they merely show how desperate the Commission's staff members were becoming.

Trying to assess psychological 'harms' is a dubious practice at the best of times, given that adults' reactions to events depend to a considerable extent upon their belief systems. Simply listing witnesses' claims regarding apparent pornography-induced damage to psychological functioning and 'sense of self', hospitalization, break-up of family relationships or 'status', and so on, tells us nothing.

Many of the examples of 'suicidal thoughts and behaviour' contain no indication of the subjects' general mental health when they saw the material, if they ever did. Cases like 65, 66, and 68, where the 'harm' of seeing pornography is in reminding childhood molestation victims of the offence, makes no more sense than out-lawing car advertisements in case a road crash victim sees one. A far more fruitful line of inquiry in these cases would be to uncover why it is that claims concerning re-trauma are far more prevalent in 'adult survivor'-type unsubstantiated 'sex abuse' cases than in sub-stantiated sex assault cases, where the cause and nature of the debilitating reaction can be quantified. Many of Meese's cases are early examples of the False Memory Syndrome, where the alleged effects such as amnesia, denial, and repression of the 'abuse' appear only after the 'victim' has been locked in a room with a fundamentalist Christian or separatist therapist and where the 'compulsive re-enactment of sexual abuse' is a morally based *theory* about effects.

In any event, even if such cases as case 95 are true, they happened so long ago that the 'abuse' could have nothing to do with the alleged recent increase in pornographic material; such cases thereby defeat the purpose of their inclusion. But given the moral motivation in cases like 94, where masturbation is equated with sexual abuse, it is easy to see how they overlooked the contra-diction. It gets so bad that a case like 99, where a woman claims she believed she cannot enjoy sex because of its association with dirty 'pornography', end up proving how debilitating the moral values promoted by the crusaders are rather than providing evidence against soft core.

If this was not bad enough, readers are then offered a number of examples of 'fear' and 'anxiety' apparently provoked by simply seeing pornography in bookstores. Apart from the fact that these separatist feminist and crusader witnesses would only have themselves to blame for that, by scaring themselves by repeating snuff movie legends and other horror stories at their meetings, what on earth are they doing in porn stores? Cases like 73, which involves the assumption that an alleged violent boyfriend *must* have once read pornography, are simply unsound. The same applies to all those cases quoted to show how pornography promotes 'feelings of inferiority and degradation', which also feature Dworkinites. Case 105, for example, thinks men see her as a slut because she is coloured – not that she can offer one single example. Case 107 does not like coffee-table books featuring classic nude art! As for cases 76, 77, 78, and 79, which simply voice disgust at pornography, who cares? Some people find separatist hate-crime literature offensive and disgusting too, but that is no ground for outlawing it.

The cases supposedly demonstrating general social harms play off feminists' complaints like sexual harassment, and imply that this occurs because of changes in pornography. In reality, sexual harassment has not increased; it has merely come to the attention of middle-class women because more of them now have to go out to work than fifty years ago. Stopping harassment will be better served through rigorous pursuit of cases through the courts than through removing *Playboy* from 7-Elevens. Even more bizarre is the suggestion that the stigma porn models suffer in society is somehow the fault of the industry rather than the double standard and moral condemnation of the industry. Like most of the other examples these general harms are nothing of the kind.

Collectively, this ideological evidence is a very good example of why social scientists do not automatically accept separatist 'authentic experiences'. While it is likely that several cases were authentic, the Report's presentation makes it very difficult for a social scientist to distinguish them from the fabricated. It is, therefore, a disservice to those who are seriously looking for the ways in which consuming pornography may contribute to such problems, and to real victims.

Detailing the evidence

The remainder of the Report lists the titles of material available without category, provides extracts from some, lists witnesses and those submitting written statements, and provides some photographs, a bibliography, and a staff listing. What is most bemusing, however, is that a welter of contradictory data suddenly begins to appear in both text and footnotes, after page 900 of volume 1. A section covering public attitudes to pornography suddenly reveals that consumption of pornographic material had *not* increased dramatically. Likewise the Commission suddenly admit that: sex offences are committed by a small number of people who commit an extremely large number of offences, and they do so regardless of consumption pattern; 'callousness', predisposition, and psychoticism are vital issues in the scientific studies; asserted links rest upon highly debatable behavioural theories; violent sexual material has never constituted more than 10 per cent of the hard-core industry, even when so-called 'degrading' practices are included; sales of soft core are falling; and the Report's references to cable violence were based on 'R'-rated rather than sex movies. Buried deep in the Report, hundreds of similar revelations keep appearing, and demonstrate that, far from being ignorant, the Commission had clearly chosen to ignore evidence that they had all along because it would have completely undermined their arguments. No wonder the reaction to the Report was hostile.

No evidence whatsoever was offered to demonstrate that soft core had become more violent or demeaning.

Reaction

As the Report simply amounted to a series of religious and politically correct justifications for the Moral Majority position on sex and their demand for new law enforcement initiatives, the media thought Meese an expensive joke. This falsified reversal of the 'not guilty' verdict of the 1970 Commission, and use of feminist justifications for outlawing pornography, when the feminist consensus had collapsed, was obvious to every media hack in the world; except those trying to import its counterfeit conclusions into Britain, encouraged by Dr Itzin, who continues to blow the Meese trumpet today.

When *Time* magazine asked Donnerstein and Straus to comment, they could not believe the way their work had been quoted. The *New York Times* faulted the questionable evidence and condemned the Report for recklessly encouraging censorship. The *Washington Post* praised the dissenting views of Dr Becker and

Ms Levine for their intellectual integrity and their refusal to be 'buffaloed' into unsupportable conclusions. The *Chicago Tribune* wanted to know why, if pornography was to be censored for inspiring violence, the Justice Department was not consistent; what about the deep religious convictions that had recently led to over 200 bombings of abortion clinics? Why was it that when a self-proclaimed religious person committed crimes, the religion was never answerable?

Reagan's attempt at damage limitation, by conferring his blessing, sounded somewhat hollow given his family history, so Alan Sears toured the country seeking endorsement; but the plan came unstuck in Maine, where the Christian Civic League was peddling the Report's conclusions in a state referendum to make it a crime to sell soft core. Maine voters spoke for the whole country by rejecting this proposal by a 3 to 1 margin.

The Christian crusaders produced their own 'report', *Pornography: A Human Tragedy*, which, by relying on Scott, meant the fundamentalist wheel had turned full circle, and their exaggerated claims placed back in their proper setting. a Christian critique of pornography. It argued that without soft core, society would not suffer the spectacle of women engaging in acts like oral sex which 'assault female modesty and represent an affront to an entire gender'. It ended with an appeal:

> Until we *know* that pornography is not addictive and, until we are *certain* that the passions of fantasy does not destroy the passions of reality, until we are *sure* that obsessive use of obscene materials will not lead to perversions and conflict between husbands and wives, then we dare not adorn them with the crown of respectability.

As that would be like *Forum* magazine demanding the separatists prove that they are not making snuff movies to discredit soft core, the Christians have still failed to see that the major reason why soft core is respectable is that those who oppose it no longer command respect. There is accumulating evidence that their horror stories are becoming more perverse and violent, and that there is a proven link between their beliefs, as opposed to faith, and the potential to look ludicrous. They do themselves, and the faith they supposedly advance, no favours by claiming that Meese proves anything else.

The Surgeon General's Commission

Following closely behind the Meese Commission came the Surgeon General's Report on the social scientific evidence, which emerged from a seminar held by various social scientists to reach their own consensus concerning effects. For the first time, they publicly admitted the limitations of research and warned against 'the inevitable tendency' of individuals to quote results which support their personal beliefs. Likewise, research needed more adult subjects and needed to take more account of 'no effect' findings, when considering cause. This, they hastily assured the public, did not mean that the social scientific data were useless, merely that *no one study or set of findings using only one method should be taken as a definitive result.*

Their own definitive statements about what was known did not amount to much either; effectively, that short-term and 'rape myth' adverse effects were recorded by coercive individuals who appeared (*sic*) to possess prior tendencies for inter-personal violence towards women. They then tried to palm this off on to 'delinquent peer groups', which was absurd given that the vast majority of studies involved students. On the other hand, even with Zillmann present, they agreed that because coercive-orientated individuals saw sexual intercourse as an aggressive act whatever the movie, this could explain why adverse effects had sometimes been found in soft core exposure subjects in the past; thereby giving soft core a clean bill of health.

In order even to make sense of the research to date and to expand upon it, the group advised: clearing up definitional problems; gaining more data about content, sales and readership, and also how consumers categorized it; gaining more data about production, distribution, consumption and patterns of usage, as opposed to widespread myths; making a serious study of arousal patterns, and the way sex education could affect development; and making documented studies of changes in viewing patterns and in the subjects' sexual behaviour, which could start with an assessment of soft core's contribution in solving some people's sexual dysfunction or phobic reactions to sexual activities. Without these crucial data, it was believed that future theoretical and applied research would be meaningless.

In other words, they had made a clear statement that there was no accumulated evidence about adverse effects from reading or viewing soft core, and that studies like the Reading Group's content analysis would be very useful. This would obviously have upset the British crusaders, if they had bothered to notice; but they now had Meese and were determined to make the most of it.

Flesh and blood

In less than a year after the Meese Report, CAP were promoting the 'new evidence' of Meese, and have never stopped. This was then hyped as proof that Diana Russell's 'Pornography and rape: a causal model', an old missive constantly reprinted in feminist collections, was vindicated; and once the theory appeared in the academic *Political Psychology* during 1988, CAP thought they had all the proof they needed. All they had to do was convince the public.

As the public would never wade through Meese, the publicity campaign took the form of waving a copy around in the air while making emotive comments about content and inflated pronouncements about the number of women assaulted because of the unrestricted availability of soft core with its 'alarming level of violence and sadomasochistic imagery', not to mention child pornography. These were reinforced by publishing a copy of the Minneapolis Ordinance Hearings.

As the Reading Report has provided a study-by-study refutation of the Baxter and Russell model, which proposes only a simplistic 'model' of the *possible* link between pornography and rape, backed up by a huge 'pick 'n' mix' of experiments and decontextualized quotations, representing methodological tools like LR scores as fact, and ignoring every caveat and warning in the Surgeon General's seminar, I need only mention it in passing.

Dr Russell's cavalier attitude to evidence, and how she seeks to pass ideology off as fact, can be seen in the introduction, where readers are told that the only reason Americans don't accept the proven link between porn and sex crime is a conspiracy by the American Booksellers Association, the Association of American Publishers, the Council of Periodical Distributors, the International Periodical Distributors Association and the National Coalition of College Stores. Proof of this? Catherine MacKinnon told her! The model also looks remarkably like one produced by Finkelhor covering paedophile seduction.

The results can be amusing, and provide an insight into typical separatist ideological manipulation of research data. At one point Russell refers to a Bryant study which, she contends, proves that college students' porn reading habits are dangerous. Bryant had other ideas:

> The generalizability of these results is somewhat question-able as is their comparability with the findings from other surveys....
>
> In fact, when the survey instrument was administered to intact college classes with 100% participation, many of the normative use data were reduced by one half.

In order to avoid the obvious problem with having only American 'evidence', the claims were domesticated by a Dr Baxter, whose tacky third-rate review 'Flesh and blood' was published by *New Scientist*. It covered the same old tired quotations about male callousness and content, from Zillmann's massive exposure study to Dr Court's correlations. The only new assertion was that magazine covers were dominated by group sex, bondage and transvestism. The conclusion and appeal that 'there comes a time when the demand for conclusive proof gives way to evidence beyond reasonable doubt' was inevitable, and made it more than an example of what sociologists Stan Cohen and Jock Young have called 'the manufacture of news', presenting unsubstantiated and ideological beliefs as fact. The article's timing was significant; coming so close to the expected release date of the Cumberbatch and Howitt Report, Baxter's review was obviously a 'spoiler', and, by gaining widespread media publicity which puffed it up as 'new' research, and which saw Baxter being touted in TV documentaries as an 'expert', it would have worked if the Home Office Report had been released earlier than it was. Baxter could then have been offered as an informed alternative, whereas his reliance on the same old rubbish suggests he knows nothing. Hence the failure to compare Zillmann's 'findings' to Linz's study, or even Zillmann's own concern about the withdrawal rate. Baxter could not even distinguish between soft-core terminology either side of the Atlantic. Being pure hype, the only issue it raised was why *New Scientist* with its 'scientific' pretensions refused to consider a refutation.

Could it have anything to do with the two prominent blocked panels designed to draw the light reader's attention to them? The first, despite admitting that women often find pornography arousing, suggested that they did not buy it in quantity, and that a survey revealed that 30 per cent found the nudes in *Playgirl* made them feel guilty, dirty, cheap or bad; it implied that the other 70 per cent did not know their own mind, and should have it made up for them. The second insert, surprise, surprise, drew attention to the MacKinnon 'new' definition of pornography, then actually over six years old, and by raising fears that massive exposure leads to less censorious attitudes among people to the extent that they put pornography in the hands of children, offered MacKinnon as salvation.

Hyping Baxter as 'new research', when its contents did not even reach the status of a review, is typical of the tactics used by the crusaders. That it found its way into so many media outlets demonstrates that far from being objective, the reporters and editors are sensation mongers or share the ideological commitment of the crusaders. Part of the problem, of course, lies in the fact that separatists do not separate evidence from ideology. Russell's latest missive, *Making Violence Sexy*, and Dr Itzin's *Pornography: Women, Violence, and Civil Liberties* are typical examples. Despite almost one thousand pages between them, you will have to look long and hard to find a real piece of original research, let alone a worthwhile one.

The same applies to the March 1988 *Cosmo* 'survey', promoted by Dr Itzin as conclusive proof that the women of Britain supported 'her' campaign and wished the government to legislate. In large numbers, the respondents did agree with her definition of, and description of the effects of, pornography, which is not surprising as the survey questions broke every 'scientific' rule about the method of sampling and answer options. The presentation of the 'results' in *Cosmo* was also confusing, making it frequently impossible to determine whether some of the percentages quoted relate to the total sample, or sub-samples. When covering the role of pornography, for example, it is not made clear whether or not the 'third' who claimed to have been raped *or* sexually 'assaulted' when porn was present was or was not a third of the sub-sample of those claiming to have been raped or sexually assaulted. Typical of the erroneous claims built upon such obfuscations was the declaration that a 'correlation' had been found between childhood 'exposure to pornography' and sexual experience below 16 years of age. Instead of presenting the necessary table of figures, the survey merely contended that it was 'more than a quarter', which, of course, is *not* a correlation! No wonder this was published in *Cosmo* rather than subjected to the rigour of an academic journal or conference presentation. The fact that the authors claimed that while 95 per cent believe some forms of pornography should be curbed, and 60 per cent wanted all forms including soft core to be outlawed, but that they 'had no difficulty in distinguishing between erotica and pornography', when no examples were given, cannot but make one highly suspicious.

Pornography politics

That CAP's hype worked despite the impossible extrapolations based upon the separatists' selectivity and the failure of Meese to prove any link suggests that apart from the poor quality of British graduates, some other factor had to be at work.

The most important was that despite being hopelessly behind current developments in feminist thought and dependent upon the non-feminist press, women from the Labour Party and the Liberal Democrats rushed to support the campaign against soft core because they thought it offered votes, rather than a solution to sex crime. This search for a token 'woman's issue' can be seen as far back as April 1984, when *New Democrat* tried to make pornography a politically correct issue by making 'pornography as immoral as anti-Semitism or sweated labour'.

Likewise, journalists passed off CAP or CPC, depending upon which hat Dr Itzin was wearing at the time, as independent groups reviewing scientific evidence rather than the typical media-based pressure groups they were, in order to secure members. Did no one else ever notice that these groups had apparently just been 'launched' every time a new article appeared, so that the hacks could convince their deputy editor it was a 'news' story, and could encourage readers to join at the same time; or that most features, like those in the *Observer* and the *Independent* in April 1989 invariably appeared immediately before a significant event such as the Liberty conferences?

Incredibly, evidence of the real intent behind the five-year publicity drive appeared in the *Independent* back in 1987. Having covered the Dworkin–MacKinnon Ordinances without any hint of the controversy amongst feminists back in the States, the report quoted Ms Dworkin who, having admitted that 'We have defined pornography as something which is a direct cause of violence against women', laid out the strategy:

> Before we could state this categorically we had to have hard clinical evidence of the harm it does. We now have this and can prove its direct effect upon people's behaviour. We now know that sex and violence can't be pulled apart.

In other words, the 'hard clinical evidence' of Meese was being deliberately selected to serve Dworkin's 'redefinition', and MacKinnon's attempt to undermine the concept of 'harm' upon which Anglo-American laws are based. At the same time Ms Short revealed that CAP was a deliberate attempt to make opposition to soft core politically correct:

> In the past anti-porn campaigners have been seen as repressive ... we are quite different. Because we can now prove that porn uses and degrades women, all kinds of people with liberal instincts will want to join us.

The allusions to 'hard clinical evidence' are, however,

merely the icing on the cake. The crusade, especially once the real feminists deserted it, increasingly relied upon mixing a pound of fear with six ounces of indignation for the non-feminist readers of mainstream women's magazines, which readily asserted that:

> Today's easily-available pornography ... isn't simply naked breasts and come-hither poses; it's women being penetrated by all kinds of objects, by animals, knives, guns, women being tortured, so-called lesbian scenes. Almost invariably, the women are smiling, supposedly enjoying it.

As more and more women realize that such claims grossly misrepresent modern soft core, the crusaders are getting more and more desperate to pretend otherwise.

Summary

Far from demonstrating a link between soft core and sex crime, the Meese Report even cleared what most British people would define as hard core. The Report did, however, offer a series of weak religious rationales as to why we should still believe it is harmful, and backed this up with ideologically motivated testimony borrowed from the separatists, because their own was not good enough.

Apart from the crusading Christians and separatists no one else, especially social scientists, thought Meese did anything other than make those associated with it look very foolish. The fact that it has since been hyped as proof in Britain just goes to show that while all the people can be fooled for some of the time, some people can fool themselves all of the time.

Chapter seven

Carry On Crusading

HAVING implied that soft core was a serious social harm, when it was not, the Justice Department were determined to use their new powers regardless by persecuting soft-core distributors. In Britain, the separatists abandoned the women's movement and joined the alliance between politically correct parliamentarians and the Christian crusaders. The battle over soft core was on.

Cleaning up America

Among Meese's 92 recommendations proposing changes in Federal and state laws and enforcement, number 12 was the most important. The Report's nonsense about organized crime had merely been an excuse to propose a Justice Department Obscenity Task Force, with the right to apply the Racketeering Influenced and Corrupt Organizations legislation, originally designed for seizing drug cartel assets, to anyone selling pornography.

Having set up the 'evidence' to secure this recommendation in the first place, the Justice Department were more than happy to oblige, and created a thirteen-lawyer National Obscenity Enforcement Unit to promote their moral agenda and try to destroy soft core, irrespective of prevailing community standards. The owner of two adult movie theatres in Salt Lake City was threatened with a tax indictment, the RICO, with Federal and state obscenity charges to follow, and was reminded that just one conviction would lead to denaturalization and the first flight back to Pakistan; he closed the theatres. Later renamed the Child Exploitation and Obscenity

Section, to elicit greater public sympathy, the team also set out to bankrupt distributors of soft core and *non-obscene* materials protected by the First Amendment, through simultaneous multiple prosecutions in different states, making it impossible for the accused to defend themselves because of the cost, and stretching the small number of defence lawyers who specialized in obscenity cases. Apart from upsetting local DAs who saw their powers being usurped, these methods quickly led to complaints that the unit was behaving in an unconstitutional manner. That was an understatement.

The unit did not even care whether the cases were viable; defendants' costs drained company resources, and softened them up for plea bargaining, thereby giving the unit 'a result' they might not have secured in an individual case, and the opportunity to offer to drop other charges in return for the defendants' agreement not to sell any sexually orientated products again. Panavue Enterprises Inc. were forced to close down, destroy their artwork and advertising, as well as agree never 'to promote, produce, sell or distribute sexually orientated materials'.

Rather than prosecute the companies in their home towns, the unit picked conservative religious jurisdictions where they might get a conviction, and solicited the material from the company – thereby adding entrapment to their dubious approach. Toa Publications from the East Coast, which specialized in female mud-wrestling videos, were prosecuted in Utah and Arkansas, making it likely they would be bankrupt before they ever got to see what a jury thought about bikini-clad grapplers.

Any attempt to challenge the legality led to further charges; by also indicting different parts or subsidiaries of the company concerned, the unit threatened individual employees with prosecution, notably owners' wives. The mail order Brussel/Pak Ventures sought an injunction against multiple prosecution; but Truman, the new head of the unit, threatened five consecutive prosecutions unless they desisted from selling soft core. With his wife and son indicted, Brussel took a year in prison and closed down.

If at first they failed to secure convictions, the unit would continue to prosecute until they did. Avram Freedberg, who faced prosecutions in Connecticut, Mississippi, Indiana, Delaware, and Utah, also sought an injunction, only to find his wife indicted. Despite holding out, and gaining acquittals, the unit replied with state prosecutions and indicted his employees. Freedberg, running out of cash, finally agreed to stop distributing soft-core material too.

When pressing forfeiture, the unit also demanded businesses' whole stock. The owner of several video stores in Richmond, Virginia, was required to forfeit over $1 million in assets including thousands of non-sexual general-release tapes after being convicted of renting only two adult tapes.

The FBI were very unhappy with this strategy, and refused the unit's offer for joint investigations; top obscenity agents like Robert Marinaro were wary of the unit's religious obsessions and secret agenda.

Unit Director Robert Showers, a former US attorney from North Carolina, and Brent Ward from Utah made no secret of their aim to bankrupt every soft-core distributor they could, despite their protection by the First Amendment and having been cleared by the Meese Report. Ward had suggested this strategy in 1985, and had been disappointed at the Commission's failure to justify it. When the Adam and Eve company were offered a plea bargain specifically referring to soft core and R-rated movies, they asked the unit to be more specific, and they were told: *Playboy*, *Penthouse* and *The Joy of Sex*! Showers told Joe Cheshire, one defendant's attorney, that as far as he was concerned 'almost anything that depicted any kind of nudity, particularly frontal nudity, male or female, and any sex act, was immoral and obscene'. Patrick Trueman, who eventually replaced Showers, appeared on David Caton's American Family Association three-hour anti-pornography radio broadcast carried by religious stations nationwide, in order to help the re-election of Florida Governor Bob 'ban bikinis' Martinez. Apart from backing the outlawing of thongs from some Florida sunspots, Martinez was offering more prosecutions of the 2-Live Crew rap group, who had featured thonged women on an LP cover and in their stage show. In order to invoke popular support, the unit also sponsored anti-pornography organizations meetings, like the San Francisco Citizens Against Pornography conference on 'protecting children from molesters, pornographers, ritual abuse and cults'.

The unit's funding and support for anti-pornography initiatives also led to 'clean-up' crusades in Kansas, St Louis, Houston, Oklahoma, Cincinnati, Atlanta, Tampa, Jacksonville, Indianapolis, Minneapolis, and Richmond. Police in Norwood, Massachusetts also took a leaf out of the unit's book: visiting their video stores early in 1991, they threatened to prosecute owners unless all the soft-core tapes were taken off the shelves. Their attempt was blocked by a Civil Liberties Union injunction but not before several distributors had agreed not to rent or sell soft core again. Similar moves were made in Georgia, Iowa, Ohio, Pennsylvania, and Nebraska. City governments in North Carolina and Tennessee sought to ban *Oh! Calcutta!* and Terence McNally's play *Frankie and Johnny* in the Claire de Lune unless nudity was removed from these productions. The LAPD even busted a lingerie show, the proceeds of which were to be donated to anti-censorship organizations. The eleven models and organizer Bill Margold were arrested after ten undercover cops had sat through the whole show before making their arrests, for soliciting, prostitution, lewdness, and pandering – the American offence of offering women for sale!

The campaign in Cincinnati, run by the National Coalition Against Pornography's Dr Gerry Kirk, Meese member Dr James Dobson, Attorney General Richard Thornburgh, and ex-FBI Director Clarence Kelly, made international headlines. In March 1989, Dr Kirk appeared on a TV special to announce that closing down the adult bookstores in one neighbourhood alone resulted in an 83 per cent decrease in rape, robbery and assault. No one pointed out that as the neighbourhood in question was undergoing a $120 million gentrification programme, not only had the bookstores closed, but everyone else had located elsewhere at the same time too.

Meanwhile, Senator Jesse Helms took the opportunity to attempt to outlaw the National Endowment of the Arts funding for exhibits he believed were indecent or were derogatory of 'the objects or beliefs of the adherents of a particular religion or non-religion', which enabled any Christian or feminist to claim that a piece of art offended them and therefore have it outlawed. Several Federal judges eventually ruled that the restriction violated the First Amendment, but not before the gay photographer, Mapplethorpe, had to appear in court for his exhibition in Cincinatti's Contemporary Art Center.

In short, the Justice Department was attempting to bypass the Community Standards Test, whereby each community was allowed to set its own obscenity standard, while buying time for moral crusaders to change those standards. Between 1987 and

1990, US obscenity prosecutions jumped by 400 per cent; but this dubious practice could not last for ever.

The first sign of trouble came with Philip Harvey, President of the Adam and Eve mail order catalogue for lingerie and sex toys, and soft-core distributors, who had faced prosecutions of one kind or another for four years since winning a case in North Carolina where the jury acquitted him in a matter of minutes. When his attorneys protested that every item listed in the offered deal was protected by the First Amendment, the Justice Department unit agreed but insisted that 'even if the entire congregation of the First Baptist Church of Plains Georgia would stand and vote they were not obscene', the unit was going ahead. But they were in for a shock.

In July 1990, Washington DC Federal judge Joyce Hens Green ruled that the unit's conduct amounted to an attempt to suppress Adam and Eve's constitutional rights. FBI agents testified that the Federal prosecutors in North Carolina had been cooperating closely with an organization known as the Christian Action League, supplying speakers for churches in order to create opposition to the company; and the citizens who had complained Adam and Eve had sent them unsolicited adult mail had actually requested the catalogue as part of an organized campaign to claim the company were being irresponsible.

Then in May 1991, the American Civil Liberties Union filed a Freedom of Information Request to obtain information about the unit and its budget. The unit stalled; but their plan was being rumbled. An attempt to prosecute several Californian video companies led to the conviction of Video Team in Dallas during July 1991; but when the unit attempted to seize the company's assets, the judge refused them: while obscene by Dallas standards, the videos would not necessarily be so elsewhere. The unit's days were numbered. The scam was finally exposed by the Civil Liberties Union during 1992.

Indecent exposure

The Justice Department's crusade was not helped by two major scandals. Alfred Regnery, who headed the Office of Juvenile Justice and Delinquency Prevention, had been hustling for government funds to attack pornography since June 1983, and Reisman's cartoon 'study' was merely part of $8 million worth. But *Penthouse* hit back at Reisman by exposing the existence of Regnery's private pornography collection in its December 1985 issue.

Back in October 1976, as Regnery sought election as the Madison, Wisconsin, DA, his pregnant wife called the police three times in the campaign's final week to report obscene phone calls. Then she claimed to have been threatened with a knife before being orally raped by two men who insisted Alfred drop out of the race. Moral crusaders had a field day, and Regnery played the 'law and order' card to the full. The local populace, however, did not elect him, and the police were suspicious. Although Christine had 73 superficial slash marks on her breasts, the rest of the story concerning the logistics of the assaults and the alleged assailants' means of escape did not add up. There was no forensic evidence either. Officers did, however, come across a stash of hard-core magazines and catalogues for sex toys!

Regnery threatened to sue *Penthouse* but he did not. Then, when the *New Republic* magazine took up the story Regnery at first denied it, then claimed that the account was a fabrication, then suggested that 'perhaps a friend had sent him a pornographic magazine' and finally, that 'he probably did have a little around the house like most people do, not that he used it or enjoyed it'. Washington, however, inhaled the publicity, and Al had to resign; but he got off lightly.

Charles H. Keating, Head of Citizens for Decency Through Law, was Mr Anti-Pornography for over two decades. Not only had he helped to create the Meese Commission, but his CDL's lawyers acted as the Justice Department's think-tank on Obscenity. CDL also supplied materials for the Department's education programmes and hired out CDL employees as speakers. Paul McCommon even became a member of the new unit. On top of that, Keating then helped fund several senators who were backing the clean-up.

People had always thought that CDL was run on the profits of the Children's Ball, an annual fund-raising binge, which from 1988 was held at Keating's own $300 million hotel complex, the Phoenix Resort. The Ball that year promised to 'bring you a wealth of updated information on the underworld of child porn and the phone sex industry'; though what diners got for their pricey ticket was a chance to see Keating's family and friends present each other with expensive crystal awards in recognition of their efforts in the porn war, while being served up with lurid tales about depravity, and appeals to further fund the fight for entertainment.

In reality, CDL had been financed from the Lincoln Savings and Loan bank in a series of sham transactions. By 1989, the bank was broke; it would eventually have to be bailed out by the Government to the tune of $2.6 billion. Keating was not the only one to use the depositors' hard-earned cash. From the Archdiocese of Phoenix to numerous Right to Life anti-abortion groups, Keating's Christian friends were able to indulge their new concept of Christian charity by taking from the poor to feed the rich. One of the biggest beneficiaries appeared to be none other than Father Bruce Ritter. As well as gaining $400,000 in direct contributions to his Covenant House, it is estimated his 'good works' were advanced no less than $30 million!

Once the scandal broke, Alan Sears, who joined CDL on a starting salary of $125,000, having worked so hard to ensure that Meese returned the right result, did his best to salvage the cause, changing the group's name to the Children's Legal Foundation Inc., while Keating was convicted of fraud.

The American family way

With the American Moral Majority's finest falling from grace amid sex scandals, including Jimmy Swaggart's motel room rendezvous with a prostitute and a dildo, and Jim Baker's attempt to pay off his violated secretary sex scandal, and with Catholics like Keating and Father Bruce Ritter in jail, one wonders how the Christian community dares continue to preach to others, before sorting themselves out; but they do. Having used the 'feminists' to secure the Meese result they wanted, they went on the offensive. Apart from the big-city clean-ups, people like Wisconsin housewife Donna Carroll even found themselves arrested under the state's ancient adultery law. Facing up to two years and a fine of $10,000 she thankfully managed to get off with forty hours' community service by agreeing to two months' counselling; but acts like these were nothing compared to the post-Meese boycott offensive.

Don Wildmon, being Mr Clean, was untouched by the scandals, and in 1991 his American Family Association mailed one million Christian households with a 'reminder' that Christmas shopping in K-Mart stores was incompatible with K-Mart's failure to stop selling soft core. Their other campaigns have targeted sponsors of TV shows featuring 'undesirable sexual material', such as a lesbian kiss in *LA Law*, a homosexual innuendo during *Pacific Station*, sexual innuendo in *The Golden Girls* and every single word in *Married with Children*. Don's crusade shows that the attack upon soft core is only the thin end of the wedge. Along with the 'We Are Outraged' campaign targeting MTV and movies like *Basic Instinct* for causing teenage pregnancy and crime, a complaint about a Madonna video led to Pepsi dropping the star from their campaigns, and the AFA attempted to block a 1989 NBC documentary on *Row v. Wade*, the Supreme Court's decision guaranteeing women a 'right to choose' an abortion. Judy Blume's sex education books and the feminist handbook on health, *Our Bodies Ourselves*, are still considered soft core by Christian groups. More recently boycotters began targeting chat shows which discuss sexual issues, nearly putting *Donahue* off the air.

Meese, despite its rhetoric against hard core, not only led to an assault on soft core by authorities determined to lay down their law, but gave the Christian crusaders like Don the impetus to carry on expanding the list of targets in the name of family protection. Together, the activities of the Justice Department's obscenity unit and the AFA clearly demonstrate that Meese put the Christians back in the driving seat, and that Dworkin and MacKinnon's side show was merely used by them to draw people to the main attraction.

Not that the separatists learned any lessons. They too have expanded their definition of undesirable material. Women's groups at Ohio University, for example, attempted to have Christie Hefner, editor of *Playboy*, banned from the campus, because, as Women's Studies Director Ann Fuerer suggested, students 'didn't need to have that validation' of her work. In 1992, a 'symposium' entitled Prostitution – From Academia to Activism, featuring Dworkin and Stoltenberg and organized by Catherine MacKinnon at Michigan

University, led to students stealing exhibits, including a video about censorship, from an art show by Carol Jacobsen. Speakers at the 'symposium' believed the exhibits 'endangered their safety', a claim frequently made by many CAP speakers in order to close down debate.

Fed up with this kind of nonsense, well-known feminists like Judy Blume, Betty Friedan, Susan Isaacs, and Erica Jong now tour the States taking the anti-censorship position to the grass roots; and when the 1991 National Organization of Women convention failed to launch a nationwide campaign against soft core because of a lobby by sex industry performers, WAP collapsed, as organizer Paige Mcllish denounced the convention as 'doing nothing about pornography' while praising her new friends in the Republican Party for adopting the feminist approach!

From Page Three to the top shelf

The British separatist capitulation to the ongoing Christians' crusade, and their appeal for salvation from the patriarchal state, had a far less spectacular history than their American sisters', but the results were just as farcical for feminism.

Clare Short's original Amendment to Winston Churchill's 1986 Bill became embroiled in the Wapping dispute over new technology. Though the Amendment effectively denied young models an established route to a good career, for the perceived sins of the male *Sun* owner, Rupert Murdoch, it also deflected attention from one of the biggest feminist disasters of the 1980s. The inability of the print unions to prevent the wholesale introduction of new technology did not begin at Wapping, with Rupert Murdoch's deal with the Electricians' Union, but followed the failure of feminist hero Brenda Dean's SOGAT to back the male NGA compositors' rearguard strike action against de-skilling. If the NGA were out the way, once new technology was installed, SOGAT could have signed up the new female staff using it. When female SOGAT members, like those at Portsmouth's *The News*, wanted to back the NGA they received no strike pay. Up and down the country the NGA frequently struggled on its own; and as a result Wapping was lost before it began.

The Page Three amendment, however, gave the separatists the opportunity to revamp their flagging fortunes; not only had all women heard of Page Three, but a *Woman's Own* 'survey' showed their readers were 'offended' by it, and blamed these young women for provoking male sex crimes. The result was the 1988 Indecent Displays (Newspapers) Bill, which denounced simple nudity as an indecency, and the creation of CAP.

Together with Catherine Itzin and Andrea Dworkin, Clare Short laid plans for a British version of the American Ordinances. *Everywoman* reprinted the Minneapolis hearings, and the WAVAW rump dropped the separatist strategy, and set out to prevent Liberty (formerly the NCCL) blocking the British version as the Civil Liberties Union had done in the States. Dr Itzin was already on the Liberty executive, and had numerous friends on the Women's Rights Committee and among the organization's staff. After CAP hawked its propaganda around the media during 1987 and 1988, Dr Itzin also founded the Campaign against Pornography and Censorship, known as CPC, shortly before Liberty's April 1989 General Meeting, to wriggle around Liberty's no censorship policy. Dr Itzin then managed to sway enough delegates by waving around half a dozen pictures from American SM magazines and two volumes on aggression research, while implying that every corner store was promoting violence against women, to commit Liberty to backing *any* parliamentary initiative against pornography. This victory now enabled both CAP and CPC to claim that 'their' civil rights approach had the official backing of the biggest civil liberties organization in Britain. This endorsement appeared in the second wave of media features, and two TV 'documentaries', during the winter of 1989–90.

By the next Liberty AGM, however, it was apparent that far from being a 'feminist' campaign, Clare's Off the Shelf initiative and the Primarolo Bill which followed was part of some kind of deal these 'feminists' had struck with the Christian crusaders, CARE.

Off the Shelf, launched in a blaze of politically correct publicity at the Kingsway branch of W. H. Smith during November 1989, consisted of demonstrators physically removing the soft core from the shelf, dumping it on the counter, and hustling the overworked staff to see the manager. Smith's, however, was not the real target. Clare hoped that victory here over the market leaders would force others to follow suit in a kind of 'feminist' 7-Eleven. But it was never going to succeed. Typical of the problems was the débâcle in Edinburgh where Scottish WAP members apparently committed enough wilful and reckless damage to one of John Menzies' warehouses to lead to criminal charges. Over-enthusiasm in shop raids also led to another two being charged with a breach of the peace, and then with attempting to resist arrest. The problem was that former WAVAW members had not learned to demonstrate peacefully; and there were not enough of them anyway. Despite endorsements from the National Union of Students, and sympathetic noises from the Labour Party's front bench, 'feminist' support simply did not materialize; which is hardly surprising given that.OTS's major sponsor was the Townswomen's Guild!

Numerous demonstrations were really dependent upon church groups, Community Standards Associations, the Church Army, and CARE, who were merely swapping the OTS label for their own Picking up the Pieces campaign started the year before, which had also targeted newsagents in a concerted effort to finish off soft core. CARE had already compiled a digest of pornography shock-horror press cuttings which Nigel Williams, who had already drafted a Bill, was going to hand to MPs. Putting their local and national lobbying power behind this 'feminist' initiative to bring the Labour Party into the crusade, when so many Tories had recently opposed extensions of censorship, must have seemed a pretty good deal to the Christian crusaders. All they had to do in return was ensure that their pro-life MP's abandon any new Private Member's Bill on abortion to avoid antagonizing the Labour Party, which, as CARE's newsletter explained, would make it easier for a Bill on pornography to proceed.

Despite the secrecy surrounding the deal, a picture of Clare at a CARE meeting, and the text of speech in which she apparently implied that Lord Longford and Mary Whitehouse were really early advocates of women's rights, alerted her opponents, whose suspicions increased during 1990, when CARE and CAP ran a joint campaign against Bristol sex shop licences. Unfortunately for the crusaders, the city councillors, once they heard the standard claims about new evidence and content, decided to look for themselves. Finding no child pornography, let alone snuff movies, just harmless

British soft core, American baby dolls, and some cruise control vibros from Hong Kong, they decided to renew the licences.

The invisible alliance

When they were initially confronted with charges of an alliance, the separatists denied it, dismissing it as a filthy smear tactic against 'wimmin' by the pornography industry. Their capacity to maintain this falsehood in the face of all the new and accumulating evidence was astounding: and as late as November 1992, Dr Itzin was still insisting that this allegation was merely an attempt to discredit 'her' campaign by people who could not answer 'her' analysis. In *Pornography: Women, Violence, and Civil Liberties* Dr Itzin asserted that:

> No such alliances exist or have ever been made, either in the USA or the UK.

Given MacKinnon's masters in Indianapolis, and Clare's appearance at a CARE political party fringe meeting, this was always a falsehood; and CARE, who are not known for a singular capacity to lie, admitted as much back in 1988, when Williams's book on soft core, *False Images*, gave supporters a rationale for not going public:

> CARE works very successfully at national level with groups and members of Parliament who hold very different views on other issues which are important to us. Sometimes we have found that these groups are happy to have a private relationship with us, but do not wish it to become too public. That is because they fear attack from libertarian groups who want to portray *the* anti-pornography campaign as a 'right-wing' Christian campaign. [emphasis added]

Some separatists are clearly suffering from the False Memory Syndrome.

Given Mr Williams's admission that there is a private relationship, there are two questions that need answering: who is the private relationship with, and why have they asked CARE to keep it a secret?

The first answer is obvious. As Williams is talking about pornography, and was clearly not referring to Mrs Whitehouse, the only other people engaged in a systematic campaign against pornography are the Campaign against Pornography and Censorship, and the Campaign for Press and Broadcasting Freedom – all of which are also listed in the campaigning section of *False Images*. As far as I am aware, this is the first time that any wholly secular organizations or humanist groups have appeared in any of CARE's publications covering joint campaigning. It is also pertinent to note that throughout *False Images* Mr Williams constantly refers to 'the' anti-pornography campaign. It would be a remarkable slip of the pen by Mr Williams to say 'the' campaign if he thought that CARE's and the separatist feminists' campaigns were not linked in some way.

What is even more ridiculous about Dr Itzin's claim, however, is that the separatists even admitted they were engaged in an alliance with CARE as far back as 1990. In an article entitled 'Pornography: The Debate Goes On', published in the December 1990–January 1991 copy of *Everywoman* magazine, the author, Barbara Norden, informed readers:

> CAP has linked up with Christian group, CARE. 'We are having a lot of influence on them,' says Barbara Rogers. 'They're starting to argue much more in terms of the effect on women. Originally, it was purely a matter of "the family", or morals in a very conventional sense, which we don't have very much sympathy with.' However, CARE also campaigns against abortion, which Barbara Rogers admits causes 'practical problems. But really it comes back to the question of where do you start in trying to get some change? To me, if something is so obvious that people coming from opposite political perspectives can agree on it that would make it particularly strong.'

The only incorrect statement in this article is that CARE have not abandoned their 'pro-family' line. CARE have simply decided that the opportunity to form an alliance with some women's groups and socialist MPs against pornography is worth the temporary suspension of their lobbying Parliament in the Christian campaign against abortion. CARE lose nothing in doing so; this tactic increases their contacts and influence in the Labour Party, and strengthens their hand against soft-core availability, while their anti-abortion allies can continue to lobby for a reduction in abortion time limits during a period when further political advance on that issue is unlikely. While CARE can only benefit from this 'devil's pact', which National VALA were far from happy with, the separatists can only lose.

By forming such an alliance, the separatists demonstrate both their political desperation and philosophical naivety by believing that CARE's temporary tactical emphasis upon pornography's adverse effects upon images of women means that CARE are adopting a feminist analysis. As we have already seen, there is very little difference between the two groups' rhetoric, but CARE are hardly likely to change their views about women's role in society or accept political lesbianism as a viable life-style choice. Consequently, not only is the separatists' judgement suspect, they clearly have something to hide, for as Avedon Carol pointed out in *Nudes, Prudes and Attitudes*:

> It seems strange ... that feminists, who have spent the last two decades criticising the family, religion, and the State as sources of sexism, now count among their number some who are unwilling to recognise the contribution of these institutions to women's oppression ... [and who fail to see that] anti-porn campaigns are always acceptable, [being] completely in keeping with sexist social conventions that stigmatise individual pleasure, instrumental sex, and sexual exploration for women.

That brings us to the second question: why keep the alliance a secret? The answer is simple. It must be kept secret to avoid splitting the women's movement still further and ensuring that most of the gay and lesbian community mobilizes against a separatist philosophy that has become little more than an attempt to promote an extremely limited form of sexual correctness.

The gay community and pornography

The lesbian and gay community is a natural barricade to CAP's Dworkinism. Gay men, and most lesbians, have always been sensitive to 'porn laws', because as well as being used in the past to prosecute gay soft core like *Him*, the Customs and police have seized serious works by lesbian and gay writers and have frequently raided respectable shops like London's Gay's the Word and Edinburgh's West and Wild.

During the late 1980s they had two other reasons. Gay men were convinced they were being subjected to harassment by the Obscene Publications Squad, and more and more lesbians were attempting to steer clear of the separatists' sexual correctness. So it came as a shock when Liberty suddenly backed CAP, whose members had publicly praised both the Spanner trail which criminalized love bites and spouse spanking, and the attempt to prosecute the arts magazine *RE Search* because it promoted tattoos and body piercing. The lesbian and gay community had seen the second case as confirmation that Spanner had placed every sexual minority at risk from police prosecution following Judge Rant's assertion that the courts had to 'draw a line between what was acceptable in a civilized society'.

The community had also been singled out for attack in several amendments to Government legislation, like Clause 28, which effectively prohibited effective discussions about homosexuality in school sex education lessons. Given this kind of experience *Gay Times* warned its readers that Off the Shelf was 'supported by a curious mixture of traditional women's groups and individuals like Jill Knight who have played a leading role in anti-gay crusades' and urged them to oppose the Primarolo Bills.

The Primarolo Bills

In November 1989, Ms Dawn Primarolo presented an Early Day Motion calling upon the Government to review the current state of pornography and the law. It gained all-party support from over 200 MPs who presumably believed the Bill's erroneous claims about soft-core sales, content, and effects.

For reasons of its own, the Government announced that it would set up an inquiry into the issue of pornography and sexual violence; but then it only commissioned a review, though at least the Home Office had the sense to hire the two most qualified British academics in this field: Guy Cumberbatch and Dennis Howitt. As Howitt had published a major review of the research only a year before, these academics took the opportunity to spell out the philosophy, nature, and content of social scientific studies, using respresentative examples to demonstrate the core issues; and the two reviews made an excellent introduction to the subject. Yet when finally published, just before the following Christmas, Cumberbatch and Howitt's report merely provoked a large amount of inane press comment from papers like the *Daily Express* and the *Independent*, while *Today* peddled fears about satellite soft core following European deregulation and attempted to link the non-sex crimes of the Montreal massacre and the London underground acid attacker to consumption of soft core.

This media blast was followed, on 23 January 1990, by the Location of Pornographic Material Bill, which canvassed support for future legislation outlawing soft core in newsagents. Anyone distributing a pin-up magazine outside a sex shop would be liable to a couple of thousand pounds' fine and could be jailed for six months! Speaking at the press conference, orrganized by the Campaign for Press and Broadcasting Freedom, Ms Primarolo justified this Bill as a means to 'save' women from being confronted by pin-ups in their 'daily lives'. She admitted that 'Page Three' constituted pornography under the Bill's definition of pornography, which was handed out at the meeting; and being culled from the Ordinances, it deemed gay pin-ups the exploitation of women too! Other speakers then launched a tirade of personal abuse against Cumberbatch and Howitt for 'covering up' the evidence of soft core's violent links to sex crime. A week later, soon-to-be-disgraced Home Office Minister David Mellor announced that the Government intended to strengthen the 1959 Act, supposedly to prevent a torrent of pornography flooding into Britain from Europe following the introduction of the single market in 1992; but this did not satisfy CAP.

At a 'Freedom from Pornography' fringe meeting at the Labour Party Conference in October, Ms Primarolo's speech sounded remarkably like a précis of MacKinnon's. Ms Short's moral tirade packed in every WAVAW slogan one could think of, and a couple of new ones possibly borrowed from CARE, the highlight of which was the indignant assertion that the effect of soft core was so bad, *it even influenced women*. When she attempted a repeat performance at a Conservative Graduates' meeting later and was asked to name just one piece of research which justified her claims, she said something the organizers found unpleasant and left the room without answering the question.

With an example of a Bill before Parliament, it now became vital for CAP and CPC to reinforce their hold over Liberty. The Bill's unpublished definition of pornography, however, having confirmed fears about sexual correctness, led a Liberty Group's weekend conference in Bristol to reject a CAP/CPC motion following a debate in which the only 'proof' that soft core caused harm was a rather pathetic personal confession by ex-MP Alfred Dubs that looking at pin-ups behind a bicycle shed had led him to form adverse attitudes towards women's sexuality.

The Bill's definition had also provoked a group of highly respected feminist academics, activists, and authors, many of whom were also Liberty members, to form Feminists Against Censorship, known as FAC. Their contributions in TV debates quickly began to change the Channel 4 classes' minds, even though CAP tried to avoid public debate with feminists, preferring to score cheap points by appearing with, and patronizing pin-up models not trained in the art of public debate. With the Labour Party's involvement exposed as a token gesture for women's rights, and a miserable means to stake a claim for the moral high ground, the 1990 Liberty AGM buzzed with anticipation. Members who wished to hold to their principles carried the day over those dreaming of Clare's false Dawn of redirecting a massive moral vote away from the Conservatives to Labour at the next election. Having rejected the Primarolo Bill, the AGM reaffirmed Liberty's former policy regarding censorship. Coming on top of the failure to pass a similar motion at the Socialist Lawyers' AGM the month before, this was a crippling blow against British Dworkinism.

Since then, while their allies in the non-feminist women's

press desperately tried to start a 'date rape' panic to provide another excuse, CAP and CPC have been reduced to denouncing a Vauxhall Corsa advert as a sadomasochistic indoctrination of the British public, and mixing in strange company. New friends have included Ray 'crusade quote' Wyre; the Obscene Publications Squad, whose feminist credentials are somewhat suspect; the National Council of Women, whoever they are; and the Labour Party's Women's Conference, which after twenty years still has not worked out that sexism and sexuality might have a reason for being spelled differently.

The first two have hung around CAP/CPC after the Christian crusaders made fools of themselves stoking up the 1987–92 Satanic panic, which involved the legalized kidnapping of hundreds of working-class children by crusading social workers, who were then forced to denounce their parents and neighbours as Satan-worshipping, snuff-movie-making pornographers, during Inquisition-style interrogations. Unlike the child pornography crusade of 1977–8, which merely exploited the horror of sexual assaults on children, the Satanic panic abused children through physical confinement and psychological torture. Yet we should not forget that the separatists were not far behind either, and that they never applied the slogan 'believe the children' to those children denouncing their jailers, and that they then touted the confessions around the country as proof of the Satanic male plot to make women sex objects through child sexual abuse and brainwashing, as well as the reality of snuff movies. This evil episode in feminist history even involved socialist feminists like Beatrix Campbell sharing platforms with the fundamentalist 'end-timers' who, having failed to realize that calendars were invented by imperfect humans, were convinced that Christ's return at the end of the century was imminent and that the Satanic allegations demonstrated that 'Old Nick' was mobilizing his forces for the final showdown as told in Revelation.

The separatists' recourse to this delusion, and the 'date rape' hype which followed, once again demonstrates the extent to which their 'empirical data' are merely a tautological extension of their ideology.

In contrast, the Christian crusaders back-peddled fast, and found other excuses for reforming the 1959 Act. In 1991, the DPP had sensibly decided not to prosecute Arrow Books' publication of de Sade's *Juliette*; but, incapable of realizing that one needs a course in Enlightenment philosophy to understand the subtleties in de Sade, only crusaders with dirty minds go on thinking the book is about sex. On 2 July 1992 they made its publication their latest 'compelling reason' to bust soft core.

Liz Lynne, the MP for Rochdale, without explaining why she bothered, told the House that immediately she read excerpts from this 'violent and horrific book', she was so disgusted she felt physically sick and had to join the campaign. This adverse effect, however, must have had less to do with the book than with herself. For if Lynne *had* read the book she would have discovered that it did *not* describe the 'murders, torture, and abuse' of 2100 children and young teenagers and 450 women, as briefing paper author Moyra Bremner might think; because de Sade does not describe the events, he leaves them to the reader's own imagination. But why bother with such major details when you can secure instant confirmation of your prejudice simply by meeting Superintendent Michael Hames? Having done so earlier in the day, Lynne appeared impressed with Hames. She told the Commons that he had a 'quite forthright' conviction that the 1959 Act's 'deprave and corrupt' test proved 'a nightmare for juries' – a little-known euphemism for 'not guilty' verdicts.

Having recently become a convert, Anne Winterton no doubt had another reason for believing that the publication of a two-hundred-year-old attack upon Catholic hypocrisy demonstrated the 'total inadequacy of current obscenity law'. Denouncing *Juliette* as a 'child sex abuse and murder manual', Anne then blew her own trumpet by castigating the Government for leaving reform to a Private Member's initiative. Throughout 1992 Anne was forever in the paper promoting 'solutions' like the Robert Spink Bill, on 27 October, which had served as the culmination of National VALA's latest Campaign to Outlaw Pornography petition.

Spink's Bill actually made some excellent suggestions, requiring Secretaries of State to submit a report every year detailing all prosecutions under the 1959 Act and half a dozen other Acts; but he promptly ruined it by also trying to pre-empt the debate that would follow each year by insisting that the Report also contained any proposals for the amendment of the 1959 Act 'with a view to improving their operations'. What made him think that once the public could see what really lay behind media sensationalism, and could make an informed decision, they would not want to scrap the Act? There again, perhaps he did.

Sexy women

What lay behind the increased urgency to find a reason, any reason, to pass a Bill outlawing soft core after the turn of the decade was that women were publicly admitting that they liked it, used it, and even wanted to join in. Women were becoming bored with playing up to the crusaders' failure to alter their nineteenth-century stereotype of shying away from sex except when they feel a twinge of their maternal instincts.

This was rarely true of the working classes, who really only ever conformed to the 'little wife' during the period 1890–1950, when a family unit was the major means by which to increase the working-class standard of living and enhance the children's chances in life; but they had also enjoyed sex for pleasure long before the Sunday supplements heard of the Chippendales. The only real change, a generation on from the 1960s, was that some middle-class girls were openly defecting from the public stereotype too. And once women realized that they could ignore the stigma the crusaders had invented for independent women, they swung the other way and took an ever-growing slice of the soft-core market.

The 1989 Media Business Group report confirmed, contrary to Primarolo's claim, that soft-core magazine sales were falling; but that *Fiesta*, the one magazine apart from *Forum* frequently bought by women, was increasing its share of the market. Since then a spate of women's soft-core publications have also appeared. The bimonthly *Ludus* sold 75,000 on launch, and *For Women* went into a third printing, shifting over 400,000 copies. The contents are similar to those of their male counterparts, with photo-sets, a news round-up, various features regarding the opposite sex and relationships, and stories which do not exclude explicit details. *Ludus* contains more fiction, women's confessions, movie stars like Patrick Swayze, and a problem page. The major complaint by women, so far, is that the pin-ups do not go far enough.

But the current female interest in sex, denied by the separatists, extends further than soft core. During the early 1990s, mainstream women's magazines like *Company* began vying with each other to produce the most explicit coverage of sexual subjects. Women were then treated to special shrink-wrapped sex supplements of a couple in twelve positions, illustrated guides to sex toys and full instructions on how to give a 'blow job', and other acts the crusaders think are degrading. Sexually explicit accounts of experiences and novels, ranging from Sheba's *Serious Pleasures* to mainstream publishers' offerings like Kathy Acker's *Young Lust*, which answer questions about relationships that separatists could not even ask, were complemented by bestsellers like Jackie Collins, and were also surpassed by the new Black Lace series.

To think that women's enjoyment stops with print and the odd picture of a hunk would, however, be a delusion, like those patronizing commentaries penned by feminist academics about Mills & Boon being 'women's pornography'. Women have been buying and watching pornography for years, and not simply because some male 'forced' them to. As Linda Williams noted in *Hard Core*, the American Triple X industry has been attempting to satisfy the women's market for some time. An *Adult Video News* 1986 survey of a thousand video stores discovered that 63 per cent of all pornography tapes were rented by couples, or women. Nor do women's interests stop at the once publicly acceptable limits of romance and film stars. Although Candida Royalle's Productions market movies like *Sensual Escape* play off Royalle's belief that women like to focus upon sensuality and touch, women like hard core too. This take-up is not solely due to the move away from the pathetic 'bimbos and bitches' style of early videos. The real reason some women like to watch as much as men, though for different reasons, comes in Royalle's own confession that she enjoyed her own pornographic career because it gave her a chance to act out what she would have been terrified, but wanted, to do in real life. Women's desire is not less than men's, they have simply been inhibited from acting out their fantasies because society's condemnation of such a choice has created the potential risks that they may run in doing so.

What the female-orientated movies do, however, is clearly demonstrate that women can be portrayed as intelligent human beings who also like sex at the same time. They unmask the crusaders' assertion about the innate degradation of explicit sex for what it is: an attack on sexually active women. But while separatists can try to explain away any ex-porn star who does not insist she was coerced as suffering from false consciousness, they are stuck with the fact that Fatale Films was established by Suzie Bright, who came out as a 'pro-sex feminist' after having organized Take Back the Night marches, and founded *On Our Backs* in 1984 with other women who had experienced WAVAW and WAP's anti-sex attitude at first hand. Along with Tigress Productions and similar efforts in Britain, these women-only productions negate the separatists' versions of the crusaders' standard complaints about male lust.

This recent explosion of new magazines, films, and books should not, however, detract from the fact that British soft-core magazines, like *Forum* and *Penthouse*, have long been run by female editors. Separatists who suggest they are merely fronts for males merely reveal their real attitude towards the intellectual capabilities of heterosexual women like Isabel Koprowski, a female corporate role-model as well as a degree-holding Latin scholar, who happens to disagree with them. The failure to face up to the fact that several leading soft-core titles have female editors, photographers, and staff writers as well as models demonstrates the frequent gap between the crusaders' ideologies and basic facts.

The same applies to all those tales about coercion. Young women entering the glamour industry generally do so of their own volition. 'The fact that these young women will pay for their own portfolio of photographs which they then have to hawk round modelling agencies in order to secure contracts, or enter the glamour competitions held on the nightclub circuit, shows the lengths they will go to in the hope of establishing a career. Separatists who dismiss this free choice in favour of standard horror stories about exploitation, have, as the Canadian philosopher Christensen points out, a hypocritical double standard, given what the ballet industry does to naive young girls with its harsh training in unnatural movements that can cripple them, and the risk of rampant anorexia or bulimia not to mention drug abuse. Just think: all this for the lustful pleasure of upper-class women! The real difference between a failed ballet hopeful and a successful soft-core model, of course, is the issue of sex and respectability. It is no longer an issue of lack of opportunity, as the expanding educational opportunities and career market for women make modelling a positive choice, whether one begins in a wet T-shirt competition or buys oneself a copy of *Get Seen*, the magazine for modelling beginners, and sends them a couple of portfolio pictures.

The horror stories and other crusading fictions which amount to the deliberate refusal to accept the reality of soft-core life never dealt with the real issuees anyway. As the recent growth of the sex trade between Eastern European countries and the Middle East demonstrates, real exploitation is a function of poverty and limited opportunities on one side, and hypocritical moral standards on the other.

Some people simply will not accept the fact that women like and want sex too. And that is why Madonna's *Sex*, and the growing number of 18 certificate sex education videos like *The Lovers' Guide*, produced such an outcry from the crusaders and the Obscene Publications Squad, whose real concern was that the public may begin to ask awkward questions about the lack of difference between this legal material and what is still prosecuted. A *TV Quick* magazine's poll which found that the viewing public not only welcomed the sex education videos, but that 76 per cent would not be offended by more graphic depictions, clearly shows that viewers agree with Sir John Wheeler MP, former Chairman of the Commons Select Committee on Home Affairs, who thinks that changing obscene publications legislation is a waste of time:

> There is a lot of humbug talked about this. I don't know what you mean by pornography, but if people want to go out and buy a video that shows two people making love, good luck to them. *It's not Mike Hames' job to act as guardian of the nation's morals; what he ought to be concentrating on is paedophile material – where the law can be enforced.*

And that is precisely why the crusaders will use every opportunity and excuse to repeat their demands for stronger laws. They now know that, lesbian or heterosexual, women are beginning to explore openly what men have done for years. What they do not know is that many always did. While some hid their desires behind Nancy Friday's respectable works, others, separatists will be horrified to learn, have been masturbating for years to feminist horror story classics, like Barry's *Female Sexual Slavery* with its white slavery fantasy fodder.

Behind the scenes

The one major weapon crusaders have left is recourse to people's fear of sex. With women openly embracing their sexual opportunities and ditching the old stereotypes, it is easy to see why the crusaders harp on about modern juries refusing to support the prosecution's nineteenth-century definition of obscenity; explicit soft core was becoming legalized by default. Worse still, in May 1993, Alan Jackson and Stephen Brown, who ran a Forest Gate (London) cinema, were even found not guilty of obscenity for showing *Highlander*, *Just One Day* and *Blue Line*, hard-core movies featuring a woman inserting a banana in her vagina, group sex, oral sex, anal sex, and even urolagnia. Unhappy about this display of contemporary community standards, various authorities will say and do anything to convince the public that current laws should be extended in order to give them more powers to save us from this sexual anarchy. Yet most of what they really seize is simple soft core, and most prosecutions amount to an elaborate ritual designed to keep the public ignorant of that fact and punish those who transgress the authorities' determination to prevent sex for pleasure or entertainment in Britain.

Neither the Government nor the police systematically release figures, which is not surprising given how expensive the unit costs of convictions are. In 1990, 174 people were prosecuted under the 1959 Act, of whom only 73 were convicted. Yet by 1991 the Obscene Publications Squad had 18 officers, costing almost £1 million; and that is before one adds up the real cost of the court cases. And for what: a grand total of 17 warrants which netted 5500 videos and no magazines, and 1300 videos and 25 magazines under other statutes between January and November 1992. *The only thing which stops the Squad being a complete waste of time is that during the same period they took out 56 warrants under the 1977 Child Pornography Act*, which netted 3,000 videos and 500 magazines, 9000 photos, 3500 slides, and 7000 negatives. Presuming all this material was child pornography, *it would make far more sense to concentrate their efforts here.*

The number of items seized reached a high point in 1983, when the Squad carried away over 2 million items; mostly videos during the 'nasties' scare. Behind these figures, however, lies a gigantic swindle. Much of the material seized had to be returned to its owners. Sullivan and the Gold brothers would regularly have their warehouses raided even though the police knew their chances of conviction against soft core were slight.

When they are not misrepresenting the nature of the material seized, the police exaggerate the size of the operation. In August 1991 Linzi Drew, the glamorous, outspoken critic of the obscenity law and apologist for soft-core models, was supposedly running a £1 million hard-core video 'ring'. Judging by one I saw, that definition all depends upon what you call couples copulating; but Linzi received four months and her partner Simon Honey went down for nine. They would both like to know where the £1 million was found, and what was done with it. They never knew they were that rich; but I hope Linzi's glossy new 18-certificate *Members Only* series will make them so.

Local squads are no better. The worst case on record is the twenty-year persecution of Dave Britton and Michael Butterworth, the Manchester-based publishers, whose authors have included Michael Moorcock and Jack Trevor-Story, by the Manchester Obscene Publications Squad. David Britton first went to prison in 1982 for possessing 'obscenity' – Grove Press and Venus Freeway novels, which were openly on sale in every other part of the country. Eleven years later, he was jailed again for publishing his own novel, *Lord Horror*. The real reason for this scandal was their company's open opposition to the arbitrary powers of Chief Constable James Anderton, whose satirical characterization in *Lord Horror* led to the second conviction. Britton and Butterworth funded their publishing enterprise through several local bookstores selling paperbacks, American comics, minority interest books and periodicals, and soft-core pornography. They have lost count of the number of raids that have taken place and the destruction orders under section 3 of the 1959 Act, which even confined the likes of *Penthouse* and *Mayfair* to the flames.

The Fiona Cooper company, which specializes in strip-tease photo-sets and videos, faced similar problems from the Halifax vice squad, and local magistrates who no doubt think Page Three obscene. The owner, Phil Sutcliffe, also found himself prosecuted for *possessing* explicit soft-core videos, which the police removed from his house, reasoning that because he owned Fiona Cooper, it had to be possession for gain. That was enough for the magistrate, who fined him £1000 and £100 costs. The BBFC gave the company grief by initially considering giving Cooper soft core an 18R certificate, even though the models merely took their clothes off, far less than you would see on a certain TV channel known among the dirty-mack brigade as 'Fuck on Four', several nights of the week. This severely restricted Cooper's distribution; though their videos have now obtained an 18 certificate and can be found in the Virgin Megastore in London's Oxford Street.

Apart from harassing individuals the authorities do not like, obscenity laws are constantly used to hassle sexual minorities. Gay soft-core magazines have always been a target, and as their simple nudes could hardly be obscene, unless one is homophobic, the intent is clear. Even though the enormous success of *The Gay Man's Guide to Safer Sex* led to a range of gay and lesbian videos making High Street stores, the madness goes on. In April 1993, police seized 16,000 copies of a gay satirical magazine called *ff*. The offending items appeared to be a safe-sex picture which accompanied an article titled 'Rubber Fuck', and an advert for the sex shop Studio 40, showing a ball weight. That same month, a Covent Garden newsagent faced a personal prosecution under section 2 rather than section 3 of the 1959 Act, for selling the gay soft-core *Him*, *Vulcan* and *Mister International*. That police homophobia is still rife is strongly suggested by the October 1991 conviction of the Bradford-based company Scene One. A fine of £130, £1500 costs, and six months for manager Kevin Haigh, followed conviction of a dozen gay magazines among the 24,000 others seized in yet another police 'nuisance' raid.

This stupid game keeps local vice squads in business and enables them to justify their budgets, by confining millions of soft-core magazines to the flames under section 3 while the media mislead the public into thinking that it was all violent hard core. That job really rests with Her Majesty's Customs.

In the year ending March 1984, the Customs boasted that they had seized over 170,000 items – books, magazines, video cassettes, films, advertising brochures and other articles – deemed indecent. Like the police, the Customs would like the public to think in terms of child pornography and snuff movies. Yet the fact that they initiated proceedings against only 65 people, less than half of whom then received a prison sentence, debunks that myth, and the feeble total of £74,700 in fines suggests it is all an incredible waste of time and taxpayers' money. Far from the 'international porn ring conspirators' we hear so much about in the media, even the case of former English soccer player Peter Storey, jailed for four weeks in November 1990 for driving off a ferry with 20 videos, is not typical. Most of the victims are people like David Webb, the director of NCROPA, who once returned from a European trip with four representative gay videos he was given for his serious research. Postal seizures have included copies of the TV documentary *The Killing of America* and two medical films concerning plastic and infant brain surgery, ordered by Christopher Berthoud. Customs officers got very excited when they then raided his house; Berthoud's extensive collection of mummified birds and animals and video collection of serial killer documentaries must have made them think they had finally found a snuff movie or two. Despite the same subject in special colour supplement detail keeping the *News of the World* readers enthralled for weeks, this 'evidence' was enough for them to proceed and he was promptly prosecuted for importing indecent material! Other crazy confiscations have included copies of the Deutsche AIDS Hilfe poster, funded by the German Government as part of its safe sex campaign, and a Dutch safe sex education video, *In the Heat of the Moment*, imported by the Norwich Gay Men's Health Project. But not everyone can have a Health Authority protest on their behalf, and the Customs get away with this every single day.

If this were not bad enough, Trading Standards Officers have now convinced themselves that our health is better safe-guarded by seizing consignments of sex than those contaminated with salomella. A media blitz in May 1982, based solely on their press release, told of the shocking trade in snuff and mutilation movies discovered after a six-month 'undercover operation' by Liverpool officers which secured the 'largest ever haul' in Britain. Balderdash.

Far from finding one hundred thousand snuff movies, as one TV news item claimed, or even infiltrating a dangerous bondage–torture movie gang dominating the video black market, as an unnamed police officer asserted, the officers had merely picked up a group of cult movie buffs who openly advertised their activities in home-produced fanzines. The group had been foolish enough to swop or sell uncertificated copies of their private video collections among themselves, and thereby had technically broken the 1984 Act. Typical horror movies included the cult classics *Nekromantic 2*, which had even received praise in the *Guardian*'s arts pages, and *Nightmares in a Damaged Brain*. They are far less violent than other movies on general release, like the excellent *Terminator*, and far less gory than the hilarious spoof horror *Bad Taste*. Even though their films came nowhere near the hype they received, the fans were duly fined several hundred pounds for these minor offences. The buffs' collection of unusual sex films, like the *Graftenberg Spot*, was then prosecuted for obscenity. Those finally offered to the court had one or more features in common. They centred around the concept of the G-spot, and/or the clinical medical condition of female ejaculation, and/or presented females as authority figures. The authorities were clearly determined to quash women-centred hard-core movies.

The only thing to surpass the nonsense surrounding these video busts has been the blather about computer sex. Every child, we are told, has now traded in their video nasties, thrown away their collection of horror comics, torn up those all-night rave tickets, scoffed at the mayhem on TV, put their pit-bulls to sleep, flushed the E down the toilet, laughed at the idea of running away to become a call-girl in Bognor or abandoned dreams of growing up to be a ram-raider, and no longer states wide-eyed at addictive violent video games. Now these playground monsters are swopping child pornography and hard core featuring bestiality on computer disks; which, according to the police journal *The Job*, look no different from those used for homework or playing (to heighten the contrast, the now conveniently innocuous) video games on.

Really? What *The Job* is asking us to believe is that all these children have suddenly saved up £1000 from their paper rounds, set up and configured their new 386 or 486 PCs, complete with a £500 Super VGA monitor obtained with an advance on their pocket money from City Bank, and plugged it into their new £200 modem, no doubt secured through selling crack to their teachers; then rung one of the American West Coast companies which supply *pin-up pictures and simulated sex scenes* on their bedroom's personal phone line funded by the sale of their BT shares; typed in the answers to the extensive questionnaire the companies insist upon, then their credit card number and expiry date; and finally persuaded their big sister to swear to mum that the resultant phone bill was due to her talking to her surfing pen-pal from California.

That explains everything: this smart example of 'children as young as eight' has now started funding his £2000 colour laser printer by selling disks to his gullible classmates who do not realize that the disks *look nothing like those on his games consul* let alone will never load, and that he will have to work out how dad's PC at work is configured, call upon his extensive knowledge of computer languages and graphics formats to load and make the files accessible, even if his dealer supplied him with the commands. Personally, I blame it all on comprehensive education and the lack of corporal punishment; you would not believe the trouble we used to get into for taking a dead horse-chestnut on a shoelace into school.

The only real problem, as PC Kevin Ives ironically made clear at a special smut spectacle at the Commons, is that most parents are 'not really clued up' when it comes to computers. Precisely. That's why computer pornography (all child porn and snuff, of course) is one of the best openings for scare-mongering tactics for decades. Parents' fears of being outsmarted by their children are as underestimated as the extent of disk swopping is exaggerated. If the Squad had any brains at all they would be more concerned at the dramatic fall in the price of CD-ROM attachments, and the 1000 per cent increase in capacity CD disks provide over the normal floppy. These are very easy to use, as you merely load the disk and press two buttons; and once American firms like PC Component, which issues a 'visual fantasies disk' containing 2500 explicit pictures selling for $100, begin selling simulated material, the obscenity law will be futile.

Prosecutions for computer porn are very rare, because

people like Vinson Pike from Swindon, who was fined £1000 after pleading guilty to four charges concerning pornographic floppy disks in April 1992, are very rare. The fact that he was also convicted under the 1959 Act demonstrates there is no need for any new law to catch and stop people breaking the existing laws. Yes, computers and modems are an excellent means to spread child pornography around the globe; but that is all the more reason to concentrate law enforcement efforts on child pornography, and increase the penalties for this offence, rather than use it as yet another excuse to outlaw soft core.

The problem in maintaining the barrier against sexual imagery has always been new technology, making the manufacture and distribution of the material easier; and given their attitude to sex, the overdue introduction of satellite TV in Britain was always going to give the authorities a headache. Though not, it turned out, the way many assume.

In the late 1980s, twelve channels including FilmNet in Scandinavia, RTL/Veronique in Benelux, and France's Canal Plus offered soft-core late-night movies to most of Western Europe; and, thanks to the sale of some half a million decoders needed to unscramble their pictures, to a lot of British viewers too. In July 1991, FilmNet even changed decoders because of the larger number of pirates available in Britain. It was also inevitable that when a station called Red Hot Dutch started broadcasting deliberately to Britain, via the Eutelsat 11-F1, the Government would attempt to outlaw it. Yet what annoyed the Government was not, as the media would have us believe, that 'Dutch' was too hot, but that the Independent Television Commission knew more people wanted to watch Dutch's American and European Triple X features between midnight and three in the morning than their two licensed stations!

What many did not realize was that the ITC had given Home Video Channel and After 12 licences to supply soft core in Britain in November 1991, after the ITC decided the material met their requirements concerning taste, decency, and transmission times. However, by also announcing that if the material was pornographic neither company would have gained a licence, the British public were encouraged to ignore the authorities' preferred option and went 'Dutch' instead. The fact that the British Government were thereby calling naked women pornographic when they appear in magazines but not after midnight on your TV screen made no difference. 'Dutch' had to go.

In January 1993 the Government attempted to outlaw the station by invoking a clause in the 1990 Broadcasting Act enabling it to proscribe any channel that 'offended against good taste or decency'. Such a ban might have been consistent with the EC's Broadcasting Directive which permits countries to prohibit material deemed to 'seriously impair the moral developments of minors'; but in order to pull that one, Red Hot Dutch's broadcasts had to be denounced as violent, as Europeans would never censor simple sex. So another of those ever-popular special screenings for MPs was laid on by the ITC. Three selective clips brought moral sound-bites from James Hill, who thought them 'pretty bad' and Michael Alison's inevitable view: 'the worrying thing about this sort of programme is that you reach saturation level and the appetite grows for more explicit material involving children, bestiality and so on'.

But when the Government demanded that their Danish counterparts shut down 'Dutch', the Scandinavians thought they were joking; why did the British want them to close 'Dutch' when the ITC had also licensed the West Drayton-based TV1000 which was transmitting highly explicit films to Denmark? The output was not just similar, it was identical: American Triple X movies. How 'Dutch' was breaching ITC codes but TV1000 was not, and why Britain is allowed to broadcast to Denmark what Denmark is not allowed to send back, remains a puzzle that only the ITC can answer; the European Satellite Society's Mr Yves Felt thinks it has something to do with British furtiveness and hypocrisy about sex. No one had told him that the ITC's own survey found that only 15 per cent of the non-quango classes completely disapproved of satellite soft core, and that a massive 63 per cent would like more explicit material. Even the majority of those who did not want to watch thought others should have the choice, as long as *hard core* was broadcast after midnight.

Unfortunately for 'Dutch', judges, for some reason, think they know better. Despite gaining a judicial review, 'Dutch's attempt to block the decoder ban was dismissed in April 1993, making sale and advertising of decoders punishable by two years in prison. Lord Justice Legatt justified this decision, and his satisfaction that the Government's actions were in the 'public interest', by saying that as subscribers were likely to record the late-night broadcasts on their videos rather than stay up, children were in danger. The crusaders' and Parliamentarians' excuse to block adult choice with an emotive appeal regarding the moral welfare of minors has now become an excuse for judges too.

Even if all this soft core really posed a threat, which it does not, and even if lagging behind our European partners did not threaten to make us look more and more ridiculous, which it does, the price of these endless exaggerations is the persecution of harmless pleasures and 'art' students. Students from the West Surrey College of Art, for example, have discovered just how far the word 'pornographic' can be stretched, when six items were pulled from their show at St Martin's Gallery. Kate Anderson's self-portraits, including one photograph of her vagina, were denounced as pornographic, and this has seriously disrupted her career and further shows. During the 1980s it became chic to have a tattoo; and why not if, as they say, Field Marshal Montgomery and Winston Churchill's mother had one too. The new craze, partly encouraged by Cher, who as far as I am aware now has six, is not, however, to everyone's liking, as Richard Waller, of the Book Inn, Charing Cross Road, discovered. A 'routine visit' by the police led to a summons twelve months later over *Modern Primitives*, which included illustrations and very informative articles on tattooing and body piercing. This strongly implies the police were attempting to prosecute these depictions of 'sexual practices' in the light of the need to associate them with sadomasochism, in the Spanner trial. Why the police feel the need to make routine visits to ordinary bookstores; why Waller was told that pleading guilty would lead to only a £50 fine, but pleading not guilty a jail sentence; and why some police officers think tattooing is now an obscenity, has never been explained. The popular Jim Rose Circus Show were bemused to discover they were obscene too. In the early 1990s, the number of their cancelled performances surpassed those of the acid-rock group Hawkwind in the 1970s and the nude male balloon dancers OddBalls in the 1980s. Typical was the February 1993 cancellation in Portsmouth, when the Licensing Committee denied promoters the use of licensed entertainment premises using standard provisions, which have not been updated for years, including: 'No profanity or impropriety of language, dress, dance, or gesture or anything which is in any way offensive to public feelings', because the local police thought the show, which includes a feat of strength featuring a penis, constitutes an obscenity.

Not to be outdone, during June 1993 the politically correct Independent Committee for the Supervision of Standards of Telephone Information Services announced that its new code of practice would restrict adult 0898 numbers to soft-core magazines. Their removal from newspapers was inevitably justified as necessary for protecting children. Crusaders, of course, want to outlaw 0898 sexual messages altogether. In 1990, Mr Hood MP proposed making it an offence to send any sexually 'provocative' or 'offensive' material on a public telecommunications system, and the operator of the services, let alone those renting the line, could be fined £10,000 and get two years in prison. This restriction on advertising, and the campaign to outlaw such material by MPs like Terry Lewis, stand in marked contrast to the refusal of the authorities to block genuine obscene phone calls. Women face up to 20,000 nuisance calls a day. There is no evidence to show whether or not the introduction of 0898 numbers increased or reduced this; but BT initially blocked the private sale of Calling Line Identification Receivers, know as CLIRs in the United States, which for £149 would identify the caller's number. A Midlands company which was planning a sales campaign in women's magazines suggested that the real reason was that CLIRs vet incoming calls before the call is answered. BT denied that losing money was the reason, claiming that the machine would not work on British systems, and infringed privacy. They then brought out their own CLIRs three years later. Meanwhile neither the crusaders nor the separatists did anything to help women avoid millions of unwanted calls.

The constant failure of the authorities and crusaders to supply real solutions to real problems follows from the way they raise sensational horror stories to outlaw each new form of soft-core distribution. As they have to escalate their horror stories with each new development, if anyone is desensitizing the public to violence it is the crusaders and the media. As the only thing worse than an allegation of Satanic abuse snuff movies is the innocently accused committing suicide, it is hardly surprising the public are less and less likely to buy the crusaders' babble; not that this stops the media trying to tar and feather soft core for the sins of others.

Typical of the constant misinformation peddled as serious grounds for changing the law was *Today*'s December 1989 article 'Soft Core with a common theme ... the abuse of women'. The reporters were appalled to be able to rent more than 80 gratuitous acts of violence and 16 rapes and no less than 35 'degrading' sex scenes in the 15 videos they hired from an average store, not to mention the fact that these movies contained 12 acts of lesbianism'. Shock. Horror, Etc., etc. The titles were offered to the seriously flawed Parliamentary Video Inquiry as proof that sex criminals strike after such 'sex' videos; when the report finally named the titles, it became obvious why crusaders never do. The alleged offenders included *Craw Space*, *Hell Hole*, and *Out of the Dark*: suspense films, not soft-core movies. When it came to the feeble apology for soft-core cassettes allowed by the BBFC, the complaint completely evaporated. Even the article's authors described *Lady Godiva Rides Again* as 'drivel: a depressing rather than dirty or dangerous film'. As it contained only three 'violent, but jokey' scenes, five topless shots, one mud wrestling scenario', and that well-known hard-core violent act of 'one character poking fun at a fat woman', perhaps someone could complain to trading standards. The only way *Today* could imply a connection between sex and violence in the rest was the silly suggestion that low-budget thrillers such as *Pretty Kill*, *Stripped to Kill*, *Call Me*, and *Body Double* were really 'sex' films because the victims were strippers or prostitutes.

Thankfully this dishonest or naive reporting could not inhibit informed debate, because that would be impossible among any prurient reader of this trash. Regrettably the Obscene Publications Squad keeps trying. Coming close on Dworkin, the world leader in hyperbole, the Squad's remarkable powers of observation appeared in a *Sunday Telegraph* feature during January 1993 lamenting the beleaguered officers' inability to 'stem the flow of filth' on a top shelf implied to contain nothing but bondage, domination, and rubberwear magazines. WPC Jackie Malins, who monitors content for the Squad and served as the article's 'expert', told readers that the women in such 'torture scenes' look 'completely out of it, drugged up to the eyeballs' – which is very perceptive given that the models are completely encased in rubber or PVC. No wonder the Squad cannot understand why juries constantly make them look so foolish. Not being blessed with such a perverse imagination, the juries see the contents for what they are, rather than what Jackie, crusaders, or separatists think they see.

Perhaps that also explains why despite the Squad's categories of 'offence' on their content checklist being restricted to masturbation, ejaculation, fellatio, cunnilingus, 'plain intercourse', 'buggery', and flagellation, we only ever hear about snuff, child pornography, and torture movies. As the first list contains only two illegal acts, it fails to 'offend', let alone corrupt and deprave, and the authorities have to pretend they are prosecuting something else. As they cannot fool a jury in a courtroom, they pump the media full of bogus horror stories and try to gain new powers. Like the crusaders, the authorities will use any excuse. The Customs' list is longer, but the additions are limited to bestiality, bondage, erection, mammary intercourse, scatology, and urolagnia. While these may be unpleasant, there are only another two more illegal acts.

When they appeared, Mr Hames even opposed sex education videos. Completely ignoring the fact that he was empowered under the 1984 Act to seek their prosecution irrespective of their 18 certificate if he wished to do so, but mindful that he would lose a court case, Hames erroneously suggested they would be illegal if they were not billed as educational, and pleaded for an increase in powers just in case some professional pornographers started to produce similar films and called them educational. As if the BBFC would fall for that, or Rodox would bother to change their lucrative formats. The only real problem, as Mr Hames correctly pointed out, was that

> sooner or later someone who we are prosecuting will say ... 'Look, I am only showing the same acts that you can see if you go into a High Street store and buy a sex educational video'.

Precisely; but the real scandal is that this head of the Obscene Publications Squad did not appear to know that the defence of comparison is forbidden under the 1959 Act. Of course the question to ask is why the same acts are permissible when viewed as education, but not acceptable when screened as entertainment. No wonder the Dutch think we are stupid, as well as poor losers.

Summary

Again and again, through trying to exercise their choice, jury verdicts, and opinion polls, the British public have demonstrated that they do not share the crusaders' or the authorities' concerns about soft core. Channel 4's *Check Out '92* and Gallup found that more than 80 per cent of the adult population *are not* offended by explicit sex videos; and it is for this very reason that the Carry On Crusaders resort to more and more bizarre horror stories, bogus statistics, and hype about content. Knowing what decision the public will make if they gain a free choice, the crusaders are desperate to gain a more coercive law to *force* their will upon others. The language of persuasion is dead.

Yet when MPs like Dr Robert Spink cite Madonna's *Sex* as a reason for 'tidying up the muddled obscenity laws', because 'there has to be something wrong when the law could not prevent the book from being sold', that law is an anachronism. When he thinks he can justify strengthening the law's powers to restrict choice by denouncing one of the world's smartest popular entertainers as an 'obviously confused and perverted woman', it is clear what crusaders think of independent women and choice. And when he claims that there is 'an unprecedented concern over pornography' in Britain, it is clear his circle of friends is getting smaller. National VALA's petition, handed in before the Parliamentary debate in October 1992, contained only a third of a million signatures, 75 per cent fewer than they could muster a decade ago. Time is running out for the crusaders. But rather than put their own faith to the test, all they offer is the same methods that have failed in the past and will never succeed in the future.

Separatists have to resort to coercion, because women do not agree with them; and even the Labour Party appears to have woken up to that fact. In August 1992, it appeared to drop its pledge to ban Page Three girls as part of its new non-loony image. It has been rumoured that their private polls had shown that Labour's stance on 'feminist' issues turned voters, *especially women voters*, off.

Chapter eight

Sex and Diversity

SINCE the seventeenth century moral crusaders have been trying to set Britain's sexual standards and boundaries; and people do not realize that the sexual practices they think of as 'normal' and 'abnormal' were merely designated as such depending upon the crusaders' success or failure.

For many thousands of years biologically 'normal' sex amounted to playing around until either a woman's vagina enveloped a man's penis, or in a significant number of cases a single-gender event occurred. Either way both parties found it very enjoyable. The only serious problem for heterosexual couples in the far past was that biology often played very cruel tricks upon women, and having babies could be deadly. Once people worked out that the completion of the act by the male inside the female's vagina had something to do with babies, more and more people began to experiment with numerous forms of foreplay and climax production. No one minded too much, the fun increased, and the risks for women were reduced.

Then in the fifteenth century, as the historian Norman Cohn has revealed in *Europe's Inner Demons*, various religious establishments began to link sexual experimentation with eating babies and social misfortune in order to label their enemies demonic and justify breaking the Second, Third, Sixth, Eight, and Tenth Commandments: in short, killing them and confiscating their property. People who did not enjoy sex, or who felt incredibly guilty when doing so (usually because they wanted their flesh and to be celibate too), either sat in very cold rooms and invented a series of justifications for denouncing those who did enjoy sex, or rode around the countryside assuaging their guilt by torturing and killing anyone who was a local scapegoat. As a result, anyone who appeared to enjoy having any kind of sex, especially when it did not involve having babies, was in trouble. Everyone began to worry, and the fun decreased. Things got so bad that even the people who did not enjoy sex then started accusing each other of doing so. Protestants attacked Catholics, Catholics attacked Protestants, and they both attacked the Jews, Waldensians, and anyone else who got in the way. Sex and evil were now inextricably linked in the public consciousness.

Once Europeans realized that if this went on too long, there would be no one left, they agreed to pick on coloured people, especially those who did not wear many clothes because they lived in hot countries, and had some gold, diamonds, and other useful minerals lying around. When the British had dressed everyone, and taken all the loot, they noticed that their own lower orders were up to their old tricks, and started all over again. Social purity was born; and because the middle-class moralists realized their obsession with cricket and cucumber sandwiches would not appeal to everyone they tried to stop women tempting them by inventing a man called Fu Manchu whose moustache was too long to be decent, smoked opium for pleasure, and had now taken over the white slave traffic – the inevitable end for sexually active women. After Fu came the Swedes, Arabs, Latins; indeed, anyone the Government had a political or economic dispute with, and who, for some strange reason, always seemed to want to rape 'our own' women – who were simultaneously appearing in the Edwardian cricket-playing classes' fantasies. By then, of course, those men in cold rooms had now invented thousands of reasons why sex was actually bad for you; they had to, because medical science could now reduce many of the biological problems previously associated with it.

Consequently, a relatively simple mental decision about consenting sex now had to take place through a complicated and confusing array of beliefs and attitudes about what was and was not permissible; and for the next seventy years women were taught to fear sexual experimentation.

No sex please

Contemporary campaigns against pornography also want to define society's sexual boundaries and limits, and enforce them through law. Yet the necessity of recourse to law in order to make social reality reflect their beliefs proves that there is nothing natural about the crusaders' ideals.

Whatever rationales the crusaders offer the public, their ultimate aim is the implementation of God's will, to avoid His judgement upon the nation. Along the way, they wish to restrict the enjoyment of sex to the monogamous married heterosexual couple, and to inhibit lust. Unless you are lesbian or gay, this is quite a nice idea – not that sexual orientation need inhibit lifelong partnerships which result in increased understanding, feelings of love, and heightened pleasure. Unfortunately for the crusaders, more people today consider sex as a leisure activity rather than a sacrament to God's design. Separatists, not believing in God, are motivated by their desire to stop women having sex with the enemy – men. Their rationales are completely self-serving, and unless you are a separatist feminist, it is not a nice idea. Along the way they want to inflame a gender war by defining all heterosexual sex as rape, and to convince women that behind every man lurks a serial killer waiting to strike; this is incitement to gender hatred and guaranteed to inhibit understanding, love, and pleasure.

Both groups, however, share two things in common. First, their attack upon soft core is premised up the *a priori* belief that women's sexual desires are diametrically opposed to men's. Second, the social evidence is against them; women can be and are just as instrumental as men. When women's sexual options were effectively limited to marriage, it made sense for them to secure the best possible deal by accommodating themselves to the double standard. As more and more opportunities now open up, women do not have to play this game any more, and they rightly demand more from partners and marriage. The Christians, having failed to spend enough time studying the real reasons for social change, still cannot understand why this has happened; and they are convinced we can go back to the 1950s if only they can stop men imposing 'their' instrumental will upon women through pornography. Fearing their inability to convince enough people to abandon self-interest in favour of 'society', they seek the declaratory law so that even if sinners escape earthly punishment they will know they are breaking a law, and public morality will be maintained. The separatists have no such justification; they want a law to prevent women who enjoy soft core from undermining separatist theories about the world. But while Christians can explain away the lack of total success on the grounds that we are all sinners, the separatists have to delude themselves that the only reason women ignore their lousy offer of sexual apartheid is that they have been coerced or brainwashed, either as adults or through having been 'sexually abused' in childhood. Hence their insistence that the Cleveland sex abuse scandal covered up the fact that all children are abused.

The ridiculous thing about all this, of course, is that the attack upon soft core is a substitute for making certain kinds of sex a crime; and once one realizes this, it also becomes obvious that crusaders and separatists could never stop there, but will have to work towards legislating against those kinds of sex. They have already started against premarital sex by demanding that the definition of rape should begin with any sexual act involving a woman who has had a drink. Meanwhile their campaign against soft core effectively asserts that good girls do not: read sex magazines and watch videos; wear high heels and sexy clothes, especially rubber or PVC; wear tattoos, or insert jewellery anywhere except in their ear; talk dirty to men; pose for Page Three; play with sex toys; have oral sex; have anal sex; have sex with more than one man, especially several at once; enjoy sexual variations and so on. By making these assertions, the crusaders and separatists are a contemporary equivalent of the nineteenth-century Social Purity crusaders, who wished not only to eradicate all proof of sexual pleasure in public, but to promote an extremely limited set of sexual options for women. Women Against Rape complained about this trend among feminists years ago:

> it is highly offensive when groups or organizations think it is their place to tell men and women that the sex they practice is wrong and bad and shouldn't be seen on public view. It is just such attempts to judge and condemn individuals' ways of living, ways of relating, ways of dressing, etc. (e.g. the

implication that to wear 'sexy' clothes or make-up is letting the side down) that put many women off 'Women's Liberation'. This kind of moralism is the opposite of fighting for the possibility of different sexual relations, a fight which in large part depends upon a different power balance between the sexes, and which in some small part can be furthered by the depiction of sexual alternatives through pornographic material.

WAR, who coined the slogan, 'Yes means Yes, No means No; However we dress, Wherever we go', unlike WAVAW, never forgot that *the right to say yes* was as important as the right to say no; and that the choice should be determined by individual women, not imposed upon them by men *or* other women.

The recent attempt to remove a print of Goya's *Maja Desnuda* from the wall of a Pennsylvania college on the grounds that its existence sexually harassed female students has to be the limit. Calling the print sexual harassment, rather than obscene or immoral, merely replaces one rationale for proscription with another; and the fact that separatists keep quiet when moral crusaders attack politically committed feminist artists, because the work is sexually explicit, strongly implies that the separatists are more determined to outlaw the explicit than to promote feminism.

Double standards

The worst legacy of social purity is the 'she deserves it' syndrome about 'bad' girls, who having 'fallen' into the 'fate worse than death' (which is a very strange way to describe sex) were unable to rise. Yet it has never dawned on any of the naive 'feminists' or crusaders who keep shouting about rape-myth pornography that the one common belief held by all those exhibiting real callousness, as well as all those rapists in the prison studies, was the conviction they had a 'right' to 'try it on' in the first place. They did so because they 'knew' the women would appreciate their attentions, because they had 'had it' before. It is not a coincidence that the authorities and the media make a much bigger fuss over 'innocent' women who have been raped, and judges still make odious references about girls who are not 'angels'. And that means that it is coercive morality, not pornography, that is to blame for this. By promoting the same sentiments, modern moralists and separatists maintain the social climate in which women who indulge themselves sexually suffer a social stigma, leaving them open to attack.

I once wrote a Master's thesis about it; but willingly admit that Mary Hayward, the secretary of Campaign against Censorship, brilliantly summed it all up in a couple of paragraphs:

The distinction between actors and prostitutes was apt to get blurred even before the arrival of photography, but the slogan 'Porn degrades women' is ambiguous. On the one hand, it is a gesture of solidarity. The women's movement were entirely right to try to abolish the Victorian concept of whores as a subspecies. But in doing so they lay themselves wide open to takeover by people who still held the very Victorian idea that every woman who undresses in front of someone else is a whore, that every picture of a naked women is pornography. And the idea of the less than human – the degraded – slips back in ... desensitisation is our old friend depravity and corruption under another name, and there is nothing modern about it ... Sensibility is, among other things, the capacity to be easily shocked. It began as a fashion in behaviour among the educated and well to do and from there moved down the social scale. The nineteenth century social climate, and his wife, were pleased to fake a delicacy they did not necessarily feel. What had begun as a fashion then became a political tool. On the one hand Victorian husbands and fathers could threaten their women with loss of 'refinement' as an excuse to keep them ignorant ... Today ... the feminist lobby continue to mistake imaginary women for real ones and assume that men do the same. But they have adopted as their own both the Victorian conservatives' idea of women as mentally fragile creatures who must not encounter an offensive picture, and the Victorian radicals' idea of women as permanent victims.

They have developed a definition of womanhood every bit as oppressive as the one their predecessors fought to destroy. I think we can best oppose them by pointing this out, and by pointing out that since sex is still less important to men than it is to women, men in positions of power and influence might be quite happy to let them talk on and on about pornography instead of concentrating on quality, justice and freedom.

This insight, which dumps twenty years of so-called feminist scholarship in the waste bin, also raises important questions about, and helps to explain, the separatist hatred of soft core:

> The spread of female literacy happened to coincide with the rise of a cult of sensibility, culminating in the prudery we associate with the Victorians. Educated women remain in ignorance of a whole area of the male imagination. This ignorance was chipped away slowly, but did not finally crumble until the 1960s. It was supposed that women would welcome this new interest. But often they didn't, because they did not understand that they were being invited to share a fantasy, to take part in a game ... Pornography is very stylised. Women coming to it for the first time found its rules so strange that they did not realise that they were rules.

The more soft core becomes available, the more women learn the rules and lose their tendency to be 'offended', the greater the separatist's necessity to crush it, and step up their horror stories of maiming and murder in a desperate attempt to maintain the shock value.

The dependence of the contemporary campaign upon the sensibility of some women, their ability to be 'distressed', 'embarrassed', 'sickened', 'horrified', 'intimidated', and 'degraded' merely by the sight of naked breasts, is amply demonstrated by the letters protesting against Page Three in Ms Short's *Dear Clare*. This selection from her mailbag also provides a good guide to the sentiments the separatists and female crusaders hold in common, and the way in which the opposition to soft core relies upon this kind of indignation. Ms Short was, therefore, deluding herself and misleading the public when she told the *Independent*, back in September 1987:

> In the past anti-porn campaigners have been seen as repres-

sive ... we [CAP] are quite different. Because we can now prove that porn uses and degrades women, all kinds of people with liberal instincts will want to join us.

There is nothing liberal about social purity in a politically correct guise or otherwise; it is the nineteenth century revisited.

Social groups and social problems

There is sadly nothing special about misrepresentation in the battle over soft core. All people with strong beliefs, especially those who join crusading organizations, have a psychological need for affirmation of their personal beliefs. They need social reality to confirm their belief system. Anything else could lead to individual 'cognitive dissonance, widespread 'alienation' or 'anomie'. And it is this search for affirmation that provokes moral crusades, which will multiply in number as we enter the twenty-first century.

In the past, the powerful were able simply to impose their will on others to make them conform. Now growing affluence, by increasing individuals' choice of social group membership, is destroying the constraints of geographical parochialism, cultural myopia, and economic constraints; we will soon be living in a pluralistic society. Unfortunately, people whose social group identity rests upon strong beliefs rather than lifestyle preference have always worried that others' lifestyles may reveal the fallibilities of these beliefs, so they have good reason to fear pluralism. Not only does choice mean that an overt claim to the superiority of one style of life is unlikely to be tolerated by people who prefer another, but pluralism also makes it increasingly difficult for a social group to control their members' access to contrary beliefs. As a result, social groups engage in moral crusades to gain wider support for their beliefs, to maintain their members' convictions, and, they hope, by defeating the other group, to 'prove' their beliefs to be correct.

During the nineteenth century, evangelical Christians were probably the most important group outside the financial and military interests who tried to persuade or cajole the Government into adopting legislation. Since the mid-nineteenth century, they faced competition from an increasing number of professional groups, especially the socio-medical lobby. Since the late 1950s, however, everyone has got in on the act; and the groups who seek official support for their beliefs range from the women's and gay lobbies to dozens of professional agencies seeking to advance their own interests. Faced with so many competitors, a social group seeking to impose its will upon others will need a good reason to justify Government support, and/or neutralize the power of other social groups. The easiest way to do this is to label an aspect of the other group's lifestyle a social problem; and if one succeeds, the Government will not only pass legislation favouring the group, they may even fund one group's 'research' and diagnosis of the problem, just like the Justice Department funded Reisman's soft-core cartoon research. If the 'social problem' can be designated a criminal act, so much the better; the police will then enforce the social group's belief for them. The problem is, the wider the pluralism, the less likely is a single social group to achieve this on its own. Hence the search for issues which can secure alliances with other social groups and agencies in a mutual campaign of self-enhancement of power and belief. This is still possible in a pluralistic society because even very different groups can hold to some common values like the desire to protect children and dislike of violence. No wonder these appeals so frequently feature in crusades and have been so profitable.

The ultimate result, however, is self-defeating. It is no accident that social problem promotion through moral crusades in Britain is beginning to resemble those crazy set-piece battles in America, which, far from helping the real victims of real problems, merely demonstrate how social groups and professional agencies exploit victims and problems to force their will upon others; their ideological imperatives destroy both the truth and any possibility of a solution. Sadly the following example, highlighted by the victimologist Lyall, is now all too common:

> A college student tells the police that she was raped outside her dormitory late one night. She identifies a graduating senior in engineering who is a basketball star as her attacker by selecting his picture from the school year book and then

pointing him out in a police line-up. The rape charge polar-
izes the campus, in part because he is black and she is white.
His supporters view him as a victim of injustice; at rallies
they argue that the woman and the police, in their rush to
find the culprit, are having trouble distinguishing one black
man from another. Her supporters march in solidarity with
all women who have been assaulted and then disbelieved
when they came forward and ask for help. He is arrested,
and then released on bail, but is barred from campus except
to attend classes and use the library. She returns to her home
to study for her final exams. When a number of credible alibi
witnesses testify that the accused was far away from the
campus that night, the prosecutor drops the charges against
him and closes the case for lack of additional evidence or
investigatory leads.

Neither group exploiting the case really helped anybody. Both have
lost sight of the real problem they ideologically exploit. Yet this
nightmare for truth and justice is precisely where moral crusading
and political correctness is leading Britain. The only way to put the
brakes on is to rigorously challenge bogus arguments wherever they
arise, irrespective of one's personal feelings. As with racism and
rape, so with soft core. If one believes in the principles of honest,
integrity and justice, one has to cry foul when moral crusaders
abandon persuasion in open debate, close down that debate, and
then seek coercive means to impose their lifestyle upon others. If
one does not, we will all lose in the end.

Creating social problems

The means by which social groups produce social problems,
in order to force their morality upon others, are fairly uniform,
though there are variations. Silly sociologists used to call this process moral panic, and claim it was an invention of the media or
government; but behind every so-called panic since the mid-1960s
there stands a social group and/or professional agency pushing for
preference of its beliefs. The reason sociologists misread the situation was because they did not move on beyond the media and

authority figures with the power to legislate. Now pluralism makes it impossible to appeal to a single official value and norm. Because there are fewer absolute standards as once marginalized groups are mobilizing, support from Government will only follow if enough of the public can be grouped around one of the few remaining common standards. Only then can one gain the Parliamentary time and/or Government funding required to make an issue a social problem. This is exactly why the crusaders spend so much time trying to tar soft core with the brush of violence against women and child pornography. Both are abhorrent.

Any social group trying to create a social problem in order to win a battle with another group has to 'typify' that problem so that the description of the problem convinces the public that the social group's readymade solution appears to make sense. If it does not, someone may notice there are no real victims, or the real victims may want to speak for themselves, or some other group will get in first; children make the best 'victims', because no one really listens to them. In the case of pornography the problem is 'typified' by asserting that there is *now* a link between changing corner-store soft-core content and sexual violence; hence the need to place controls on something that has existed for thirty years.

Having determined the 'threat', described the problem, and offered a solution which enhances their interests, a social group or agency now has to supply evidence. As real evidence is obviously hard to find in a clash of beliefs, it has to be transcended by the generation of horror stories, and reference to 'experts' who will verify both the truth of 'the evidence' and the efficacy of the solution. Most horror stories are generated by the social group itself, as a means to affirm group beliefs. Peddling such stories to a wider public is aided by the way in which the news media like to present dramatic stories to their customers. Exaggeration and distortion have always been endemic in sensational reporting. It is secured, as Stan Cohen noted many years ago, by: misleading headlines; use of the generic plural, where one example is passed off as many; the repetition of false stories; stereotypical images of the alleged 'criminal'; the reporting of opinion as if it were fact; the promotion of dubious casualties, such as the mere correlation of 'facts'; a disaster orientation, whereby we are sold the crusaders' solution as the means to avert the disaster; and an implied consensual model of society that all decent people would agree with, in contrast to the actions of the deviant social group.

Tabloid sensationalism is a breeding ground for social problem horror stories; but, as the pornography 'debate' now makes clear, tabloid journalism is not restricted to the tabloids. Such 'stories', for stories they are, have a clear and overt social function: to convince the wider public that the crusaders' analysis of the situation is correct and that the public should adopt their solution to the alleged problem rather than an alternative.

The most consistent crusader and separatist horror story has been their 'snuff movie' fantasy, illustrated by this version penned by Ms Corcoran:

> I want to describe it to you in detail. But I cannot, because my mind won't let me. What I can tell you is that on that night I watched a man participate in the act of sex with a women, and during that act he plunged a large hunting knife into her stomach and cut her open from vagina to breast. He then withdrew the knife and stuck it into her left hand, removing the first three joints from her fingers, which fell from the bed. The woman's eyes remained open, she looked at the knife and said 'Oh God, not me'. It took her approximately three minutes to die. The camera was left running. The film was then canned and put on the commercial market as entertainment.

This version, from her *Pornography: The New Terrorism*, took the snuff movie story to Ireland to invoke a crusade against soft core over there. The real problem was that when Corcoran called a press conference to expose this movie, she was unable to show it, let alone play it, because of a fault on the VCR. How convenient. Upset by the media's negative reaction to this pathetic failure to deliver her 'evidence', Corcoran now tells us that she has lived in fear ever since, with a stun gun at her bedside, knowing 'that while rape, degradation and dehumanization of women are filmed and sold as entertainment, women's status in society is worthless ...'

Unfortunately for Corcoran, she was too late; between 1977 and 1990 crusader horror stories suffered from hyperinflation.

Now that no doped-up, Satanic, abortion-delivering, sadomaso-chistic, bestial-rape full, snuff movie featuring a crucified six-month foetus which is then eaten by the participants has been produced, despite *Dispatches*' attempt to pass off an Orridge movie as something like it, the public are getting a wee bit sceptical. They are certainly not going to buy Dworkin's sick 'skull-fucking' substitute either.

As for snuff: this is an urban legend. Its origins lay in the crusader's belief that the gruesome spectacles of the Colosseum would inevitably find their way into pornography. The first known snuff story actually appears in the Bible's Judges 19, where a husband cuts up his wife after having handed her over to a mob to be gang-raped instead of face up to them himself! American crusaders spread stories about Mexican snuff movies during the late 1970s, and the rumours grew upon the back of a low-budget horror movie *Snuff*, ironically made to exploit the hype. *Slaughter*, as it was originally called in 1971, was purchased by Alan Shackleton of Monarch Pictures, who added an extra scene, depicting an actress being murdered. With the new title *Snuff*, it was released in 1975 with publicity material included the slogans 'Made in South America Where Life Is Cheap', and 'The Picture They Said Could Never Be Made'. It fooled a lot of people, not least a cop, who then retold the story in a 1975 news release:

Latest Porno: Actual Murder

New York (UPI) – Police are investigating the circulation of a bizarre brand of pornographic movies which show the actual murder and dismemberment of an actress on screen.

Viewers at private screenings reportedly pay up to $2000 to witness the filmed killings, Detective Joseph Horman of the Police Department's Organized Crime Control Bureau said Wednesday.

Horman said very reliable sources say there are eight movies – called 'snuff' or 'slasher' films – being circulated.

'I had first heard about them from a reporter,' Horman

continued. 'As a result of that initial inquiry I sought out my sources in the underworld, sources who have proven to be very reliable in the past. They said that in the end, the climax depicts the actual murder of the female.'

He indicated the films begin with an actress and several actors engaging in a variety of sex acts. Soon, however, a knife appears, and the actress – obviously unaware of the nature of the film – is stabbed to death and dismembered.

He said a number of films simulated death, but the eight he is after show real killings.

'We came closest in Miami. This was where we actually pinpointed them as recently as seven days ago,' said the detective, who is working on the case with four other members of the bureau. 'It's such a secret operation, that these things are well guarded. In Miami I had a source who had access to it, but apparently the FBI is putting quite a bit of pressure on in Southern Florida and that killed it.'

This cop clearly was no film buff; he did not even know what slasher movies were! And as for Miami: where else? If this were the 1930s, they would have turned up in Chicago. The moral crusaders played this up for all it was worth, and the growing legend was even incorporated into the plots of major films like *Blue Movie* and *Videodrome*.

Though snuff movies have long since been dropped by the crusaders, separatists like Liz Kelly do not seem to be able to resist it. In her 1990 speech to the Scottish WAP, she not only claimed that there was a European syndicate targeting single women travelling alone for their movies, but insisted that the Obscene Publications Squad had 'recently seized videos which record the murder of children'.

The only snuff movie report that comes anywhere near the truth to date concerns those made by a certain Mr Ng, a rabid anti-communist, who having made himself a nuclear survival bunker went around kidnapping couples in the 1980s. The men were shot after being hunted down for sport, and the women were killed in the bunker, having apparently been made to watch the video of the previous victim. While we wait for details to emerge in court, it should be noted that these movies were not made for, and never appeared in, your local video store.

Snuff, of course, is hardly soft-core pornography; but by insisting that *Penthouse* and *Escort* promote attitudes that lead to snuff, they can then be tarred with the same brush.

Apart from their horror stories, social groups need an 'exppert' or two to validate their claims about the 'social problem'. This obviously presents a difficulty when the target is a new problem, as there cannot be any 'experts' – though crusaders can always find one. If no 'expert' is found from among the crusaders themselves, there are many people from professional bodies seeking to take advantage of the issue to further their own interests. Police personnel, social workers, unknown psychiatrists or unemployed therapists will queue up to fulfil this role, especially if a fee or TV appearance is involved; though their only credibility rests upon the media which offer them exposure owing to the need for an 'expert opinion' for sound bites.

In the case of pornography, Christians resort to Dr 'Correlation' Court, and the separatists call upon a gaggle of ideological academics palming off their political beliefs as 'research'. When someone points out that an English literature or theology degree is not the kind of qualification one expects from a pornography 'expert', they can call in a buzz-box billy or rat-psychologist who hopes to secure another research grant by pandering to political correctness.

Armed with a typification, a solution, a suitable horror story and a resident expert, social groups now have to find a suitable tabloid TV 'documentary' or sensation-mongering chat show to promote their beliefs as a concern about a new and dangerous social problem to the public, and then persuade an ally in the Commons in need of a few votes to demand legislation; and there are always hundreds of those.

If all else fails they may appeal to 'common sense'. Though outlawing soft core is peddled as the solution to violence against women, Meese and company have to overcome the lack of evidence about effects and content by promoting bogus separatists' accounts of soft-core crimes, and by appealing to 'common sense' about half a dozen features of soft core which demonstrate its harmfulness. Far from describing soft-core content, however, these descriptive definitions tell people how they *should* interpret the content, and make no sense at all unless they are also designed to tell people how to behave sexually.

Degradation

Soft core is supposed to degrade and humiliate the women who appear in it; but to be degraded requires that one be graded or graced in the first place. As these charges only ever appear to apply to the female models it appears to have something to do with what they are doing. While such a charge *does* make some sense from the Christian perspective in which one is degraded through lustful sex for the godly state of grace humans enjoy, to suggest that pornography degrades women is somewhat sexist; why not men too? Clearly Christians think there is something extra special about women engaging in non-marital sex. As this mystery is surpassed by the separatists who never tell us by what standard they are judging, all we are left with is the idea that it is degrading for a woman to be portrayed as a sexual being. As this is a patriarchal belief, designed to promote a sense of shame in women who desire sex, it could hardly make sense from a 'feminist' point of view.

If we then look at the specific acts listed in the 'feminist' Ordinances or Meese's Christian Report which are deemed to be degrading, we see they all relate to non-procreative and non-monogamous sex acts: oral sex, multiple partners, dressing in fetish clothing, and so on. While this clearly implies that women can avoid being degraded by restricting sex to private, monogamous, procreative acts, we are not told whether the degradation follows from the public display, the non-procreative aspects, or the fact that women may be getting pleasure from such acts. Both groups do, however, imply that for a woman to concentrate on giving pleasure to men is degrading; they thereby imply that a failure to ensure simultaneous pleasures in equal proportions (in an unspecified way) is also illegitimate sex. What we appear to have, therefore, is that the crusaders have an ideal about the way women should behave sexually, and that they think anything else is undesirable, deviant, or ethically wrong. But who are they to judge? Given their complaints about lesbian pornography, separatists clearly do not approve of public display at all; but as their core complaint is that women are *de facto* degraded by having sex with men, this certainly is not common sense either.

One way to examine this problem is to look at a second complaint that pornography 'misrepresents' what women are. Women, we are told, are not 'panting playthings with no mind of her own' or the 'insatiable uninhibited nymphomaniacs' they are shown to be, because they have a different sexual nature. There are three problems with this kind of common sense.

First, 'misrepresentation' is an imported American charge based upon explicit soft-core actions so very different from the British fare that it would require one to add this interpretation to a pin-up. Crusaders are good at this. They even assert that soft core divides women into Madonna or whore stereotypes, when *Escort* and other British bestsellers are popular precisely because they dismissed that dichotomy, and actively reduced the gap between 'pin-up' and partner over a decade ago. The only people maintaining the dichotomy today are the crusaders, patriarchs, and rapists.

Second, how on earth can soft core simultaneously represent a woman as a panting man-eating nympho when the separatists' major complaint is that women are presented as passive objects? Either/or maybe; but to accept that possibility, the crusaders would have to abandon their insistence that pornography presented a single message.

Third, to say that an image misrepresents women's real nature is also to assert that women only have a single sexual nature. The crusaders obviously wish they did: the Christian's – a wife for a husband; and the separatist's – a political lesbian. The major problem with this interpretation is not that they are ignoring over a hundred years of anthropology, psychology, sexology, and sociology, but that as Christians and separatists cannot even agree among themselves what this single nature is, their convictions about that 'nature' clearly reflect their belief systems rather than biology. Ultimately this accusation is a demand that women should adopt the crusaders', or separatists', preference, and their real complaint is that soft core offers an alternative to their own view of women's 'nature'.

In reality, soft core and hard core offer several 'natures', witnessed by the different genres which present a multitude of perspectives on sex and women. Admittedly, most pornographic imagery does not do this in depth; but then neither does a soccer match philosophize about soccer. The meanings are left up to the spectator. Pornographic texts can diverge widely. One only has to compare a copy of *Forum* to one of *Debbie Does Dallas* to see this. But the lack of depth does not negate the fact that the arrival of female-orientated material has brought dozens more possibilities to the top shelf's diversity of sexual images and ideas. What the crusaders are really condemning is sexual pluralism rather than a single 'male' message. The lengths the separatists will go to to impose their single view upon this diversity can be seen in their absurd assertion that gay male pin-ups are substitute 'women' from the point of degradation, in an effort to cover a glaring gap in their theories of 'the role pornography plays in women's oppression'. No doubt many Christians still subscribe to the erroneous Freudian twaddle that 'passive' gay men *are* acting a woman's role; but separatists have no such excuse. In sum, while the Christian complaints make sense in Christian terms, they are not widely accepted; and the separatists' arguments make no sense at all.

Humiliation

When they are not used to prove that soft core is degrading, the same lists of sexual activities are offered as proof that women are 'humiliated' in pornography. This is a very odd charge for Christians to make, given that to be humiliated is to be humbled; though I can understand why separatists dislike the idea.

To claim, as Dworkinites do and Meese did, that performing oral sex on a male is *de facto* humiliating for the women requires one of two assumptions: that the act itself is a humiliating thing to do, or that the woman is merely *serving* the man, and not receiving pleasure herself. The latter could hardly be the case given the standard format whereby the male always performs a similar service. To avoid this embarrassing fact, and to justify their interpretation, crusaders always redefine the act to suit their case, so that pornography only ever consists of men doing things to women, or women having to do things for men. If a male is being *serviced* by several women, they are his harem; yet if a woman is being *serviced* by several men, they are gang-raping her. But to 'prove' that this is the only possible perception, they have to fall back on the idea that the depiction of an active women is a degrading misrepresentation of woman's true nature, but this being a self-referential circular argument is no proof at all.

The fallacy that soft core degrades and humiliates women suggest that crusaders will say anything to put the clock back, and avoid the issue of sexual pluralism in pornography. Some pornography *does* show women as mindless, some as insatiable nymphos, and some as intelligent human beings who simply enjoy sex; but as British soft core is not explicit enough to depict the activities listed, upon which the imported American charges are based, we are ultimately left with the idea that female nudity is degrading or humiliating.

Separatists constantly deny that simple nudity is a target, but this is belied by Ms Short's Bill to outlaw 'indecent' newspaper pin-ups, pin-ups which are alleged to turn women into 'sex objects' and to offer stereotypes that create impossible expectations in men's minds. Apart from the obvious contradiction in these complaints, the latter makes no sense given the pluralistic beauty displayed in the pages of *Escort* and *Fiesta*, or gay magazines, where models come in all shapes; soft core sells precisely because it caters for multiple tastes rather than imposing a standard.

Christian crusaders' concerns about nudity are easier to understand, given their rent-a-quote approach to the Bible, from inferences about 'nakedness' in Genesis onwards. Their real problem, however, is the failure to consider the extent to which the conflict between an adherent's faith and desires can play in this. Caton, for example, while only too aware of swimwear catalogues, is completely oblivious to the fact that others do not have his problem, so he blames the conflict between his secret illicit desires and his high religious standards on everything from bra adverts to *Playboy*. Those who do not aspire to Caton's impossible standards, who do not believe they are committing a sin by joining a naturist club, will never become 'slaves to compulsive hedonism' like Caton did. A strong faith coupled with a healthy approach to sex should not cause a Christian any problems. Despite my having seen Linzi Drew's body a hundred times in magazines and on video during my research, sexual desire, let alone obsessive compulsions, never entered my head when I finally met her during a TV programme in Manchester – though I did spot a moralist salivating. Christians who find themselves suffering from such problems should avoid Caton, and instead try John White's excellent *Eros Defiled: The Christian and Sexual Guilt*.

Once again, recourse to deceptions and misrepresentations, while ignoring other factors, means there is no 'common sense' in the charge examined; this is merely another demand that women should not engage in public display.

Objectification and instrumental sex

The implication behind the charge of 'sex object' is the dumb politically correct ideal that one human being should never objectify another. This could never make any sense given how quickly modern society would collapse if we all tried to avoid objectifying one another.

When I lecture to a class, I objectify the students, and they, sensibly, objectify me; if we did not do this together we would never start the lecture, let alone finish it. When I tutor students, I personalize the individual; if I did not do this, I could not help to improve their performance. With the exception of the separatists, who make a virtue of always objectifying men, everybody slips in and out of numerous states of mental focus to objectify one minute and personalize the next, a thousand times a day. So if soft-core readers objectify, they are doing nothing unusual, merely judging by a temporary and transitory standard. Like the charges that soft core shows only one dimension of life, or misrepresents the 'whole person', the sin of 'objectification' ignores the fact that very few media products do not objectify. All magazines and TV programmes specializing in subjects like sport, food, fashion, hobbies, and politics depersonalize those presenting and appearing in them; in doing so they, like novels, do not rob individuals of an essential something because they are *not* discussing sex, despite the fact that if people did not have sex, the planet would soon be depopulated – which makes sex a very important part of everyone's lives. Likewise, all pictures objectify their subjects whether it is Micky Quinn scoring a goal, or one of those anonymous anorexic ballerinas in the line at Covent Garden. Why should we have to consider a TV cook's sex life, or a topless model's taste in food to appreciate their particular role at a particular time? The only reason for denying sex any public place is the silly notion that we should elevate the mental over the base physical aspects of humans, and that sex should be completely private.

In turn this notion rests upon two other beliefs, or rather obsessions. The first is the neurotic Christian one that fleshly desires and functions are dirty. Has anyone else noticed that those who like to quote Matthew 5: 28 (which actually requires one to be lusting after the woman to have committed the offence) never carry out the command in Matthew 5: 29 to pluck out the eye that offended them. The second obsession is the neo-secular class-orientated cultural imperialism which insists upon transforming 'dirty', degrading sex into clean 'erotica'. This one has always bemused me; as I must confess I never saw anything elevating about less-than-half-dressed people bouncing around a stage pretending it has something to do with a fairy story at a subsidized £40 a ticket, or a couple of squiggles on a canvas priced at £400,000. Anyone who dichotomizes the mind and the flesh is hardly promoting the search for the whole person anyway, which means there is little common sense in this charge.

Christian crusaders have stronger arguments when insisting that soft core is an instrumental, non-reciprocal form of gratification; not being sacramental, it is obviously sinful. But once again we are left to ponder why they concentrate upon instrumental sex, rather than all those other instrumental acts in modern society like making money and buying houses or cars. Separatists have no arguments. They do not think sex should be for fun either; but at least they do not discriminate against sex. As demonstrated by Corinne Sweet's list of all the other elements of patriarchal culture separatists counsel against because they are addictive (read: pleasurable) and designed to glue people to the system (read: why people like the system), separatists are consistent. After pornography, separatists wish to abolish: birthday parties, sugar, chocolate, fizzy drinks, cream cakes, credit cards, gambling, soap operas, tobacco, wedding breakfasts and funeral wakes, and, in order to get more feminist therapy fees, agony aunts. For separatists nothing is to be treated lightly, frivolously or hedonistically. In their canon, everything, including sex, has only one purpose, and people must be made to conform. But whereas Christians would limit women's choice to honouring their husbands, the separatists think they should be living in a wimmin's commune, with one of them.

Callousness, violence and rape

The recent claims that soft core makes men have callous thoughts and actions about women owes much to Zillmann's research, which, as Alison King's critique in *Good Girls and Dirty Pictures* has shown, is simply untenable. The fallacies upon which this research was based included: redefining male violence against women, so that, for example, having sex with a woman who has drunk alcohol becomes a callous act, on the presumption that women would say no if they had not done so; and a study which claimed that 23 per cent of American males cannot stop themselves – which, of course, means that 77 per cent do. Ironically, the theory ultimately requires one to believe that pornography's powerful effect is all due to its vivid and capitivating content, which is an odd thing for Zillmann to say given that his most famous study's results rested upon the assertion that it was the soft-core-induced 'boredom' that led people to seek out other more violent or bizarre forms! It also conveniently requires one to bury the females' results in order to maintain the stereotype of men as instrumental, and to label the subjects' rejection of the double standard as callous. One would have thought that if soft core encourages men and women to abandon this kind of double standard it should be welcomed; unless one wants to keep it.

As soft core reduces aggression levels in those predisposed to anger, I need only to say two things about the crusaders' charge of violence here.

First, crusaders' and separatists' examples of alleged soft-core violent imagery invariably come from splatter movies, or Fem-Dom material. Some separatists are correct to point out that this is also a male fantasy, and most models are paid; this raises the awkward question of why men would like being dominated: it means that many men would not wish to see women being degraded, but themselves. Thus crusaders now have to explain away the possibility that when we see men in dominant roles in fantasy pornography, or 'willing' women in pin-ups, this may reflect the consumer's real experience of powerlessness with women. At the very least, the fact that men seek out different kinds of material suggests there is no single message, and down goes a core foundation of 'pornography effects' theories.

Second, Dr Zillmann a well-known opponent of pornography. He holds the ideals of love and marriage in high regard. He is not an advocate of instrumental sex. He is, however, highly regarded as an expert on sex and aggression, which is not surprising. Having spent a lifetime researching aggression, if anyone knows anything about the mechanism of the eroticization of 'pain' in mammals, it is Dr Zillmann. I have all his books. My favourite is *Connections between Sex and Aggression* in which he tells us:

> As the arousing capacity of novel partners is *likely to fade* and acute emotional reactions such as fear and guilt are improbable accompaniments of sexual activity, what can be done to combat the drabness of routine sexual engagements that is expected to result from excitatory habituation? *Roughhousing, pinching, biting* and *beating* emerge as viable answers. In terms of theory, it is the *controlled* infliction of pain that holds promise of reliably producing excitatory reactions for transfer into sexual behaviour and experience. The excitatory capacity of acute pain is not in doubt. Moreover, *pain is extremely resistant to habituation.* Acute pain then always can be counted on to stir up excitement. It is the habituation fighter par excellence. [emphasis added]

While Zillmann is hardly advocating heavy sadomasochism, he does provide an acceptable reason why so many couples take to and love a little 'roughhousing'. What is more, this world expert destroys thousands of crusaders' assertions about addiction in the process. Indeed, he expands upon what he means in such cases, and thereby helps those not versed in the psychological or medical use of terms like 'acute', 'aggression' and 'pain', to get the full picture:

It appears that there is no substitute for pain as a reliable standby for the creation of excitedness, in case it is lacking. *Pinching, scratching, sucking, biting, squeezing, pulling, shoving* and *hitting* constitute the bulk of the arsenal of aggression-related arousers that can be exploited for the enhancement of drab sexual endeavours. And in exploiting these means, receiving tends to work better than giving. [emphasis added]

Who am I to disagree? To spell it out: violence and playful biting and squeezing are not the same thing; and the vast majority of so-called 'violent' pornography is sex-play, not harmful aggression.

Exploitation

Of all the charges against soft core, that of exploitation has to be the most hypocritical.

Christian crusaders like to suggest that, ethically, pornography exploits sex. They are correct; but as the Canadian philosopher Christensen pointed out, it does so in exactly the same way that *The Waltons* exploits families and family life. Charges that soft core is unrealistic and not true to life are true. Yes, and truly hypocritical too; for if pornography *is* unrealistic fantasy then bang goes most of the other complaints against it. Unless, of course, one wants to outlaw fantasy.

The worse form of hypocrisy arises from those charges concerning economic exploitation. Soft core modelling is no different from other forms of modelling where the lion's share of the profit goes to those who pay the model for signing over the total rights to the product. This is unfair, but not unusual. I have to sign a similar form, throwing away all rights to the film, when I am interviewed by the BBC or a film company. But if the crusaders are so concerned about structural social and economic disadvantage being the cause of soft-core employment (which it rarely is), why are they not doing something about these wider problems, or unionizing the modelling industry? The answer is they are not really worried about the conditions that could lead to exploitation.

My advice to those who are going to model is to start by

demanding double what you are offered, and strike out those 'no claim on further use' clauses.

Diversity

From degradation to exploitation, the crusaders' complaints, far from making common sense, only amount to saying that soft core offers an alternative to their own view about sex, and that it appears more common than their own; that is why they want it outlawed.

National VALA's complaint that soft core is the propaganda of permissiveness is correct. The real 'effect' of soft core is the promotion of a *laissez-faire* approach to sex: the idea that some men and some women like instrumental, gratuitous, and non-discriminatory sex, when they feel in the mood. It is no more than that.

What crusaders refuse to accept is that this approach to sex does not mean that all soft core viewers will consequently see all women merely as 'sex objects'; it is obvious that separatist feminism will make sure of that. Nor will all men become callous and violent towards all women; because soft core does not promote those values. Soft core does not even promote paraphiliac (sexual minority) behaviour. As John Money's lifelong research at Johns Hopkins University makes perfectly clear, people's sexual orientations have been formalized long before they get to soft core. And as paraphiliac fantasies are not socially contagious (you can't catch urolagnia from watching a movie), those who seek out minority sexual material do so and are attracted to them because the behaviour depicted already interests them.

Soft core merely presents a slice of modern life, and by buying it, some people are saying 'no thank you' to the crusader and separatist lifestyles. It does not mean that consumers then automatically subscribe to everything else National VALA fears. Like the rest of us, soft-core readers also want the Government to do something about juvenile crime, the growing recourse to interpersonal violence, rape, mugging, ram raiding, school bullying, noisy neighbours, and so on; they simply do not believe that these problems are caused by perusing the top shelf. And if they have read this book, they will now know that hard core does not lead to violence either. Where pornography is freely available in Europe it has had little impact upon the crime statistics either way, whereas if Dr Court was correct there should not be a woman alive in continental Europe by now; and the fact it has little impact is simply because pornography is not a major factor in sex crime.

The real choice facing Britain, therefore, is not between legalizing soft core and sexual violence on the one hand, and outlawing soft core to achieve sexual harmony on the other; but between sexual diversity and a coercive law which indiscriminately punishes all material from nudity upwards, with no secular justification whatsoever, so that crusaders can be happy in the knowledge that the public do not have the choice to make the 'wrong' decision, and may continue to ignore the social harms caused by the lack of sensible sex education.

Sex crimes

The real problem facing Britain is that those who complain most loudly about sex crimes have no solutions. They have none because they have deluded themselves about the cause, by constantly lying about content, research, and the real aim of their crusade. As a result, they merely promote sexual prejudice in particular and misinformation about sexuality in general. This philosophy, of more controls by any excuse, has led to a shame morality at any price, which apart from the police harassment of sexual minorities has led to the Satanic panic which, by tearing hundreds of children from the family home of their innocent parents, has done far more to destroy the family in the last decade than council queue-hopping by teenage mothers ever did. Meanwhile, the crusaders have done nothing for sex crime victims personally, nor have they contributed to society's understanding of the origins and consequences; quite the reverse.

Sexual violence, unfortunately, has been around for a long time, but as pornography did not exist until very recently, 99.99 per cent of history's rapists never saw a soft-core magazine, let alone listened to 2 *Live Crew* or visited a Mapplethorpe exhibition. For people so predisposed, anything is capable of justifying their actions, as Supreme Court justice William O'Douglas once made clear:

> There is no 'hard core'. Everything, every idea, is capable of being obscene if the personality perceiving it so apprehends it ...
>
> Heinrich Pommerenke, who was a rapist, abuser, and mass slayer of women in Germany, was prompted in his series of ghastly deeds by Cecil B. De Mille's *The Ten Commandments*. During the scene of the Jewish women dancing around the Golden Calf, all the doubts of his life became clear: women were the source of the world's trouble and it was his mission to punish them for this and to execute them. Leaving the theatre, he slew his first victim in a park nearby.

On 3 September 1988, Douglas Hurd, then Home Secretary, sensibly acknowledged that while sex criminals may watch blue movies, a three-month police monitoring exercise, recording any evidence of the perpetrators' collection or use of pornographic material, discovered a miserly 48 cases in which offenders appeared to have viewed pornographic videos or magazines before committing crimes, and most of these charges were for indecent exposure. In a letter to Mrs Whitehouse, Mr Hurd apparently revealed that further investigations suggested that there was no evidence that pornography had been the cause of the offences, for these perpetrators would have committed them anyway. Mr Hurd thought that it would be surprising if among all the other influences, pornography was not sometimes a factor; after all, failing to find a connection did not mean that there was not one. And in doing so he made an important point.

Given that modern technology can enable those who seek out sexual images to obtain them, and prevent those who wish to control them from doing so, it is time we began to reformulate and initiate some means of encouraging allegiance to moral values which abhor and inhibit sexual crimes, rather than wasting our time whining about soft core. Rather than ideologically exploiting the victims' misery and encouraging fear, or allowing the police to try to justify the crusaders' perverse psychotic fantasies about snuff, sex, and Satan, we need a systematic assessment of the way in which some materials may be used by some people to promote interpersonal crimes. As the vast majority of people who purchase and read soft core never think of engaging in sex crime, let alone commit it, we need to explore seriously those factors and beliefs which encourage some people to do so.

We can start with the research studies that crusaders love to quote, while failing to realize that they provide accumulating evidence that sexual aggression and callousness are exhibited by people who have a cluster of predispositions including authoritarianism, sexual ignorance, strong guilt at arousal, conservative values and attitudes towards women, belief in violence as conflict resolution, no ability to emphasize with anyone, and so on. You will not find any of these values being promoted by soft core; for only those who see sex as defiling, or active women as 'fallen', could possibly see sex as a means to hurt women.

To blame soft core for sex attacks makes no more sense than claiming that women provoke attacks if they dress in mini-skirts or skimpy blouses. So we also need to explore the Victorian moral, political, and ideological beliefs which still promote such attitudes. If we had spent just a tenth of the money wasted on pornography aggression research in this direction we might understand a lot more about sex criminals from the Yorkshire Ripper to the Putney rapist. If we banned soft core tomorrow, they would still be out there. And as sex criminals who blame their actions on God and the Devil clearly lack an allegiance to a sensible moral code, as do coercive partners who sometimes seek to copy what they may see with an unwilling partner, we need to look at that question.

As pornography cannot have any adverse effect upon people who have a moral code and who maintain a balanced perspective on life, we need to place greater effort and energy upon reviewing the upbringing and beliefs of the predisposed, to discover what may have led to their compulsions in the first place, and then to improve our civic education accordingly. Though this make take longer than outlawing soft core, it certainly will be more useful.

This will, of course, require Christian crusaders to face up to the fact that there is a fundamental contradiction between a free-market economy and their dream of imposing a single lifestyle upon society, and that any attempt to reconcile the two is doomed to failure. Hopefully, the Christian community will drop those stones, and discover why so many of pornography's worst 'effects' appear among those who had a 'religious' upbringing. A little thought about counter-productive activities could go a long way; God is hardly going to be fooled by an odd law here and there, for He knows there are far greater sins around.

As the separatists will never face up to anything, they are unlikely to realize that there is a contradiction between the promotion of gender equality and the fantasy that the women who benefit will not adopt instrumental attitudes to life. Nor will their politically correct friends grasp the ethical contradiction between promoting equal opportunities and telling people how to behave. So these people simply have to be stopped; there is no hope for them.

Some members of the anti-censorship lobby cannot afford to be smug either; decriminalization is one thing, but encouraging recklessness is another. As things stand at the moment, I certainly would not advise simply opening the Pandora's box of pornography in a free-market free-for-all. Any liberalization of the law would require a simultaneous overhaul of the UK's grossly inadequate sex education. To this end, the recent introduction of sex education videos serves a useful purpose; but it would also prove useful if all 'hard-core' material produced or imported into the UK carried a couple of detailed educational pages, akin to the advice given in the *Forum* Comment published in every issue of the magazine.

It is up to the rest of us to try and ensure that the Government stops taking advantage of the existence of sex crime to seek cheap votes with 'moral values' conference speeches every September. Where is the detailed inquiry into the way British courts approach cases of sex crime in general, and rape in particular? The need for reform here should not be side-tracked by opposing those trying to exploit the issue of 'date rape' to further their own ends, and to redefine premarital sex as rape. It is very easy to see which beliefs and assumptions can place women (and gay men) at a disadvantage in these situations; and that anyone who claims they did not realize that the victim's 'no' meant 'no' clearly did not know them well enough to be having sex with them in the first place.

Likewise, when is the Government going to sort out sex education programmes for schools, which continue to fall between the two stools of the 'condom culture' and the 'just say no' brigades? While we continue to underestimate the level of children's curiosity about sex, we worry far too much about giving children appropriate sex education lessons. The Dutch have a simple system which appears to work very well. During his or her school career, a child receives three blocks of age-appropriate sex education lessons which cover no more, but no less, than is needed at each particular stage. The effect is drastically to reduce the growing child's uninformed guesswork and needless worries, so that, by the time they leave school, teenagers know everything they need to know about both the mechanics and the ethics of sex. The ultimate result is not, as some would have you believe, a completely liberal society, but a nation of people who, like myself, are somewhat conservative in their own habits, but extremely tolerant and practical when it comes to others' preferences.

More powers

The simple solution to the supposed obscenity problem has been offered by solicitor Patrick Stevens. If the 1959 Act is to be amended, the Government should build on the real consensus that exists in Britain and outlaw any material involving children or real sexual violence. His first step would be to bring mainstream pornography into the existing certification system with a category 'P'. A second step might be to initiate a consent form system to enable companies providing material for sexual minority interests to document that they are not engaged in any form of coercion. The police, closely advised by someone who knows what they are talking about, can then concentrate upon any material which involves a real crime – the supply-side sickos; and where possession of such material would be a crime – the demand-side demented.

Unfortunately, as I write, Kenneth Clarke, the current Home Secretary, and the Prime Minister, John Major, have announced that the police are to be given greater powers of search and arrest in a 'major crackdown' on pornography. In a letter to Ann Winterton, and later at the Party Conference, they were seeking to 'streamline' the 'complex and time consuming procedures for seizing pornographic material', and to end the 'court delays' which have apparently hindered the 'fight against pornography'. This will not come as a surprise to anyone who has been on the wrong side of the Obscene Publications Act. The justification that the police have problems gaining convictions against porn-filled warehouses when the 'incriminating documents' are held elsewhere will certainly bemuse the May family, for it did not stop them being charged. Yet the proposal is to give the police more powers to search and arrest without a warrant, and to give the same powers to Trading Standards Officers. This will merely ensure that more police time will be wasted on the easy task of handing out criminal records to people whose only crime is watching sex for pleasure, while less effort will be spent on the more difficult task of putting rapists behind bars; there is new and accumulating evidence that the British public gets the law and consequences it deserves.

Me? I'm going to learn Dutch, and get the first plane over there.

Further Reading

IN a popular book of this kind it is impossible to cover in any great depth all the arguments and issues that have been raised over the years. Readers who would like to pursue some of the themes covered will greatly enhance their understanding of the issues by reading the following:

Feminism

Assieter, Alison and Carol, Avedon. 1993. *Bad Girls and Dirty Pictures*. London, Pluto Press. An exciting introduction to British anti-censorship feminism.

Bouchier, David. 1983. *The Feminist Challenge*. London, Macmillan. Covers the contradictions and problems in the movement that opened the way for the anti-pornography strategy.

Burstyn, Varda, ed. 1985. *Women against Censorship*. Vancouver, Douglas & McIntyre. An interesting collection of essays covering early justifications for anti-censorship feminism.

Ellis, Kate *et al.*, eds. 1988. *Caught Looking: Feminism, Pornography and Censorship*. Seattle, Real Comet Press. A very interesting presentation of half a dozen seminal anti-censorship feminist essays.

Roberts, Nicky. 1986. *The Front Line*. London, Star. Covers sex industry work.

Rodgerson, Gillian and Wilson, Elizabeth. 1991. *Pornography and Feminism: The Case against Censorship*. London, Lawrence & Wishart. The initial FAC arguments against censorship, and the need to question single-issue crusading.

Segal, Lynne and McIntosh, Mary, eds. 1992. *Sex Exposed: Sexuality and the Pornography Debate*. London, Virago. A collection of essays from the academic members of FAC. Worth persevering with, despite its academic approach.

Criminology and sociology

Greek, Cecil and Thompson, William. 1995. *PornWars*. London, Aldyne. Based on ten years' scholarship, this provides detailed discussion about the motivations and consequences of pornography legislation, especially in America. Academic, but very readable.

Lyman, Stanford. 1989. *The Seven Deadly Sins: Society and Evil*. Revised and expanded edition. Dix Hills, NY, General Hall. America's best sociologist covering the philosophical issues involved.

Thompson, William. 1992. 'Britain's moral majority', in Wilson, B. *Religion: Contemporary Issues*. London, Bellew. Instant introduction to the rise of Britain's moral majority.

Law

Feinberg, Joel. 1985. *Offence To Others: The Moral Limits of the Criminal Law*. Oxford, Oxford University Press. Uses the issue of obscenity to discuss the function of law in public morality.

Robertson, Geoffrey. 1979. *Obscenity*. London, Weidenfeld & Nicolson. Still the best book on the legal aspects.

Sutherland, John. 1982. *Offensive Literature: Decensorship in Britain 1960–1982*. London, Junction. Covers the major court cases, item by item.

Separatist feminism

Barry, Kathleen. 1979. *Female Sexual Slavery*. New York, New York University Press. An excellent collection of horror stories for urban-legend students, with the odd disturbing case of men's exploitation of women.

Itzin, Dr Catherine, ed. 1992. *Pornography: Women, Violence and Civil Liberties: A Radical View*. Oxford, Oxford University Press. The attempt to justify the import of the Ordinances to Britain. As most articles strongly reflect the views of the American movement, this will save you having to plough through Dworkin, MacKinnon, and the rest.

Rhodes, Dusty and McNeill, Sandra. 1985. *Women Against Violence Against Women*. London, Onlywomen Press. A collection of papers charting WAVAW's self-delusion, and ideological exploitation of real social problems.

Short, Clare. 1991. *Dear Clare ... This Is What Women Feel about Page 3*. London, Radius. Plenty of examples of people's irrational fear of topless pin-ups.

Christian perspectives

Johnston, O. R. 1979. *Who Needs the Family?* London, Hodder & Stoughton. The original defence-of-the-family text.

US Department of Justice. 1986. Final Report of the Attorney-General's Commission on Pornography. Nashville, TN: Rutledge Hill Press.

White, John. 1977. *Eros Defiled: The Christian and Sexual Guilt*. Leicester, Inter-Varsity Press. For anyone who has a problem with pornography.

Whitehouse, Mary. 1985. *Mightier than the Sword*. Eastbourne, Kingsway. Instant guide to National VALA actions and rationales.

Whitehouse, Mary. 1977. *Whatever Happened to Sex?* Hove, Wayland. Mary at her thought-provoking best.

Wildmon, Donald. 1986. *The Case against Pornography*. Wheaton, IL, Victor Books. A good summary of the major American complaints and fears.

Williams, Nigel. 1991. *False Images: Telling the Truth about Pornography*. Eastbourne, Kingsway. CARE's latest justifications for opposing pornography.

History

Bristow, Edward. 1977. *Vice and Vigilance*. Totowa, NJ, Rowan & Littlefield. Despite his prophecy we would never see their like again, the best coverage of moral crusades prior to 1960.

Gabor, Mark. 1978. 5th ed. *A Modest History of the Pin-Up*. London, Pan. Also 1984. *The Illustrated History of Girlie Magazines*. London, Harmony Books. A pleasant introduction to the world of soft core.

Pornography

Christiansen, F. K. 1990. *Pornography: The Other Side*. New York, Praeger. An extensive rebuttal of major criticisms of pornography.

Cumberbatch, Guy and Howitt, Dennis. 1990. *Pornography: Impacts and Influences*. Home Office Research and Planning Unit. Also 1989. *A Measure of Uncertainty: The Effects of the Mass Media*. London, John Libby. Excellent detailed introduction to all media effects researches, and pornography in particular.

Hebditch, Dick and Anning, Nick. 1988. *Porn Gold*. London, Faber & Faber. The best coverage of the American and European products.

Nobile, Philip and Nadler, Eric. 1986. *United States of America vs SEX*. New York. Minotaur Press. A very detailed and amusing account of the Meese Commission's history.

Stoller, Robert. 1991. *Porn: Myths for the Twentieth Century*. New Haven, CT, Yale University Press. Naive but intriguing insight into the work of the American pornography industry.

Thompson, William and Annetts, Jason. 1990. *Soft-Core: A Content Analysis of Legally Available Pornography in Great Britain 1968–1990 and the Implications of Aggression Research*. Reading University Sociology Department. The original Reading Study.

Williams, Linda. 1989. *Hard Core: Power, Pleasure, and the 'Frenzy of the Visible'*. Berkeley, University of California Press. Despite its title, an arty introduction to 'soft-core' American movies.

Books, articles and papers referred to

Abel, G. G. *et al.* 1977. 'The components of rapists' sexual arousal'. *Archives of General Psychiatry*, **34**.

Abel, G. G. *et al*. 1978. 'Differentiating sexual aggressiveness with penile measures'. *Criminal Justice and Behavior*, 5.

Amendolia, M. and Thompson, W. 1991. 'Survey of sexual attitudes concerning data and acquaintance rape'. Unpublished study, Reading University.

Baron, R. A. 1979. 'Heightened sexual arousal and physical aggression: an extension of females'. *Journal of Research in Personality*, 13.

Baron, L. and Straus, M. A. 1984. 'Sexual stratification, pornography, and rape in the United States', in Malamuth, N. M. and Donnerstein, E., eds, *Pornography and Sexual Aggression*. New York, Academic Press.

Baron, L. and Straus, M. A. 1985. 'Legitimate violence, pornography, and sexual inequality as explanations for state and regional differences in rape'. Unpublished manuscript.

Baron, L. and Straus, M. A. 1986. 'Rape and its relation to social disorganization, pornography, and sexual inequality in the United States'. Unpublished manuscript.

Baxter, D. J. *et al*. 1986. 'Sexual responses to consenting and forced sex in a large sample of rapists'. *Behaviour Research and Therapy*. 24.

Buchman, J. G. 1989. 'Effects of repeated exposure to non-violent erotica on attitudes towards child sexual abuse'. Unpublished dissertation, Indiana University.

Carol, A. Forthcoming. *Nudes, Prudes and Attitudes*. New Clarion Press.

Carr, S. and Thompson, W. 1993. 'Culpability and sexual aggression'. Unpublished study, Reading University.

Check, J. V. P. 1985. 'The hostility toward women scale'. Unpublished dissertation.

Court, J. H. 1976. 'Pornography and sex-crimes: a re-evaluation in the light of recent trends around the world'. *International Journal of Criminology and Penology*, 5.

Court, J. H. 1981. 'Pornography: an update'. *British Journal of Sexual Medicine*. May.

Court, J. H. 1982. 'Rape and trends in New South Wales: a discussion of conflicting evidence'. *Australian Journal of Social Issues*, 17.

Dermer, M. and Pyszczynski, T. 1978. 'Effects of erotica upon men's loving and linking responses for women they love'. *Journal of Personality and Social Psychology*, 36, 1302–10.

Dietz, P. E. and Evans, B. 1982. 'Pornographic imagery and prevalence of paraphilia'. *American Journal of Psychiatry*, 139, 1493–5.

Dietz, P. E. *et al.* 1986. 'Detective magazines: pornography for the sexual sadist'. *Journal of Forensic Science*, JFSCA, 31 (1).

Donnerstein, E. 1984. 'Pornography: its effect on violence against women', in Malamuth, N. and Donnerstein, E., eds. *Pornography and Sexual Aggression*. New York, Academic Press.

Donnerstein, E. and Barrett, G. 1978. 'The effects of erotic stimuli on male aggression towards females. *Journal of Personality and Social Psychology*, 36.

Donnerstein, E. and Berkowitz, L. 1981. 'Victim reactions in aggressive erotic films as a factor in violence against women'. *Journal of Personality and Social Psychology*, 41.

Donnerstein, E. and Hallam, J. 1978. 'Facilitating effects of erotica on aggression against women'. *Journal of Personality and Social Psychology*, 36.

Donnerstein, E. *et al.* 1986. 'Role of aggressive and sexual images in violent pornography', unpublished manuscript cited in Donnerstein *et al.* 1987. *The Question of Pornography*. London, Free Press.

Donnerstein, E. *et al.* 1987. *The Question of Pornography*. London, Free Press.

Fisher, W. A. and Grenier, G. 1988. 'Failures to replicate effects of pornography on attitudes and behaviour: the emperor has no clothes'. Unpublished manuscript.

Greendlinger, Virginia and Byrne, Donn. 1987. 'Coercive sexual fantasies of college men as predictors of self-reported likelihood to rape and overt sexual aggression'. *Journal of Sex Research*, 23 (1), 1–11.

Kant, H. S. and Goldstein, M. J. 1978. 'Pornography and its effects', in Savitz, D. and Johnson, J., eds. *Crime in Society*. New York, Wiley.

Kelley, K. 1985. 'Sexual attitudes as determinants of the motivational properties of exposure to erotica'. *Personality and Individual Differences*, 6.

Kelley, K. 1989. 'Prosocial responding and affect induction: sex differences following exposure to sexually explicit slides'. Quoted in Kelly. K. *et al.* 'Three faces of sexual explictness', in Zillmann, D. and Bryant, J. *Pornography: Research Advances and Policy Considerations.* Hillsdale, NJ, Lawrence Erlbaum.

Kelley, K. and Musialowski, D. 1986. 'Female sexual victimization and effects of warnings about violent pornography'. Paper presented at the Eastern Psychological Association, New York.

Kenrick, D. T. *et al.* 1986. 'Influence of popular erotica on interpersonal attraction judgments: the uglier side of pretty pictures', in Donnerstein, E. *et al. The Question of Pornography.* London, Free Press.

Krafka, C. L. 1985. 'Sexually explicit, sexually violent, and violent media: effects of multiple naturalistic exposures and debriefing on female viewers'. Unpublished doctoral dissertation, University of Wisconsin, Madison.

Langevin, R. *et al.* 1985. 'Are rapists sexually anomalous, aggressive, or both?', in Langevin, R., ed. *Erotic Preference, Gender Identity, and Aggression in Men: New Research Studies.* Hillsdale, NJ, Lawrence Erlbaum Associates.

Leonard, K. E. and Taylor, S. P. 1983. 'Exposure to pornography, permissive and non-permissive cues, and male aggression toward females'. *Motivation and Emotion,* 7.

Linz, D. 1985. 'Sexual violence in the media: effects on male viewers and implications for society'. Unpublished doctoral dissertation, University of Wisconsin, Madison.

Linz, D. *et al.* 1984. 'The effects of multiple exposures to filmed violence against women'. *Journal of Communication,* 34.

Malamuth, N. 1984. 'Aggression against women: cultural and individual causes', in Malamuth, N. and Donnerstein, E., eds. *Pornography and Sexual Aggression.* New York, Academic Press.

Malamuth, N. and Ceniti, J. 1986. 'Repeated exposure to violent and non-violent pornography: Likelihood of Raping ratings and laboratory aggression against women. *Aggressive Behavior,* 12.

Malamuth, N. and Check, J. V. P. 1980. 'Penile tumescence and perceptual responses to rape as a function of victims' perceived reactions'. *Journal of Applied Social Psychology*, 10.

Malamuth, N. and Check, J. V. P. 1981. 'The effects of mass media exposure on acceptance of violence against women: a field experiment'. *Journal of Research in Personality*, 15.

Malamuth, N. and Check, J. V.P. 1985. 'The effects of aggressive pornography on beliefs of rape myths: individual differences'. *Journal of Research in Personality*, 19.

Malamuth, N. M. and Donnerstein, E. eds. 1984. *Pornography and Sexual Aggression*. New York, Academic Press.

Malamuth, N. and Spinner, E. 1980. 'A longitudinal content analysis of sexual violence in the best-selling erotica magazines'. *Journal of Sex Research*, 16.

Marshall, W. L. 1989. 'Pornography and sex offenders', in Zillmann, D. and Bryant, J. *Pornography: Research Advances and Policy Considerations*. Hillsdale, NJ, Lawrence Erlbaum.

Marshall, W. L. *et al.* 1986. 'Sexual offenders against female children: sexual preference for age, victims and type of behaviour'. *Canadian Journal of Behavioural Science*, 18.

Meese, E. 1986. Attorney General's Commission on Pornography: Final Report. Vols 1 and 2. Justice Dept., Washington, DC.

Milgram, S. 1963. 'Behavioral study of obedience'. *Journal of Abnormal and Social Psychology*, 67.

Palys, T. S. 1984. 'A content analysis of sexually explicit videos in British Columbia'. *Working Papers on Pornography and Prostitution, Report No. 15.* Department of Justice, Ottawa, Ontario.

Palys, T. S. 1986. 'Testing the common wisdom: the social content of pornography'. *Canadian Psychology*, 27 (10).

Przybyla, D. P. 1985. 'The facilitating effects of exposure to erotica on male pro-social behavior', Unpublished doctoral dissertation, State University of New York at Albany.

Rada, R. T. 1978. *Clinical Aspects of the Rapist.* New York, Grune & Stratton.

Scott, J. E. 1985. 'Violence and erotic material: the relationship between adult entertainment and rape'. Paper presented at General Meeting of the American Association for the Advancement of Science, Los Angeles.

Scott, J. E. and Cuvelier, S. J. 1987. 'Sexual violence in *Playboy* magazine: a longitudinal content analysis'. *Journal of Sex Research*, 23 (4), 534–9.

Slade, J. 1984. 'Violence in the hard-core pornographic film'. *Journal of Communication*, Summer.

Smith, D. D. 1976. 'The social content of pornography'. *Journal of Communication*, 26.

Thomas, M. H. *et al.* 1977. 'Desensitization to portrayals of real-life aggression as a function of exposure to television violence'. *Journal of Personality and Social Psychology*, 35.

Thompson, W. and Annetts, J. 1990. Soft-Core. Unpublished manuscript, Reading University.

Walker, C. E. 1970. 'Erotic stimuli and the aggressive sexual offender'. *Technical Reports of the Commission on Obscenity and Pornography*, 7.

Weaver, J. B. 1987. 'Effects of portrayals of female sexuality and violence against women on percentages of women'. Unpublished doctoral dissertation, Indiana University.

Winick, C. 1985. 'A content analysis of sexually explicit magazines sold in adult bookstores'. *Journal of Sex Research*, 21.

Wydra, A. *et al.* 1983. 'Identification of cues and control of sexual arousal by rapists'. *Behaviour Research and Therapy*, 21.

Zillmann, D. 1989. 'Effects of prolonged consumption of pornography', in Zillmann, D. and Bryant, J., eds. *Pornography: Research Advances and Policy Considerations*. Hillsdale, NJ, Lawrence Erlbaum.

Zillmann, D. and Bryant, J. 1984. 'Effects of massive exposure to pornography', in Malamuth, N. and Donnerstein, E., eds. *Pornography and Sexual Aggression*. New York. Academic Press.

Zillmann, D. and Bryant, J., eds. 1989. *Pornography: Research Advances and Policy Considerations*. Hillsdale, NJ, Lawrence Erlbaum.

Zillmann, D. and Weaver, J. B. 1989. 'Pornography and men's sexual callousness towards women', in Zillmann, D. and Bryant, J., eds. *Pornography: Research Advances and Policy Considerations*. Hillsdale, NJ, Lawrence Erlbaum.

Index